A Passion for Running

A Passion for Running

Scott Ludwig

iUniverse, Inc.
New York   Bloomington

iUniverse books may be ordered through booksellers or by contacting:

iUniverse
1663 Liberty Drive
Bloomington, IN 47403
www.iuniverse.com
1-800-Authors (1-800-288-4677)

ISBN: 978-1-4401-7835-1 (sc)
ISBN: 978-1-4401-7836-8 (ebook)

Printed in the United States of America

iUniverse rev. date: 10/19/09

To mom and dad, who worried I might run with the wrong crowd.

I didn't

Table of Contents

Part Three Thanks for the Memories (The Nineteenth Hole)

Everyday Heroes

In my autobiography *Running through My Mind* I mentioned one of my future goals was to write a book about the amazing runners—my personal superheroes I've grown to know throughout my running lifetime. After all each one has their own unique story to tell and my dream has always been to be the one to tell them.

It is my honor to tell you that time has arrived, and these are the stories I've wanted to tell.

Soon you will be reading about 18 of the most fascinating people I have ever had the pleasure—the *privilege* of knowing. They come from all walks of life and in many ways are as different as night and day.

Yet they are alike in many ways, as they all:

- are experienced, veteran and lifelong runners.
- are passionate about running.
- are supporters of running.
- are promoters of running.
- encourage and motivate others to run.
- have many stories to tell—some inspiring, some downright amazing, and in most cases both.
- are much too modest to tell their stories themselves.

The last bullet point is where I come in. They have all graciously allowed me to be the one to tell their story, thus making my dream come true.

The 18 portraits will all be presented in its own chapter and will include a short introduction and photograph of the runner, my biographical sketch of the runner, the runner's personal insights on the sport of running, and their personal accounts of the more memorable running events in their lives. Each portrait will lead you to the exact same realization: they are all truly passionate about their craft, and all serve as proud ambassadors for the sport of running.

You will understand their passion for running not only through their written words, but I dare to say more vividly through their *actions*.

My first book was a labor of love. It would be fair to say that this, my second book is a labor of passion.

Scott Ludwig
Peachtree City, Georgia
July 2009

Foreword

To be physically **active**—to run is the nature of man. Our Stone Age ancestors had to run in order to eat…and to avoid being eaten. This way of life went on for millions of years and since that time our bodies have changed very little. It's what we are: their legacy to us.

Even in today's culture there are those who understand this and live by it. Most of us probably never really thought of it in that way when we started; it just felt right, very natural and so we decided to give it a go.

We read about and watched others do things we considered to be next to impossible for us, but we eventually came to realize that most of these people were no different than we are. They were just ordinary people for the most part; ordinary people who were accomplishing extraordinary things in their lives.

Scott Ludwig has managed to assemble just such a group of ordinary people as his subjects. As you read their stories you will realize these people have one thing in common: a passion for running! You will also discover just how powerful this passion can be. They have acquired a special gift—one that adds a new dimension to their lives. They are lucky indeed.

It has been my good fortune to personally know most of these runners and count them among my best friends. They are a truly diverse group. Some have run in the coldest places and some in the hottest places on earth; some have even done both! Another has run races on all seven continents, another hasn't missed a day of running in over 11 years, and one, 85-year old Lloyd Young has set pending world records in his age group!

Each one of these people has a unique story—a legacy that can be passed on to others for inspiration. I can only imagine how many lives have been enhanced by knowing them. They are some of the most interesting people I have ever met.

Al Barker
Nantahala, North Carolina
June 2009

Scott and Al, 2008 Atlanta Marathon

PART ONE:
Ladies First
✦
(The Front Nine)

Chapter One

Anne Rentz

Anne Rentz is a source of inspiration for many people.

Taking up the sport of running at an age when most people would be more inclined to observe than participate, she has achieved goals that once-upon-a-time she considered to be nothing more than dreams.

But that was then, and this is now. Anne Rentz is living the dream.

I first met Anne in 2004 at an 8-hour run I was directing at a local quarter-mile track in Peachtree City. I advised the runners at the start of the event that they could run the entire eight hours if they would like (most would opt to simply quit after running a complete lap on the track). If they chose to continue running past the start/finish line, I would measure their additional distance by rolling a measuring wheel to the point on the track they stopped.

Only one runner that day opted to run every precious second of the entire eight hours.

Anne officially covered 32.7 miles and finished in second place among the women. I was so impressed with her that I ran a lawn chair out to her on the track so she could get some well-deserved rest. I then measured the distance from where she had stopped *back* to the start/finish line (instead of the other way around).

Anne Rentz is a source of inspiration for many people.

I'm one of them.

Anne and Bill, Runner and Mentor

RUNNING FOR FUN

Before running, there were books to be read…jigsaw puzzles to be assembled… cigarettes to be smoked. What more could you expect from an admitted couch potato?

Then one day Anne Rentz gave up the life of a couch potato and ran… and walked…and ran some more. She thought it was fun.

Anne Rentz is admittedly not a fast runner. Once upon a time she tried speed work, but it just didn't work out. You see, Anne didn't find it to be fun. Running *is* supposed to be fun, isn't it?

Running (and walking) led to other activities. Cycling. Parties. Traveling (primarily to races!). Listening to books on tape in the car took the place of reading on the couch. There was no longer time for jigsaw puzzles (or a desire for cigarettes). After all, who has time to put together a 1,000 piece puzzle of a mountain scene when you could be spending an entire day walking and running up and down a *real* one?

Anne's self-professed claim to fame is her stubbornness. She simply 'loves to run and walk a long way.' For someone who claims to be a non-athlete, Anne has compiled quite a resume over the past 13 years. Among her credentials:

- 43 Marathons
- 27 Ultramarathons (including three 50-milers, one 100K, and one 100-miler—more on that later)
- 70 Marathons/Ultras completed in 23 States + D.C. + Berlin

Anne's personal best in the marathon is a 4:53 in Cleveland, a race she ended with an exclamation point by tripping over the finish line and winding up with a black eye.

Her one DNF ('did not finish') was at the Oak Mountain 50K in Alabama *('pesky time limit')*. Anne has one DNS ('did not start') as well: She was planning on running the Great Wall of China Marathon but had to cancel her trip as she was diagnosed with 90% coronary blockage that had to be repaired. Immediately.

Anne has shared her enthusiasm for the sport with others. She has been with the Jeff Galloway Training Group for twelve years; the last ten years as a Group Leader. Anne's group is known as the MRA (Moving Right Along) Runners. She's inspired other runners ('back of the packers') to achieve their goal of running a marathon and others to do things they never imagined— like discovering running is *fun*.

On a personal level, Anne is proudest of her finish at the 2008 Umstead Endurance Run—a race of 100 miles—in under 30 hours. The special belt buckle she earned for her accomplishment is the crown jewel in her collection of running memorabilia. She attributes her success to following Umstead Race Director Blake Norwood's Training Program. But Anne is short-changing herself, because it is her stubbornness, determination and love for the sport that can be credited with an assist.

Anne is a single 56-years *young* woman with 'a supportive significant other, a beautiful daughter, a marvelous grandson, a super son-in-law, two best-friend sisters, one fun older brother, a bad cat, and a huge family of running partners and friends.' With a supporting cast like that, it's no wonder Anne is realizing her running dreams at this point in her life.

Anne says her favorite race is 'any race with a long time limit.' She believes the McKenzie River 50K and the Tahoe Rim 50K to be the most beautiful she has found during her extensive travels.

Occasionally, Anne will put on her *own* race if there isn't one that suits her schedule. Two that immediately come to mind: (1) The Mamasan 50 X 50, where Anne ran 50 miles on Atlanta's Silver Comet Trail to celebrate her 50th birthday, and (2) the Run to Alabama 100K, where Anne and several of her supporting cast members ran 62 miles from Smyrna, Georgia to the Alabama state line on the Silver Comet Trail (and a small section of Highway 278 in a spot where the Trail wasn't yet completed).

Anne is a member of several running clubs and groups:

- Jeff Galloway's Training Group, because Anne loves to run and walk with others at her pace. She finds the program is perfect for social running and getting people involved in exercising. Anne enjoys helping beginners achieve their goals and finds their progress to be inspiring.
- 50 States Marathon Club, because Anne likes to run in different places and finds President Tom Adair and the other members motivating.
- Darkside Running Club, because Anne loves to run in the dark and appreciates the fact that the members take their running seriously, yet don't take *themselves* seriously.
- Georgia Ultrarunning and Trailrunning Society (GUTS), because Anne loves to run trails and she finds President Janice Anderson and the other runners so supportive. Anne considers it a bonus that she lives next to the trails of Kennesaw Mountain, a favorite haunt of the GUTS members.

- Atlanta Track Club, because the Peachtree Road Race captured Anne's imagination early in her running career. Plus, she heard that you could actually *walk* the race, so she signed up only to find that she actually had the ability to *run*.

Besides her membership in these clubs and groups, she also has assembled quite an entourage of support comprised of family and close friends:

- Bill Cox and Katie Crockett, her favorite crew.
- Becky Rentz and Terri Hayes, her favorite pacers (and in some cases, 'draggers').
- A Medical Team comprised of Josh Glass (chiropractor), Charles Peebles (podiatrist) and Nan Webb (sports masseuse). Anne calls the trio her 'duct tape.'

With Anne's extensive network of support, family and friends as well as her personal level of commitment, dedication and intrinsic ability to *enjoy* the sport, it's no wonder that this 'non-athlete' is accomplishing things in the running world that many *athletes* would be proud to have on their resumes.

Despite her accomplishments, Anne continues to harbor several dreams:

She dreams of running the Boston Marathon, although she doesn't think she'll ever have the speed to qualify.

She dreams of competing in the prestigious Comrades Marathon, but fears that she wouldn't be able to finish within the mandated time limit.

She dreams of testing her mettle in the Badwater Ultramarathon, but doubts she'll ever have the credentials to receive an invitation.

But as long as Anne's dreams are alive and her running remains fun, there's still a chance. A very good one, in fact.

STARTING SLOWLY

By Anne Rentz

In 1992 I was 40 years old, recently divorced with a 15-year old daughter, overweight and out on my own for the first time. I moved into a nice little condominium next to Laurel Park in Marietta, Georgia. There was a tennis park next to me with a ¾ mile paved path for walking. One day I decided to check out the park and take a walk. I always liked to be outside and I liked to walk but never did it on a regular basis except occasionally when I was dieting. I wondered if I could use the trail to lose some weight even though I was not currently on a diet. On my walk, I met some folks who said they walked every day and invited me to join them. If I only knew what that would lead to. One of the walkers eventually became my biggest supporter and support chief, Bill Cox. At the time he had been walking four miles every day for six years. The reason he started walking was following a heart attack his doctor told him if he wanted to live he needed to exercise. I began to look forward to going for a walk every day to meet my new walking friends.

Sometimes I had to run a bit to catch up with Bill and the other walkers because they walked so fast. At some point if I went out by myself I would try jogging just a bit. There are ¼ mile markers on the track and I made it a goal to run for a complete ¼ mile; then when I was able to do that, I set a goal to run a mile. Whew! That was fun. I have an Uncle (Capt. William O.K. Rentz, Ret.) who came to Atlanta to run the Peachtree Road Race every year. I thought that sounded cool but would not have ever considered it-- the distance was 6.2 miles! However, someone told me that you could walk Peachtree and since I was walking four miles a day, I thought maybe I could do it. With encouragement from Bill who was certain I could do it, I signed up for the race and also signed up for the Atlanta Track Club 'In Training for Peachtree Clinic.' That was scary because I would have to drive into Atlanta from Marietta at night to attend the classes once a week and then go into town on the weekend for the weekly run – by myself. Scary proposition!

But I loved that Clinic. The volunteers were supportive, upbeat and friendly. The training consisted of starting at Lenox Shopping Center (the start of the Peachtree Road Race) and running down Peachtree as far as you could go, and then catch a bus back to Lenox, every week going a little bit further. One week, I had gone as far as I could and was walking up to the bus stop when a volunteer said 'Anne, you seemed pretty strong on your run; now that you have rested by walking a bit, why don't you run some more?' I did and ran another mile. After that it seemed real easy to finish up the six miles in training and then to run my first Peachtree in 1995. During the clinic, I heard about a book by Jeff Galloway, *Galloway's Book on Running*. I bought the book and became an avid runner! The track club published a training schedule for the half marathon on Thanksgiving Day and I trained for it and ran the event the same year. By this time, my sister Becky had gotten the bug so we were two former couch potatoes on the run! After the half marathon, we had heard about Galloway's marathon training groups and we joined that program. Jeff's program consists of a combination of running and walking, gradually increasing your distance to the 26.2 miles of a marathon. During this time I was able to slim down and felt better physically than I ever had in my entire life. Becky and I trained with the Galloway program and 'graduated' to our first marathon: the 1996 Marine Corps Marathon in Washington, D.C. As we were running the last few miles we were already talking about doing another marathon.

Becky has since gone on to run many long distance races, adventure races and an Ironman distance triathlon. I have stayed with the long run events as my primary activity but I also love to ride my bike and have completed several BRAG (Bike Ride Across Georgia) events. At some point I realized I was never going to be fast but my thought was that I could run forever. I have completed numerous marathons and ultramarathons (any distance over 26.2 miles). My longest distance to date is 100 miles at the Umstead 100 mile Endurance Run in 2008: my goal is to complete 100 races of marathon distance or longer. I am also attempting to complete a marathon in all 50 states.

I am now the grandmother of an 11 year old grandson, David Brannon Crocket, IV. I'm not doing too badly for a granny! Life is indeed very good!

Important things I have learned about running/walking/exercising:

- Find a training group. There is nothing like the camaraderie and the commitment to meet with a group of folks once or more each week. I have met the most interesting people and they are all so supportive and entertaining at the same time. There are many training groups and clubs for all interests and abilities.
- Don't limit yourself by what you think you can do. In long distance running the majority of the effort is mental, not physical. If I plan to run five miles and that is mentally what I am prepared for, that is pretty much as far as I can run. With the same conditioning, if I plan to run 26.2 miles, that is doable. I almost never run more than I am mentally prepared to run. Most runners who run 50 miles and 100 miles do not do training runs of that length. You add mileage to your weeks but don't generally run the distance beforehand. For a

50 miler, I might do 35 miles in training and for a 100 miler, I might do 50 miles. The mileage between your training and the event itself is mostly a mental exercise.

- Be an ambassador for your sport. I think sometimes if people only knew how much fun it can be, more folks would be out there hiking, biking, walking and running. When I used to see runners I thought they weren't having much fun. They always seemed to be frowning. Now I know it is more because they are concentrating or just enjoying the run while thinking of other things. I try to remember to smile and wave as I pass others and talk to people about the benefits of running, including its social implications and how much fun it can be. While there are some who look down on those who are not competitive, fast 'athletes,' I have found many elite athletes are very encouraging and supportive.

- Exercise is a great way to lose and maintain weight BUT you still have to watch your diet and eat appropriately. You can run long distances and still gain weight! Bummer! When they say weight loss is successful through a combination of a healthy diet and exercise, they are absolutely right.

- Cross Train: Find an exercise to give you a break from your main activity. It adds variety and enhances your conditioning.

Not so important but helpful tips for running:

- Prepare your running clothes and gear the night before a race or training run.
- Do not try something new (food, clothes, shoes, etc.) during an important event.
- When flying to an event, always carry your running shoes on board with you! You can replace most everything else, but not your broken-in lucky shoes.
- Always keep an extra set of running clothes in your car. You never know when a run might break out and you never know when you might forget something like your socks!
- In a big race, don't take water from the volunteers at the first table; go further down to the end where it is not so congested.
- Carry your own water in a bottle for races over distances of 10K. You never know what might happen. In my very first marathon, they were out of cups at the first stop and one race major race there was no water for the first six miles…and it was very hot that day!

- In a race do not go to a porta pottie with a line. Be sure to get there early enough to visit the porta pottie well before the race begins. When you need to make a pit stop during an event, wait until you run across a porta pottie with no line. Most of the time, you can hold it a bit longer! Whether you are trying for a new PR (personal record) or just trying to finish by the time limit of the event, stopping or lingering at porta potties or support tables can eat up your time in a hurry!
- Thank the volunteers and remember they are not there to hear complaints; they are taking their time to help.

If at First You Don't Succeed

By Anne Rentz

The first time I attempted to run 100 miles, it didn't turn out too well. Why, you may ask? Well, let me count the ways:

- I didn't have the necessary respect for the distance.
- I didn't adequately train—physically or mentally.
- I was wearing clothing that was insufficient to combat the cold, rainy conditions.
- I had an undetected 90% coronary artery blockage which I did not learn about until *after* my failed attempt.

OK, enough with the whining. I built on my failure—which could actually be considered a 'successful' 62 mile run (it all depends on whether you perceive the glass to be half full or half empty) and I decided to give 100 miles a second chance. My race of choice? The 2008 Umstead Endurance Run near Raleigh, North Carolina.

Here's how it went.

Training

There are many 'How to Run 100 Miles' programs out there. I elected to utilize Umstead Race Director Blake Norwood's training program since it was specifically designed for his course and based on his experience. Plus, it didn't appear to be overly complicated, which I particularly liked. My training consisted of increasing my mileage from 25 miles a week to 60 miles a week. The 60 mile weeks consisted of one long run, two shorter runs, one day of speed work, one day of speed *walk*, and two days of rest. I started my training on October 1st, 2007 (the race would be held on the first weekend in April 2008). I admit I didn't follow the program to the letter, but I was pretty dedicated getting in my mileage.

For the record I am a slow runner who doesn't like speed work. I run for fun, not work. My speed work consisted of half-mile downhill repeats. I only built up to four miles but thought it was pretty fun running down the hill. It gave me the feeling of what it might be like to be fast. I could raise my arms and say 'WHEEEE' as I barreled down the hill. My speed work coach and friend Bill Cox diligently recorded my times, cheered me on and brought me snacks to give me energy. I completed one of the recommended overnight runs as part of my training with my sister Becky and good friend Susan Kolbinsky at the Kennesaw Mountain Battlefield Park. We ran from 8:00 p.m. until 3:00 a.m. Many of my training runs were Galloway Group runs and I pretty much ended my training with the Iron Horse 50-Miler in Orange Park, Florida on March 1st, a race where I lowered my 50 mile best from 14:09 to 12:42. However, the Iron Horse was an easy, flat course; Umstead is somewhat less flat with its 8,000 feet of climb.

Was I ready? I hoped so. If the weather was good and I didn't hang out too long at the support stops...and nothing disastrous happened, I had a legitimate shot at completing 100 miles. Now whether I could do it in the 30-hour time limit was another question. However, I was prepared to continue after the time limit to finish the distance...*unofficially* if I had to.

The Night Before

The forecasted weather for the day of the race called for a 100% chance of heavy rain and thundershowers—all day long. However, the *actual* weather proved to be a comfortable long-distance running temperature with a couple rain showers and sprinkles thrown in throughout the day. In other words, perfect.

My supporting cast was at the ready:

- My crew, consisting of friend Bill Cox (aka 'Eagle Bill') and daughter Katie Crockett (aka Kitty Cricket)
- My pacers (aka 'draggers'), consisting of friend and ultra mentor Terri Hayes and sister and friend Becky Rentz
- My fans, consisting of son-in-law David Brannon Crockett, III and grandson David Brannon Crockett, IV

My game plan was simple: my crew would anticipate my every need and get me in and out of the aid stations without allowing me to lounge around for any significant length of time. I would run and walk like the wind with no thought in my head except finishing 100 miles as fast as I could, and of course to have fun while doing it.

We attended the prerace spaghetti dinner and meeting. I learned there was an award for the last place finisher. I would be honored to win that one since it would mean I had finished the race in less than 30 hours. This race is particularly nice because if you're unable to complete 100 miles but do finish at least 50, you are credited with a 50-mile finishing time. However, for me *this is not an option!*

The Start

Although the race didn't start until 6:00 a.m., I was up at 2:30 just to be certain I would be on time with every single piece of equipment I would need. My entourage and I arrived early enough to park, put drop bags in the proper area, visit the restroom, greet friends (the ultrarunning community is very close!) and get a bit to eat. Did I mention visiting the restroom? With a forecast calling for rain, Becky taped both of my feet…with waterproof duct tape. Before I knew it the gun sounded and we were off running in the dark for the first of eight 12 ½ mile loops through Umstead State Park. The first part of each loop is a short out-and-back used to make the lap an accurate 12 ½ miles. The course terrain can best be described as groomed trails with hills—lots of ups and lots of downs. It was neat in the dark to see the frontrunners coming back toward me on the out-and-back with their headlamps on. It looked like a herd of giant fireflies bobbing along. Before long the darkness dissipated and while it seemed like rain was imminent, the downpours never happened and we settled for a few sprinkles and a fair share of humidity.

I completed my first loop much faster than I thought: two hours and 49 minutes. Was that bad for my strategy? I usually do better when I can put some time in the bank. We'll see.

100 Miles of Fun

I completed my first 50 miles in 13:35, which was 35 minutes slower than I felt I needed to run to complete 100 miles in less than 30 hours. But I thought that if I just stuck with my original game plan, I had a fair shot at achieving my goal.

Again, the plan was that if I missed the 30-hour time limit I would still continue to reach my goal to run 100 miles. Period.

An *official* finish would be the icing on my cake, of course.

My very seasoned and talented ultra friend and mentor Terri had driven up from Aiken, South Carolina to run with me as I started my 5th loop. When we run together we spend a lot of time catching up with our lives, and this occasion was no different. The time passed quickly. However, in the midst of the 6th loop I started falling asleep. I just could not stay awake. All of a sudden I would 'blank out' and drift off the trail, only to be saved by Terri who would grab me and wake me up. We met a friend of hers who shared some caffeine tablets which helped me gain some semblance of consciousness.

My strategy was to run the flat and downhill sections of the course and walk the steep inclines. My definition of a 'walkable' hill became more and more generous throughout the day. I knew that Terri was trying to trick me in the dark by saying 'here's a flat section; let's run.' It didn't work.

The 5th and 6th loops both took over four hours and I realized we had to pick up the pace to break 30 hours. My sister Becky joined us for the 7th loop. Before long I was having problems with sleep deprivation once again. I was mumbling and wandering, and Terri and Becky stayed on either side of me and held my arms up to keep me moving forward. Another caffeine tablet and a double espresso GU got me back on track.

Once I regained consciousness Becky said 'Anne, remember all your training; you can get this done!' At that point I started thinking about all the training I had done and the fun running down hills and walking strong up hills. Terri kept after me about my posture and arm swing and just kept encouraging me to run. After we finished the 7th lap—or 87.5 miles, my elapsed time was 25:48, which was just under the 26-hour cutoff. I had a little over four hours to finish the last 12 ½ miles. At the turnaround the volunteers said 'you can do it, but it will be tight!'

We had already decided that I would not go into the aid station but simply go through the check point and head back out for my 8th and final loop. Terri and Becky took my water bottle and got soup and stuff to bring out to me on the course.

On the 8th loop I was still running, and we were actually passing other runners as we made our way around the park. I had suggested that Becky bring her camera on the last loop as it would again be daylight and I knew she would want some pictures of a really scenic bridge that was surrounded by beautiful wisteria. As we approached the bridge we passed a runner on the side of the road who was experiencing stomach problems. We checked on him and he seemed OK so we continued and took pictures at the bridge. The aforementioned runner joined us so we were able to get a nice picture of the three of us at the bridge. We finally passed the last aid station with about six miles to go and realized we should make the 30-hour time limit! Once I realized that, I tried to relax but Terri kept pushing.

I, however was being very cooperative. We finally passed the runner that I thought was the only one in contention for last place. I thought about *not* passing her so I could win the 'Last Person-Female' award but it really was more important to get to the finish line within the time limit.

WE DID IT!!! Twenty-nine hours, 37 minutes and 38 seconds. We had a little bit of a cushion, but I know that if my crew hadn't done their job and gotten me in and out of the aid stations quickly, I could easily have lounged around and missed my goal.

Afterwards

One hundred miles! Was it fun? You bet! At least 96.7 miles of it was fun, anyway. The staff and volunteers were so supportive and dedicated you felt like they were really pulling for you to do well (and they were!). Of course my crew and pacers were absolutely the reason I was able to finish. The camaraderie of the other runners on the course also made it more fun. I was able to chit-chat with runners for miles at a time. I saw people I already knew and met many new people who I now am proud to know as friends. I saw one man that I couldn't place who called me by name a couple of times. I asked him where I knew him from and he said he works at a running shoe store and even sold me the Super Novas I was wearing. I ran for a while with a Galloway runner from Cincinnati, Suzelle Snowdon. She finished her first 100-miler that day as well. I met with Fred (the 'caffeine guy') and chatted with Angela Ivory and the Race Director from Iron Horse, Chris Rodatz. Scott Ludwig helped push me up a steep hill as he passed me on one loop (the hardest hill on the course, by the way which Becky named the 'Whee and the Whoa... Whoa...Whoa').

It was just a fun, memorable day.

Chapter Two

Amy Yanni

I ran into Amy Yanni somewhere between the 19 and 20 mile mark of the 2007 Museum of Aviation Marathon in Warner Robins, Georgia.

As runners are inclined to do during a marathon with only a couple hundred participants, we struck up a conversation. Amy was wearing her Marathon Maniacs uniform. I was unfamiliar with their club, so Amy provided me all of the relevant information about it.

Amy and her husband had traveled from their home in Rapid City, South Dakota to Georgia to enjoy a short respite from a rather cold winter back west. Plus, she needed to add Georgia to her ever-increasing list of states in which she completed a marathon.

I maintained her pace until the 25-mile mark at which point it was obvious she had more left in her tank than me. Amy went on to finish a couple minutes ahead of me but more importantly ahead of all the female runners in the field. She not only escaped a cold South Dakota winter and added another state to her marathon resume; she won a marathon as well.

She also won over a new admirer.

Me.

Amy Yanni

MARATHON METRONOME

By definition, a metronome is a clicking pendulum used to indicate the exact tempo of a piece of music. If one were to apply the word to running, it would mean something—or some*one*—used to indicate the exact tempo (or pace) of a run.

If one were looking for a running metronome to adhere to an eight-minute per mile (plus or minus five seconds a mile to allow for variations between routes) pace during a marathon, then look no further than South Dakota's own Amy Yanni.

Amy, who began her marathon career in earnest during the fall of 2003 after bravely fighting through a bout with breast cancer and recovering from a double mastectomy — has been quite the human metronome. With well over a hundred marathon finishes under her belt in her first five years as a runner (she won't run ultras because she says they're 'too far'), over two-thirds of her finishes have been in the sixteen-minute window between 3:24 and 3:40; which is essentially an eight-minute per mile pace...plus or minus five seconds a mile, which with Amy's consistency *must* be indicative of the variations between marathon routes). After all, Amy is a virtual lock to run eight-minute miles...as many as 26 in a row at times.

In her debut marathon in Bismarck, North Dakota in September of 2003, she announced her presence to the marathon world with a convincing 3:32 finish, which was good enough to win not only her age group but the Female Master's trophy as well. Only eleven marathons later Amy won her first *overall* (yes, she beat all the men in the field) title with a fine 3:27 in Brookings, South Dakota (May of 2005). And she's been adding to her victory total ever since, with an amazing total of 77 age group victories (in 107 marathons).

But Amy isn't always content with age group victories. She also touts nine overall marathon victories, several of which were in some of the more offbeat marathons: 'Running from an Angel' in Nevada; 'Swan Lake' in South Dakota; 'Zoom! Yah! Yah!' an indoor 150 lap January marathon at St. Olaf College in Minnesota; 'Frank Maier' in Juneau, Alaska; and 'Running with the Horses' in Wyoming. In some of the more prominent marathons, she has won her age group, e.g., San Francisco, California (2008); Denver, Colorado (2007); Louisville, Kentucky (2007); Myrtle Beach, South Carolina (2007); Gasparilla in Tampa, Florida (2006); and Seattle, Washington (2005).

Thus far it's been quite a successful running career for someone whose first race was of the three-legged variety at the Michigan State Fair. But to be fair to Amy, she admits that she's been running all her life, because she always had to race home before the streetlights came on when she was young--because she would be in *big trouble* with her mom if she were late.

To explore her true roots in the sport of running, you have to delve deep into her first love: baseball. As a child, she rooted for the Detroit Tigers, but eventually her cheers were for another team—a rival team of the Tigers, no less: the Boston Red Sox. Her 'grampa,' a semi-pro catcher advised her to 'always root for the home team.' So when Amy moved to Boston between 1967 and 1968, she switched her allegiance to the Red Sox. Her untimely move caused her to miss the Red Sox 'impossible dream' season of 1967 (she was still in Michigan) and the Tigers winning the series in 1968 (she was now in Boston). However, she's more than recovered from that double whammy since her beloved Sox finally broke the 'curse of the Bambino' in recent years.

How did baseball lead to her affinity for running? Amy always favored the infielders who made the tough fielding plays, then got on base by bunting, drawing a walk, or getting a bloop hit, then stealing a base or breaking up a double play with a hard slide into second base, and then scoring by quickly rounding third base and heading home to beat the throw to the plate. To that Amy says 'You can see where running was important.'

As a teen, Amy was co-captain of the girls' softball team, but it got harder and harder to find 17 other people to play with after school. She took up tennis for a while—after all, running was a pretty important component of the sport—but even then she had to find someone else to play with, locate a free tennis court, and have a fresh stash of tennis balls. In time, she found that running was just…well, simpler. She started out running in her old reliables, a pair of Tretorn running shoes (which she now will quickly tell you is *not* recommended).

Today, Amy is one of the most energetic and enthusiastic supporters of the sport of running. She writes a semi-regular column for the local newspaper, the *Rapid City Journal,* which is loosely based on the joys and challenges of running.

She is a member of the Marathon Maniacs (she's number 130) and the Black Hills (S.D.) Running Club and the 50 States Marathon Club, having just completed running a (Boston-Qualifying) marathon in each of the 50 states and DC.

In Dean Karnazes' famous '50 marathons in 50 states in 50 days' tour of 2006, Amy was the sole companion to run the entire course with Dean in his marathon along the Mickelson Trail in Deadwood, South Dakota. In his book *50/50: Secrets I Learned Running 50 Marathons in 50 Days*, Karnazes mentions running with Amy and that she was named MarathonGuide.com's Female Outstanding Runner of 2006 after posting top-three finishes in fifteen separate marathons. He goes on to say 'upon hearing this, I briefly considered inviting (Amy) to finish out the (50 marathons in 50 days, the marathon with Amy being his 10th) Endurance 50 with me. Possibly to carry me, if need be.' After Amy finished her pacing duties with Dean, she went to work. 'After all,' as Karnazes says, 'it was Tuesday.'

That is to be expected from a person who says that out of all the races in the world, the one she would most like to run is 'the one I'm signed up for next week.' And with Amy, the next marathon is usually exactly that: *next week!* If life's little irritants—obligations and finances--weren't an issue, she would run 52 marathons a year. At least. When asked which race she would never run again and why, she asked if it was a trick question, because there *wasn't* one she would not want to run again.

In November of 2008, Amy ran the New York City Marathon wearing a Red Sox shirt and hat while carrying 'Wally,' the Red Sox mascot. She's been a proud member of the Red Sox Nation for over four decades. She predicted that her attire would present 'a real possibility to inspire some very fast running, especially in certain parts of the city.' Indeed, the plan worked and she ran a 3:29 while discovering 'The Nation' is very much alive and supportive in all five boroughs of New York City.

When Amy is not busy running her 50 miles a week, she enjoys reading contemporary fiction, doing crossword puzzles, and playing with her cats Spencer and Kate and her dog Frank. And then there's her vocation as a public defender. She says that running is an excellent balance to the demands of her workday. Being able to get out and run over the lunch hour gives her a chance to reflect, regroup, and recharge. Given that Lady Justice holding the scales is the symbol of her profession, it is only natural that balance is an integral factor in Amy's life. Perhaps that helps explain why she also follows her beloved Red Sox in any manner possible, whether it be via the *Boston Globe* online, XM radio or any other forum or outlet she can get her hands on. After all, she's been their number one fan for over 40 years.

Amy's short term running goals are to continue having fun and staying healthy, and in that same vein, her long term goals are for the running to never end and for it to remain 'fun.'

With Amy, how could it not be?

LAST THINGS

By Amy Yanni

Last things, last times. Some life events are marked by observances so that you remember them as being 'the last.' You may recall your last day in high school or the last Christmas your kids believed in Santa. Perhaps you've given up a bad habit but still vividly recall your last cigarette, double scotch, trifecta bet or banana split.

There are so many other things or occurrences we enjoy for the last time without the knowledge that indeed, this is the last. When was the last time you spent a summer afternoon lying in the grass looking up at the clouds or the last time you swung on a swing? The last firefly or butterfly you caught in a jar and tried to keep alive?

One of my favorite pieces on running, *I Remember Running*, was written by Darcy Wakefield. At 33, Darcy was diagnosed with ALS ('Lou Gehrig's disease'), a fatal condition. Before long, she was unable to run. After recounting some of the places and times she had especially appreciated running in her life, she went on to describe herself as 'continuously mourning running.' Reflecting back, she tells us she wished she had known those were her last runs because 'I would have appreciated every hill, every post-run high, every minute my legs moved in that way we call running.'

Even for those of us who love running, there are days when we head out for our regular jaunt with more of a sense of obligation than joy. Sometimes it is because the weather threatens, or maybe we'd rather knock off and stay in bed, or accept that invitation to lunch with office colleagues. Sometimes it is because following a training schedule can become tedious or confining ('but I don't want to do speed work today!'). Still, anyone with a 'runner's soul,' as Darcy Wakefield portrayed herself, will soon miss running if prevented from doing it for too very long.

A good run can provide you private space for pondering a work-related issue or a personal dilemma. You think about things a little differently when your body is in motion and you are taking in the features of the season: warm summer breeze, crisp fall air, sparkling winter sun on white snow, the greens of spring, and the waters of March. At other times, it's pleasant to create an escape and listen to music or a book as you put in the miles.

For those of you reading this that do not run, take a moment here and try to remember the last time you ran. I don't mean running to catch a bus or plane, or running after your child or dog that got away from you. I mean running the way you see children run in an open field. Not running for a purpose, but just running for running's sake. Running because it felt good… because walking wasn't enough…because it made you happy just to be running.

Now that you remember that last time, just think: it doesn't have to remain the last time. It is *so* much easier than you might imagine to start running regularly again. How will you know whether or not you have a runner's soul if you don't at least try running for fun? (*Being a lawyer, I am duty-bound at this junction to interrupt myself and put in the necessary caveat here about consulting a doctor before you take up any exercise program. But you knew that, didn't you?*)

Two of the beauties of running are that you need not invest a lot of money in equipment and you can start a running program by stepping right outside your door. Before you take that step, however, you do need to spend *some* money. This is not the time to do what I did years ago, which was to start running in my Tretorns. These were fantastic shoes for playing tennis but all wrong for running. Your running shoe selection needs to be based upon the size of your arch, the way your foot lands when you run, and your size. Do not buy your shoes at a discount mart and do *not* buy them by color! Running in cheap or ill-fitting shoes is an invitation to injury.

Once you have your shoes, you need a place to run. We are blessed with the bike paths near my home in Rapid City. If you cannot think of where to start, ask around—there's certain to be a suitable spot in your area. I love the rose garden near the Berlin Wall memorial, and so appreciate the flowers and herb garden by the sundial. There are mile markers built into the pavement for your convenience if you run by distance. The other way to run is by time; then of course, you just need a watch. Running near your home is an option; just use the odometer in your car (or perhaps on your bicycle) to measure out a route. For a beginner's plan, a three-mile loop (or 1.5 mile out-and-back) would be sufficient.

To minimize the possibility of injury, you should follow a plan of some sort. 'Hey! Wait a minute,' you're thinking, 'what about all that joy of running? A plan sounds like work, or a diet.' No, that's not the kind of plan I mean. Think of it as a guideline. If you can walk two or three miles at a stretch currently, a plan will help you to reach a level of running three miles in about 8 to 10 weeks. Really.

A good plan should start with alternating jogging and walking, at least at first. It should have you taking periodic rest days. At a minimum, you need to devote 20-30 minutes a day on no less than three days a week. You'll want to alternate an active day with a rest day. If that seems too light, by all means, cross-train on some of the alternate days; e.g., bike, swim, walk—or participate in any other low impact activity.

There you have it; all you need to start running again. While I know that some run in my future will be my last, I am hoping it is in the far distant future. In the interim, I try to remember to appreciate each day I am able to run; I know that running makes my life more balanced and joyous. It could add an extra dimension to yours.

After she could no longer run, Darcy Wakefield goes down to the beach near her home one night, takes off her shoes, and starts moving along the cold sand in circles. She relates that if you had seen her, you wouldn't have called what she was doing running, but it was good enough for her. She confides that this is what she thought that night as she gave thanks: 'We are so lucky to be able to do this, all of our nerves and muscles working together as we move ourselves forward to do this thing we call running.'

ARE YOU RUNNING WITH ME?

By Amy Yanni

Are You Running with Me, Jesus? is not a running book, but you might want to read it anyway. This slim volume of prayers influenced many of us when it was first published in 1968. In it, Reverend Malcolm Boyd carries on a seemingly one-on-one conversation with God in everyday language. He talks about justice, freedom, and the pressures of contemporary life in a frank and honest manner.

The title prayer begins: *'It's morning, Jesus. It's morning, and here's that sound and light all over again. 'I've got to move fast...get into the bathroom, wash up, grab a bite to eat, and run some more.'* Boyd goes on to explain he doesn't feel like it, and wants to go back to sleep. Then he asks: *'Where am I running? You know these things I don't understand. Its not that I need to have you tell me. What counts most is just that somebody knows, and it's you. That helps a lot.'*

'So I'll follow along, OK?' he concludes, praying, *'But lead, please. Now I've got to run. Are you running with me, Jesus?'* While I was in my teens when I read this, I think of it often. Not surprisingly, it comes to mind during many of my long runs.

I like to think of Jesus as a runner. I imagine that some of the more conversational prayers he had with God might have happened when he was running. After a day of listening to peoples' cares and worries all day, of teaching and addressing crowds of followers and being patient with skeptics, slipping away for a solitary run would have been a tremendous relief for a young, active man.

Or perhaps he was a morning runner, rising early to carve out a bit of time for himself. Running as the sun rose, clearing his head for the days work, sorting out how best to address the problems and issues ahead. Talking with God for guidance and for all the reasons we seek out a parent—for comfort, joy, and just to know they are there, caring for us.

At the risk of being labeled a heretic, I confess I feel closer to God at times when I am out running than I ever have in a church. Meditation is enhanced when you fall into the good rhythm of a run outside, experiencing weather on your face, feeling your heart beating and, if you're lucky enough, having some birdsong in the background. Perhaps it is because I read Reverend Boyd's book at a young and impressionable age, but I sometimes think of Jesus as my running partner. As I contemplate things I would discuss with him, I often find insights that I would not have come to on my own. Even when I do not, I feel more able to cope and a better sense of perspective.

More than a century before Reverend Boyd published his book, our revered American Transcendentalist, Henry David Thoreau, wrote about walking alone in woods or fields. Even on a cold, bleak day, when others would be thinking of a warm spot indoors, he found *'I come to myself, I once more feel myself grandly related, and that cold and solitude are friends of mine. I suppose that this value, in my case, is equivalent to what others get by churchgoing and prayer. I come home to my solitary woodland walk as the homesick go home.'*

Whether you are running or walking this weekend, I hope you find something spiritual or meaningful along the path you follow.

RUNNING WITH DEAN

By Amy Yanni

I consider myself an advanced runner and I primarily run for hobby. Dean Karnazes chose the Deadwood Mickelson Trail Marathon course for the 10th run of his Endurance 50 tour (50 marathons in 50 days in 50 states) during the fall of 2006. Since it was early on in his quest and fell on a weekday, there weren't a lot of people signed up to run with him. I had only run the half-marathon at Deadwood, and saw this as a great opportunity to do the entire 26.2. (I was running a lot of marathons in 2006 and was ready to go.)

I don't follow a specific training program when preparing for races. I just run marathons on a regular basis, so I'm pretty much *always* ready to go. As a member of the Marathon Maniacs, I was intent on earning the highest level of 'achievement,' which is ten stars. To do that, I needed to run at least 30 marathons in 30 different states in one calendar year. I'd already run South Dakota in 2006, but not Deadwood, so it was a great experience.

In terms of marathoning advice, I've heard people say you can't run more than four marathons in a year without hurting yourself. Obviously this is something I don't agree with based upon the fact I ran 36 marathons in 2006 and all but two were Boston Qualifiers for me.

The 2006 Deadwood Mickelson Trail Marathon was better than expected. We showed Dean many of the things that make South Dakota special: a gorgeous setting in the hills, a challenging course (yet on a rails-to-trails course, so gentle on the bones), enthusiastic, a talented race director, lots of wildlife and the serenity of a setting without the madding crowds.

I've never run a marathon where I've gotten such fantastic individual attention--when there are only two of you, there are no porta-potty lines and the water stops are total replenishment stations (Dean eats a lot along the way. Even so, it doesn't make his butt look big). In fact, the organization was tremendous--from his people, and from Jerry Dunn, the race director of the Deadwood Mickelson Trail Marathon, who ran with us at several points. We had mile markers, crowd support, porta-potties and unique finisher medals made from Black Hills alabaster. We also had Jerry's remarkable wife Elaine, who brought along a bevy of 8th grade girls to offer crowd support (for all of us) and swoons for Dean ('is he a model?' one asked Elaine).

Maybe this won't seem like much to non-runners reading this, but my experience was that of running a regular marathon (albeit with lots more individual attention--I ragged on Dean a bit, telling him he's going to get spoiled) with all the ups and very few of the downs. I run a lot of smaller marathons, where after the initial miles the crowd thins out and I'm left running solo or, on a good day with a person or two who'll talk as we tool along. Dean and I just chatted the way you do in any marathon. Our conversation ranged from shoes (of course) to courses we've run to raising kids. (Yes, we also touched on the obligatory runner gastro-intestinal issues topic.) This was my 24th marathon of the year, and I offer this observation as real praise. When I find good company to pass the time with in a marathon, then it's a special race.

I left soon after we finished (for work--I had a hearing at 3 p.m.) feeling great that I'd finally run the Deadwood Marathon while in the company of a fellow runner who appreciates and shares the lure of taking to the trail or road and just covering the distance. The first 13 miles of the course are uphill at altitude, so instead of running Deadwood I've headed out to Casper the past two years, feeling really guilty for doing so.

So while my experience was not on the actual day of the marathon, the course remains as beautiful as it was when I was on it. Jerry was Jerry, which means the attention to runners and the details that matter most are all there. Then there was the chance to run in God's country with some of the friendliest, warmest people around. What more could you ask for?

I also ran the race slower than usual--my times in 2006 averaged 3:30 with several in the 3:20s (then there *was* the five hour trail marathon in the Rockies). The Mickelson Trail is a lovely 'tame trail' I recommend, and I am so NOT a trail runner!

Amy is a member of Marathon Maniacs and was named the Outstanding Female Marathoner of the Year in 2006. In 2006 Amy ran 36 marathons with 15 top three finishes. Amy ran this particular marathon with Dean Karnazes during the North Face Endurance 50.

Chapter Three
Bobbi Gibb

A friend of mine suggested to me that a lady he knew might serve as a nice addition to the book I was writing about my personal heroes. He explained that this lady he knew, Bobbi Gibb, was someone very unique and had that 'something special' he just couldn't put his finger on.

Although I've never met her in person, I'm proud to say that I've known Bobbi Gibb for just over a year now. We've communicated frequently during that time—primarily about her contributions to this book but just as importantly about her passion for running, and I can whole-heartedly support my friend's contention that she indeed does have that 'something special' that I just can't put my finger on.

Once you've met Bobbi Gibb through these pages you'll understand exactly what I'm talking about…but you won't be able to put your finger on it. But you will most definitely *experience* it.

Bobbi's sculpture, 'Marathon Man' personifies the triumph of the human spirit. It is with her gracious permission that it serves as the cover of this book.

Bobbi Gibb 2008

THE FIRST LADY OF HOPKINTON

I spoke with Bobbi-Lou (as she was known growing up) for the first time on May 25, 2008. We had been introduced by a mutual friend several days earlier in a 21st-century-kind-of-way: E-mail. Our first conversation was more 20th-century as we communicated by more conventional methods: over the telephone. I'm glad we opted for the give-and-take of an actual conversation, because I would have hated it if Bobbi-Lou's enthusiasm and love for the sport of running had been lost in translation had I simply read her written words. Her motivation is simple: *'I just love to run'*—no truer words were ever spoken. When she told me that in her world 'running is a spiritual experience,' the sincerity and enthusiasm in her voice during our 90-minute conversation made me realize that Bobbi-Lou has the purest love for the sport of anyone I have ever met.

Most of you know Bobbi-Lou as Roberta Louise Gibb, recognized by the Boston Athletic Association (BAA) as the first woman to complete the Boston marathon. Bobbi, the name most of us know her by, accomplished this feat in 1966—six years before women were officially allowed to enter the most prestigious marathon in the world. Prior to 1972 it was common knowledge that 'women were physiologically unable to run distances greater than 1 ½ miles.' However, Bobbi's training runs—which would have been legendary had they been known—quite frequently were of distances between 30 and 40 miles. She knew in her heart that she had what it took to complete the Boston Marathon, a race she first watched and 'fell in love with' in 1964.

The Long Road to Hopkinton

Bobbi knew the instant she watched her first Boston Marathon that one day she wanted to traverse the 26.2 mile route from Hopkinton to Boston. She trained fiercely for two years, running through the fields and mountains of America with an assortment of neighborhood dogs who served as her friends and protectors during her long hours on the trails. In the mid-1960's there were no women's running shoes, so she opted to run in nurses' shoes. There were also no training books on running, so everything Bobbi learned was through first-hand experience.

Bobbi discovered a fondness for long training runs. Many days she and her boyfriend would go on motorcycle rides, and on the way home Bobbi would ask to be dropped off along the way so she could run home. She traveled across the country in 1964 and used the experience to complete long training runs (with Moot, a white malamute) in various cities along the way.

When she arrived on the west coast, she still did not realize *how* long her runs were until meeting a local running hero. Bill Gookin noticed Bobbi's running prowess and asked about her routes; he quickly calculated that she was regularly covering distances of 25 miles or more. But Bobbi was not concerned with distance; after all, she just loved to run.

In 1965 Bobbi considered running Boston, but injuries to both her ankles postponed her hopes for another year. She attended Tufts University during the day and worked as a nanny at night, all the while maintaining her training regimen for the day when she would finally make her initial appearance in Hopkinton. In the fall of 1965 she traveled to Vermont to watch a 100-mile equestrian event. Wanting to make the best use of her time, she decided to run alongside the horses the first day of the event, covering 40 miles over rough terrain. As she entered the town of Woodstock, a spectator gave her a carrot, the same thing given to the horses. While it may have been given in a humorous vein, it was also given out of respect for what Bobbi had done: run 40 miles on a difficult course in a single day. The next day she ran another 25 miles.

Bobbi married the gentleman who introduced her to cross-country running at Tufts University in January of 1966 and they moved to San Diego, California. Three months later she would return to her home state of Massachusetts to fulfill an appointment with history.

At Long Last

Early in 1966, Bobbi wrote to Will Cloney of the Boston Athletic Association (BAA) for an application to April's Boston Marathon. Her request resulted in more than a rejection: the now-famous response from Cloney detailed women's physiological running limitations.

Officially Bobbi was refused entry as it was thought that women were not capable of running more than a mile and a half, and therefore were not allowed to do so under AAU rules due to safety concerns. Bobbi realized this made her quest even more important as she wanted to demonstrate that a woman could run marathon distances. She felt that once everyone knew the truth, the rules could be changed and the Boston Marathon would allow women to enter. However, she was facing a Catch-22: how could she prove something she was not allowed to do?

Undeterred, Bobbi took a three-day Greyhound bus ride back to Boston. Once she arrived in town, she called her parents and told them of her plans to run the marathon. They both thought she was nuts; in fact, her dad thought she may very well kill herself running.

On Patriot's Day (the traditional day for the running of the Boston Marathon) Bobbi's dad left the house to preside over a sail boat race. Once he left the house, Bobbi asked her mom to drive her to Hopkinton. By giving Bobbi a ride her mom also left her mark in history.

Bobbi was attired in a black bathing suit tank top, boy's size six running shoes, her brother's Bermuda shorts, and a blue hooded sweatshirt which she wore with the hood up to hide her long hair. The hood also covered something else: her femininity.

Bobbi arrived in Hopkinton two hours before the start of the race. Feeling a bit anxious—or was it *impatient?*—she opted to run several miles behind a row of houses before the marathon started. She then hid in the bushes to await her appointment with destiny. Once the race began, Bobbi slipped into the race somewhere near the middle of the pack. After running alongside several men for three minutes, one of the men turned to her and asked no one in particular, 'Is that a girl?'

Once Bobbi made her gender known, she feared that they would force her out of the race. She even thought that she may end up in jail. After all, women were prohibited from entering this prestigious 'men only' event.

Fortunately just the opposite occurred. The men thought running alongside this brave and endearing woman was great. And not a minute too soon, as the hood was making her really hot. She now felt more comfortable letting her guard down, especially since the men reassured her that they wouldn't let anything happen to her.

During the course of the race, word spread that there was a woman competing in the field. The crowd began supporting her. Radio broadcasts were fascinated with the developing story that a woman was not only *running* in the Boston Marathon but might actually *complete* it. History was being made, and it was evident that Bobbi had captured the imagination of an entire city.

Bobbi maintained a sub-three hour pace for most of the race, but the ill-fated and ill-fitting running shoes were taking a horrible toll on her feet. She was also becoming dehydrated as she had not been drinking fluids along the course. In 1966 it was a popular misconception that drinking water during long-distance events caused cramps. While her pace slowed in the latter miles of the race, she found herself becoming increasingly afraid of failing. Bobbi *had* to succeed, or face the possibility of personally setting women back decades.

Bobbi crossed the finish line three hours and 21 minutes after she darted out from behind the bushes in Hopkinton. She made history and provided scientific support that the so-called 'weaker sex' could indeed run farther than

1 ½ miles. A lot farther, in fact. She even beat more than half the men in the field!

While Bobbi's performance had captured the imagination of the city (and later the entire world), that was not the case with the officials of the marathon. Bobbi was denied the traditional finishers' beef stew. She was not awarded a medal. After all, she was still a woman. And women didn't have a place in this prestigious 'men only' event.

Bobbi took a taxi home to Winchester, only to discover that the streets were full of cars. She figured that many of the neighbors were having Patriot's Day parties. She was wrong. The cars were there to celebrate an historic event: *little Bobbi-Lou had just finished the Boston Marathon.*

The next day her accomplishment made front page headlines throughout Boston and the neighboring towns. One newspaper, in an effort to portray Bobbi as feminine (even though she could run a 'masculine' 26.2 miles), took pictures of her in a dress making fudge in her parents' kitchen. The next day, most of the local papers featured Bobbi's accomplishment on the front page. *Sports Illustrated* did a story on her. *Sports Illustrated!!!*

She'll Always be the First

Bobbi ran the Boston Marathon again in 1967 and 1968. During this pre-sanctioned era, Bobbi was the first woman finisher on both occasions, extending her unofficial winning streak to three years. In 1967, she finished in front of Kathrine Switzer by over an hour. In 1968, Bobbi finished in front of the four other women in the race.

In her autobiography Switzer promotes herself as the first woman to officially enter and run in the Boston Marathon, one year after Bobbi's Hopkinton debut. Bobbi questions the 'official' status of this endeavor since Switzer failed one of the primary qualifications to be an official Boston Marathon entry: she was not a man. Although some deception merited Switzer a race number, Switzer, like Bobbi Lou was a very 'unofficial' participant in this legendary race. (An historical footnote: There were no official women entrants in the Boston Marathon until 1972 when the BAA created a women's division race.)

The reason Switzer has received even more attention is that by being an unqualified entrant and running with an invalid number she posed serious accreditation issues to the Boston Marathon. Her 'official' participation threatened to invalidate the finishing times of the qualified male entrants. This was the primary motivation for Jock Semple, a man whom Bobbi describes as 'a great man who doesn't deserve to be misrepresented' when he made his infamous attempt to physically remove Switzer's number during the race.

But for the sake of historical accuracy, Roberta Louise Gibb will always be 'The First.'

Immortality

It took 30 years for the Boston Marathon to recognize Bobbi's accomplishment. In 1996 Bobbi was officially recognized by the Boston Athletic Association as the winner of the Boston Marathon three straight years in what is now called 'the pre-sanctioned era.' To commemorate this accomplishment the BAA presented her with a medal emblazoned with those three memorable years: 1966, 1967 and 1968.

As importantly, Bobbi Gibb's name has been permanently engraved on the Boston Marathon memorial in Copley Square, an enduring tribute to the First Lady of Hopkinton.

Lasting Impression

In the short time I have known her I have found Bobbi to be a woman who is not only generous with her time, but generous in bearing her soul as well. To hear her speak—for an hour, for a minute, *for just a few seconds*—is to hear the words of someone who absolutely cherishes the freedom to run through the fields and mountains in the company of her four-legged companions. She epitomizes—truly—the spirit of running.

Roberta Louise Gibb was the first woman to finish the Boston Marathon. There will never be another like her, and I am proud to have this opportunity to tell her story…to pass on a piece of history that bears telling time after time.

I Love to Run

By Bobbi Gibb

I love to run.

I love the sensation of wind on my face. I love the way the world whirls by picking up the rhythm of my body running. I love knowing that my own body is naturally at one with the earth. I love the sensation of breathing in and out and knowing that the same air which I breathe surrounds the globe and brings life to every living creature. I love watching the patterns in the road beneath my feet and seeing the sky arching above.

Running centers me and brings me back to basics. Running is the way I express my joy at being alive and the way I celebrate the mystery of the source of all being. Running relieves all the stresses of the day, relaxes and energizes me. I love the sense of freedom and independence that running cross-country long distance gives me. I love glorying in the beauty of all creation.

Running returns me to some deep human potential, some irreducible wildness, which is as primal as birth, and as mysterious as death. Running expresses something fundamentally human and reconnects mind, body and soul into its original unity. Running makes me feel whole. When I share this with others I feel doubly grateful.

In 1964 when I saw the Boston Marathon for the first time I fell in love with it. There is no other way to explain it. Surely there was no rational explanation for the decision that was made inside me, not by my rational mind, but by something much deeper. There was no money in it, no reason for doing it. At that point I had no idea of the stir my run would create. I didn't know that women weren't allowed to run. I just saw a bunch of incredible people who shared my love of running, my vision of what it means to be human, the courage and strength it takes to lead a life of integrity, to keep on putting one foot in front of the other, to be mortal and to embrace the brevity of life along with its gift. To me the Boston Marathon was a celebration of life, a spring ritual and a supreme challenge, all of which I firmly embraced.

At that time I was attending the Tufts School of Special Studies and the Boston Museum of Fine Arts School. I loved to run through the woods with the neighborhood dogs. I found something there in the peace of my woodland retreat, something that was being lost from modern civilization, some reconnection with an ancient potential, a mystery and wonder, and a sense of the incomprehensible love out of which all existence flows. All I saw was unimaginably beautiful to me, from the infinite cosmos stretching away into the evening sky to the tiniest detail of the smallest speck of dust shimmering in the sun.

In the summer of 1964, following that sense of wonder I journeyed across the entire continent in a VW microbus with my malamute puppy, Moot. During the days I ran; each day in a different place all across this amazing country, and at night I slept out under the stars. This is the way I trained for the Boston Marathon. I had no coach and no books on running, no idea how to train. I was wearing nurses' shoes because women's running shoes weren't made then. Hardly anyone ran. As far as I knew the Boston Marathon was the only marathon in the country. Only a few men ran and certainly no women.

Each day I'd run in a new place and at night I'd sleep out under the stars. I loved looking into the night sky out into the infinity of space, the peaceful velvety darkness sprinkled with stars.

The further west I traveled the more amazed I became at this marvelous planet on which we live. It was all new to me. I had never seen it before. At night I looked up and saw more stars than I ever had before. There were more stars than there were dark spaces, and they kept going on and on forever.

By the time I got to Nevada I was strong. I'd see a pale blue mountain peak on the horizon and set out across the broad valley following no road. I'd spend the day running to the top of the mountain and back.

I was in complete awe that all of this exists. Why not just some empty vacuum? Why bother with all this immensity of space and time, and all the glory of creation? Why so big? I felt very close to the creative source of all being, as if it were all around and within me. It is beyond words, so I won't try to describe it. But somehow I felt as though I'd found what I was looking for and it felt like pure love. The experience gave me a perspective on life that I have never lost. The universe is a miracle beyond anything imaginable. Every seemingly ordinary thing is beautiful and every seemingly ordinary person is extraordinary.

Then I went on into California over the Sierra Nevada Mountain Range (where I thought of John Muir, one of my childhood heroes) and into San Francisco. As I drove across the Golden Gate Bridge tears of joy were running down my face: for the first time I saw the western sun sparkling on the vast Pacific, which spread out like a shimmering cauldron of molten gold to the horizon.

I drove up Route One through the Muir Woods, where I felt the mystery and grandeur of the giant redwood trees that had been seedlings a thousand years ago. Finally we got to Stinson Beach, where I ran at full speed down the beach and plunged into the crashing surf. Moot waited for me on shore and then we made camp for the night. She mooched hotdogs from picnickers who joined around our campfire. One of them had a guitar and we sang into the night while stars glittered above and surf thundered on the beach. I felt a sense of freedom and happiness unlike anything I'd ever known. I had fallen in love with the Pacific Ocean and knew that someday I'd come back.

I thought that I would run the 1965 Marathon, but a few weeks before the race I fell and sprained both ankles. Boston would have to wait another year. I continued to train, and in September of 1965 I went to Woodstock, Vermont and ran in the annual hundred mile equestrian event on foot. As I trotted along beside the horses, I'd converse with the riders. The first day I arose at dawn, set out and ran the 40 mile course, up and down mountains on old logging roads, across fields, and along the many hard dirt roads of rural Vermont, finishing around one in the afternoon. The next day I ran 25 miles, but my knees were hurting. I didn't want to risk injuring myself and not being able to run Boston, so I hitchhiked back to the barn. After running 65 miles of the Woodstock Hundred Mile, I figured I was ready for Boston.

In January of 1966 I moved to California and continued to train, running 20 and 25 mile courses along the beaches, across the sagebrush covered valleys, and up the mountains. In those days the country north of San Diego was essentially open pastures, sage and wild lilac. It was like paradise, with exotic palm trees and sandy beaches. I was in love again and very happy.

Finally in February I wrote for my application to get a number. I was dumbfounded when I received a curt reply back from the race director that women were not able to run marathons, and that furthermore they were not allowed to do so. Here it was again, those unbearable constraints, that mind-numbing and body-binding prejudice that kept women down for millennia. I'd seen it eat away my own mother and I vowed that it would not happen to me.

In those days very few options were open to women. If you were a woman you could be a factory worker, a phone operator, a secretary, a nurse, or a schoolteacher, but you were expected to give up any career once you got married. I chafed against this injustice and here it was again telling me that I couldn't be all that I was, that I couldn't do what I most loved, that I couldn't be a whole person, that I was living in a world where I would never get to be all that I could be and never get a chance to fulfill my dreams. Why? Simply because I was a woman.

The thought of giving up my dream felt like dying. I couldn't do that. Whatever was compelling me to run was too deep in my soul to give up. It was something inside that from the outside made no sense and was very far outside the social norms of the day. So I took the Greyhound bus back from San Diego to Boston and arrived the day before the race.

My parents thought I'd gone mad and that somehow I was delusional in thinking that I was going to run the Boston Marathon. My father was very worried that I might actually try it and injure or perhaps kill myself trying. But I convinced my mother that I had to do this to set women free, and that once everyone saw that this false belief was wrong it would throw into doubt every other false belief about women. My mom drove me to Hopkinton and let me out.

My first problem was how to get into the race without being stopped. My biggest fear was that someone would stop me and I would be prevented from proving what I had to prove. I was sure that once everyone knew that women could run the marathon that it would open up to women. And I knew if I could prove this widely held false belief about women was wrong that it would throw into doubt all the other prejudices that had kept women down for so many centuries.

It was a double bind: how can you prove you can do something that you're not allowed to do? I hid in the bushes near the starting pen disguised in my brother's Bermuda shorts and a blue hooded sweatshirt. The crowds were milling around, popcorn and balloon venders were selling their wares. Children were laughing. It was a great celebration. Stiff and tired from three nights on the bus, I warmed up by running for 30 minutes or so out behind some buildings.

When the starting gun fired, I waited until about half the pack left, and then I jumped in. In a matter of minutes I could hear the guys behind me talking and I could feel them studying my anatomy from the rear.

'Is that a girl?' one of them said to the other.

I turned around and smiled.

'It is a girl!' They exclaimed. I knew that they could force me out or call the police or the officials and have me dragged off the course. I was alone and unprotected. I knew that I had to keep it upbeat and inspire people with the love I felt. I wanted to inspire people to find in running the same wonderful sense of freedom and peace that I felt. I wanted to settle the so-called war between the sexes so that men and women could share all of life's challenges and rewards as friends and equals.

To my great relief the men were friendly.

'I wish my girl friend would run,' one of them said.

'I wish my wife would run.'

'Are you going to go the whole way?'

'I hope so,' I replied.

'I'm getting hot in here,' I said, 'but I'm afraid if I take off the sweatshirt, they'll see that I'm a woman and throw me out.'

'We won't let them throw you out,' one of the men said.

'It's a free road,' another said.

So I took off the sweatshirt and its restricting hood and then everyone could see I was a woman. I was apprehensive about the reaction of the crowd. People can sometimes be hostile when one does something far outside the social norm.

One of the spectators cheered and said 'At a go girly!' A woman shrieked. I'm a shy person and here I was in front of thousands of people. Jerry Nason, a newspaper reporter from Winchester (my hometown) and reporters from the *Record American* spotted me and saw a story in the making. I hadn't thought about the media: in fact, I don't think I'd ever even met a reporter. Soon my progress was being broadcast over a radio station.

Alton Chamberlain and I ran along stride for stride for many miles. We were on a sub three hour pace, running easily and talking. I was surprised at how soon we were in Framingham, then on into Natick. As we ran into Wellesley I could hear women screaming up ahead. It sounded like a day at the beach.

'This is the best part,' one of the men confided.

'The tunnel of love.'

I wondered what they were talking about.

Up ahead I could see a tangle of people in the road and hear screaming and laughing.

Many years later the President of Wellesley College, Diana Chapman Walsh wrote a moving article about that event. She said that the women knew I was coming and were scanning face after face looking for me. When I finally came into view they let out a shriek of joy. They knew, she said, that the world would never be the same.

I followed the other runners as they ducked down and passed through a tunnel of women who stood facing one another in two parallel lines, holding their hands high to make a roof. Women were screaming, crying, laughing.

Over to one side a large middle aged women, with several children around her screamed 'Ave Maria! Ave Maria!' As I looked up and met her eyes, I felt a rush of tears. Did she know that in my heart I wanted children and I admired her for undertaking without thought of fame or reward the most important job of all?

On we ran, downhill and crossing the Charles River. I could smell its dank coolness and remembered the times my Dad and I had kayaked together on that river. We pushed up a hill and over a bridge. I could hear fast moving tires whining on pavement and smell exhaust. It seemed strange to be running over route 128 as if we were a primitive tribe lost in time that had somehow ended up running in modern America. We ran along route 16 through Newton. As we turned onto route 30, we began to sense Boston up ahead and I felt excited.

I could hear the men around me muttering about Heartbreak Hill.

'It's a killer,' one of them said. I wondered what they were talking about.

Then the road started to climb. For the first time, instead of slowing myself down to conserve energy I was pushing myself. My breath shortened and I could feel my legs tiring. But I was used to hills.

Finally the road flattened out.

'That wasn't bad,' I thought to myself. 'No where near as steep or as long as Black Mountain.'

But then the road started going up again. I dug in and pushed trying not to lose my pace, but for the first time felt the edge of fatigue beginning to creep in. Ah, finally: the top.

But just as I was relaxing and catching my breath, the road went up again. This time I began to wonder if there was going to be a top, or whether this would just keep happening.

Finally, the *real* top. I felt exuberant. I could see Boston in the distance and could feel the road descending beneath me as we careened down past the spires of Boston College into Brighton, thick with close-packed apartment buildings and thousands of spectators.

The fronts of my legs were hurting and the blisters caused by my new running shoes were rubbing through. As we ran through Brookline we could sense the finish up ahead.

My pace was dropping off. My feet were burning on the bottoms. I wasn't used to running on pavement. The roast beef and apple pie my mom had cooked for last night's dinner, which I'd gobbled down after four days eating only apples and bus station chili, felt like a cannonball in my stomach. Thinking that drinking water while racing would give me cramps I politely refused all the water and orange slices offered along the way. I didn't realize that I was severely dehydrated.

My bleeding feet hurt and throbbed with each step. Up ahead loomed the huge red Citgo sign in Kenmore Square, indicating a mile remained until the finish. I was tiptoeing along as if I were running on broken glass. The last two miles took me longer than the preceding eight. My three hour marathon was left dead on the course; my hopes of winning had long ago died a hero's death. I began to wonder if anyone would still be at the finish by the time I got there. It was here that I learned the true meaning of fortitude, to keep going on even with your hopes dashed, to keep on doing the best you can even though you feel defeated and disappointed.

I turned the corner onto Hereford Street where hundreds of people were hanging out of windows, drinking beer, cheering, and laughing. Then I made the last turn onto Boylston Street and to my astonishment thousands of people cheered as press trucks rolled along beside me. I picked up my pace and crossed the finish line in a time of three hours, twenty-one minutes and forty seconds, ahead of two thirds of the pack. Some kind person threw a wool blanket around my shoulders. My new friend Alton grinned and put his arm around me. The war between the sexes was over: now we could all be friends and share life together in a spirit of mutual respect and love.

The Governor of Massachusetts came down and shook my hand. I felt supremely happy. The press surrounded me and whisked me off to a nearby hotel where they interviewed me. I was as interested in them as they were in me, and wondered how it would be to be a reporter.

Using the money my mother had given me, which I'd pinned to the inside of my bathing suit, I took a taxi home. When I got to Sargent Road, the entire street was filled with cars. I wondered if someone was having a giant party.

Then I realized that the press was at my house.

My poor confused parents were standing in the living room looking absolutely bewildered. The phone was ringing as people called to congratulate them on their daughter. What has she done now? Reporters were scribbling. Photographers took photos of my parents and I grouped around a chair, then one of the reporters asked me if I'd put on a dress. So I donned a polka dotted dress and the photographer took a photo of me and another woman making fudge in the kitchen, which is, after all what women were *supposed* to do.

Unbeknownst to me I was the first woman to ever run the Boston Marathon, and evidently one of the first women to ever run a marathon in the history of the world. For the most part, documentation of the few previous marathons by women was hazy at best and for the most part obscure.

The evening front page headlines read, 'Hub Blonde Runs Marathon.' The next day the front page headlines read, 'Hub Bride First Gal to Run Marathon.' In one article a spokesperson for the Amateur Athletic Union came out in favor of changing the rules so that women could run. *Sports Illustrated* ran an article entitled 'Game Girl in a Man's Game.'

I'd changed forever the way the world thought about women and I hope helped to end the prejudice and to open up the beginning of new opportunities for women and a new consciousness for people everywhere.

I was to run my beloved marathon again in 1967 and 1968.

In 1967 I finished first among two women. The other woman had obtained an illegal number and incurred the wrath of race officials who accused her of subterfuge and tried to remove her from the race. In 1968

I finished first among five women runners. Later, in 1996, on the thirtieth anniversary of my first run the Boston Athletic Association awarded me a medal for my three wins and carved my name with the names of the other winners on the Marathon Memorial in Copley Square.

Over the years I've continued to run, day in and day out. My love for running, for nature and for people is as strong as ever. The last time I ran Boston was in 2001. I ran to help raise money for research on neurodegenerative diseases. I was sick with bronchitis and it was a tough run. By the time Boston was in view, it was cold with a brisk east headwind. Dusk was falling as I turned the corner onto Boylston Street, where 35 years before I'd made history to throngs of cheering spectators.

The stands were empty. Work crews were cleaning up. Just as my friend and I headed down the final stretch, two huge street cleaners started up and accompanied us to the finish. We doubled over with laughter. I glanced up at the dark face of the stopped clock; it stopped a little past six o'clock. I muttered the words, 'The first shall be last and the last shall be first.' What a fitting end this was to my Boston Marathon history.... And then I thought.... well maybe someday I will run this again...

I've learned from running that however humble you are and however limited your finances, you can always put on a pair of shoes and just start running, slowly at first, but eventually you can get anywhere. I've learned that great things are accomplished in small steps and that if you just keep doing it a bit each day it adds up and finally with persistence you succeed. I've learned that you always start from where you are, and that tomorrow is another day. I've learned that you can set goals that seem impossible, but that if you take it a bit at a time you can do most anything.

I've found in running a key to happiness and health that is so simple. I've found a doorway to a sense of the sacred. Everything, every moment, every person is of inestimable worth. Every speck of sand is a diamond sparkling in the sun. Running helps you find and keep a sense of openness and wonder which makes you happy for no reason. You feel full of love for everything. I've learned to linger as well as to race. Lingering allows the present moment to unfold in all its glory and subtle beauty. I've learned that beauty is all around: in patches of drying mud, in people's faces, and in simple things like friendship.

Life is like a marathon. You start rested, eager, and full of energy, restless to go. Although you are all running together, no one can do it for you. Those who cheat are stealing someone else's victory and lying about it. I've learned that in the end the truth will come out, that the truth will heal the human mind. Those who cheat will be found out and discredited. Those who run the straight race are those we admire, those who advance the human spirit.

I've found that love is the only meaningful basis of human endeavor.

As the race proceeds your strength and integrity is tested.

True morality consists in treating others as you would want to be treated. This is a timeless truth. The basis of morality is empathy, being able to stand in the shoes of others. Those who lack this capacity are immoral and require restraint to keep them from harming others in a misinformed effort to advance themselves. All justice is based on fairness, and this yearning for fairness is fundamental to the human spirit. All just societies are based on the principle of fairness. In order to build a successful nation the good of the whole must be linked to the good of each and every person. When we all are working for the good of the whole we are also working for our own highest good. This is the basis of ethics. Without ethics an economy will fail. To create a healthy flourishing society we must create trust, and this can only be done when ethics are enforced and fairness is the norm. Greed is a form of human illness.

The just person is the balanced, healthy person. Running helps to keep us healthy and balanced in mind, body and spirit. Running also keeps us in tune with our mortality. Running brings us back to our oneness with nature from which our lives derive. Staying in tune with the source of our being, which is the source of all being keeps us whole. We are naturally whole, born in unity of mind, body and spirit; this means we are naturally innocent. Only when we depart from our original integrity do we become sick and only when we return to wholeness are we healed. Running helps us to reintegrate mind, body and spirit and to remain whole even in the face of life's disintegrating challenges.

At the end of the race you are tired. You may feel victorious or defeated depending on how you look at it. You realize life's brevity, your own vulnerability and the vulnerability of others, even in the moment of your triumph.

Suddenly the poignancy of endings overtakes you and the friends you have seem evermore precious. Just as in life, you have come together to celebrate and to share, you've done your best, you've run your race, and now it is over. The race is being dismantled, everyone is leaving, and stiffly, you pack up your satchel of belongings and walk away, full of memories, which are now all you have of what once was but is no more. Time races on, leaving all awash in its wake.

And yet there is the anticipation that slowly begins to build of next year's race and the reunion with old friends that it will bring.

Footnote

It should be noted that prior to 1972 when, following a change in the rules governing the Amateur Athletic Association and the Boston Marathon opened its first women's division, no women's race over 800 meters was officially open to women, and there could be no official women entrants in the Boston Marathon.

It was true then as it is true now that a man cannot officially run in a women's division race and a woman cannot officially run in a men's division race. Prior to 1972 there was only a men's division race in Boston so all women running Boston were considered unsanctioned runners running the course unofficially. These years are now referred to as the pre-sanctioned era.

If a woman were to run in a men's division race or vice versa, that would jeopardize the accreditation of the race and would invalidate the official running times of the sanctioned runners. This explains why race officials were enraged when in 1967 a woman obtained an invalid number and why they tried to throw her out of the race. The woman was alleged to have finished an hour behind Bobbi, although there was no official record of her having completed the entire course.

The race officials accused the woman of cheating and subterfuge and pointed out that in order to obtain a number a woman would either have to have a man get a number for her, conceal her gender on the application form and falsify the required medical records and/or have a man take the required physical exam for her, and that any number so obtained would be invalid. This explains why race officials were upset and tried to remove the illegal number from the second place woman finisher in 1967. After that incident all thought of opening the race to women was squelched for another five years.

Through the work of hundreds of men and women, including the Road Runners Club of America, the New York Road Runner's Club, other running organizations, and Congress, which passed Title IX, the AAU rules were finally changed and after the summer of 1971 official marathons for women were organized and sanctioned, so that women could finally officially run as sanctioned runners in races over 800 meters.

Nina Kuscsik was the first official women's winner of the Boston Marathon in 1972. Bobbi, who was beginning law school and starting a family, did not run in 1969, 1970 or 1971. Sara Mae Berman was the unsanctioned women's winner in all three of those years. The Boston Athletic Association ultimately (and officially) recognized Bobbi's three wins and Sara Mae's three wins and the women were given winner's medals for the years they won.

To Boston with Love

The Story of the First Woman to Run the Boston Marathon

by Bobbi Gibb

I ran the Boston Marathon out of love.
I believe that love is the basis
of all meaningful human endeavors.

Running expresses my love of Nature,
my delight in being alive.
Yet it was a love that was incomplete
until it was shared with others.

When I started running,
I knew no other runners, male or female.
I had not heard of the Boston Marathon
and had never seen a track meet.

I ran as a way of reaffirming some
semiconscious ancient bond
between the Earth and
myself as a human animal.

I came to running from a feeling that
something was missing in my secure
suburban existence and in the life plan
the 1950's had in store for me.

At a deeper level, I sought to come
to terms with my own mortality,
with the relationship between mind or
soul and body or the physical.

I was groping for a synthesis
in my life and found comfort in running
long-distance through field, forest and city.

I was looking for the bare reality of things,
people, and the world.

That comprehension
excited and awed me.

My running companions were my dog
and her canine friends.
I found peace in the solitude and
exquisite perfection of Nature.

As a student at Tufts University
School of Special Studies and the
School of the Museum of Fine Arts, Boston,
I met a man who ran cross-country.

'Five miles!' I exclaimed in disbelief
when he told me how long the meet was.

But within six months
I was trotting right along
as he ran five, six, ten miles.

I seemed to have a knack for it
and a lot of stamina.

'Twenty-six miles!'
I gasped when the father
of a friend told me about
the Boston Marathon in 1964.

'Sure. Why don't you go out
and watch it since you like running
so much,' he suggested.

At that time I was commuting
eight miles from Winchester to
Boston, running, every day.

So I went, and I saw people running.
They looked like wonderful people,
like some kind of exotic animal running
so strongly, quietly, patiently.

I knew they felt the same bond as I felt

with some ancient human potential
all but lost in modern society.
I recognized a kindredness
with these runners and some
internal decision was made to run
with them in a mutual expression of
our belief in what it means to be human.
I started to train but had no coach,
no notion of how to train, no encouragement,
no role models. So I just kept running farther
and farther, curious to see
how far I could go and how fast.

Some days I could fly like a bird,
other days I felt tired and discouraged.

My friend and I explored the
architectural wonders of Boston,
New York, and New Haven together.
We ran out along the railroad tracks,
across frozen lakes. He would take me into
the country and drop me off to run home.
That summer I took my dog and VW bus
across the continent to California and back,
running every day in a new place.

The hills of Pennsylvania and West Virginia,
the lush forests of Indiana,
the plains of Kansas and Nebraska,
the streets of Denver,
the high meadows of the Rockies,
the Sierras and the Coastal Mountains
of California all became my friends.

Miles and miles of nameless trails
I ran, and at night
I slept under the stars.

The next April, 1965,
I stood almost in tears
watching the Marathon
with two sprained ankles.

It would be another year before I ran.
That autumn, still training,
I ran sixty-five miles of the
Woodstock Vermont hundred-mile
equestrian event, in which the horses
run 40 miles the first day,
40 miles the second day and
20 miles the third day.

The first day I arose at dawn
and set off with the first horses.
All day we ran over rugged terrain,
dirt roads, mountain trails.

The horses and riders passed me
and at lunchtime they stopped
and I passed them.
The riders were friendly.
Often we would converse as
I trotted along beside their horses.
We finished around 1:00 p.m.

The next day I set off again at dawn
and ran 25 miles before my knees started hurting.
Many years later
I was to discover that running on my toes,
as I did, strained my knees.

A good coach is invaluable to a runner.

I hitchhiked back to the barn with a trucker
who accepted my 'eccentric' passion for running
with the usual Yankee understatement.
'Better luck next year,' he smiled
as he dropped me off,
as if running 40 miles in one day
and 65 miles in two days
over rough terrain, old logging roads
and incredible hills was some kind of failure.

Finally, in February 1966,
I wrote for my application

for the Boston Marathon
from California, where I had moved.

I received a curt reply that women
were not physiologically able to run
such distances and, furthermore,
were not allowed to do so.

I was stunned.
I'd heard that the Marathon
was open to every person in the world.
It had never crossed my mind
to consider myself different from the other runners.

My outrage turned to humor
as I thought how many preconceived
prejudices would crumble
when I trotted right along for 26 miles.

I knew nothing of the formal world of athletics.
No doubt people of the time,
both men and women, simply didn't know.
Women in sports were not allowed to run
more than one and a half miles.
Women not in sports
would have little reason to do so.

My running of the Marathon
thus became a feminist statement.
I believed that once people knew women
could run marathon distances,
the field would naturally open up.
I even dreamed of running
an Olympic marathon.

Boston is my home
and the Boston Marathon has
a special significance to me.

I'll never forget my first run in 1966:
popcorn vendors, balloons,
kids, crowds of people!

Still tired from riding the bus
four days and three nights
from California to Boston,
I had disguised myself in a blue
hooded sweatshirt and was wearing
new boys' size six running shoes.

The look on my mother's face
as she dropped me off in Hopkinton
reflected pride and concern, a combination of
'I know you can do it' and
'will you be all right?'

The other runners were clustered
in the starting pen.
I was crouched in the bushes.
'Bang!' the starting gun fired.
I stumbled from the bushes
into the midst of the runners
wondering how many other women
writers, artists, scientists, and soldiers
had had to disguise
their femininity; so well that history
has still not discovered.

I have since come to see
how history can be distorted
merely by repetition of a non-truth
by a person or group
with a financial or egotistical
reason for doing so, or simply
through carelessness.

My heart was beating double time
as I began to realize the implications
of what I was attempting.
I tend to be shy,
and here I was in front of
thousands of people. A pang of loneliness
shot through my gut.

After a few minutes,
I noticed a studious silence
behind me, and murmurs.

'Is that a girl?'
'Hmmm.'
'It is a girl!'

I turned and smiled over my shoulder.

They laughed and so did I.

'Hey, fantastic!' they said.

'Are you going to run the whole way?'
they asked.
'I hope so,' I replied.

'That's great! I wish more women ran.'

'I wish my wife would run,' one man said wistfully.

I felt these men were my brothers.
I could see how much they wanted to share
their passion for running with
the women in their lives.
As I warmed up, I began to want
to take off my sweatshirt
and its constricting hood.

'Go ahead,' the tall man
from Connecticut said.

'I'm afraid if they know I'm a woman
they will throw me out,' I confessed.

'We won't let them throw you out,' one said.

'It's a free road,' said another.

As soon as the crowds saw I was a woman
there was a great commotion.

People yelled and cheered, calling
out to me, wishing me good luck.

I wanted to respond, to say 'Thank you,'
and to smile and wave back.

'How rude to run right by,' I thought.

Mr. Chamberlain, the tall man
from Connecticut, ran stride
for stride with me for many miles.

We chatted on and off.
His presence gave me comfort.

My dream was that men and women
could run together and share the consciousness
of the common bond of humanity
based on a mutual commitment and
sharing of what they love in life.

Hatred, war between the sexes,
exhausts both and leads to nothing.

We were churning off each
mile in a little less than
seven minutes.
As we passed Wellesley College,
women waved and shouted in exultation.
I felt as though I was setting these women free.

I was touched that my running
meant so much to them.

One woman, with several children
clinging to her ample coat,
called ecstatically, 'Ave Maria, Ave Maria!'
I felt a surge of tears come
to my eyes at the contact.

Did she know that in my heart
I wanted children; that I respected her

for her devotion, patience and her strength?
She had undertaken,
without thought of fame or reward,
the most difficult,
most important human endeavor of all.

Twenty miles and I felt splendid.
I was conserving my energy now,
aware that if I failed to finish
I would end up disproving exactly
what I had set out to prove
and would support rather than demolish
the then-current prejudices and
preconceptions about women.

So I didn't push
but ran comfortably
until the bottoms of my feet
began to burn.

I wasn't used to running on pavement
and my new shoes hurt.
Each step sent a searing jolt of pain to my brain.
I do not like pain one bit.
My pace dropped off.
I set each foot down as if on tacks.

'Only six miles to go,'
I had thought smugly as I breezed along.
'Six miles is nothing.
I can run six miles in my sleep.'
But the Marathon is not a place for smugness.
Respect for that distance and
for the human body that runs it
is essential.

My respect returned
as my pace dropped.
The last two miles
seemed interminable.

I began to feel like a failure.

And this is where I learned
the real meaning of fortitude,
to keep on in the face of disappointment,
to continue to do your best
even when others are passing you.
To see your hopes crushed and yet to continue.
This is why I have as much respect
for those who run and do not finish first
as I have for the ones whose strength,
endurance and training brings them first place.

At last I turned the corner
and there was the finish line.

Newspaper reporters and TV cameras
crowded into the streets.

The crowd was wild.

I had finished 126th out of about
five hundred entrants in three hours,
twenty-one minutes and forty seconds.

Bus loads of runners
who had dropped out of the race
passed waving, cheering, laughing.

I loved that crowd.

I loved my fellow runners.

I was supremely happy.

The Governor of Massachusetts
himself appeared
to shake my hand.
I was honored.
The feeling that emerged
from the crowd was that I was special
not just because I had run the Marathon,
but because I was a woman.

I don't think of myself as special,
or rather, I think everyone is special
in his or her unique way.

What I wanted was not
the acclaim for myself,
for I would rather have
love, peace, good health,
outlets for my creativity,
and children.

What I want and wanted
is a better world for all.
A better world begins with
individual integrity.

As I turned to follow the other runners
to the traditional post-marathon stew,
the doors were shut.

I walked across the damp,
cold parking garage alone.

That old lump came to my throat again.
I knew there was more to be done
to break down the subtle barriers
of which I had so recently become aware,
to restore harmony and end ignorance and fear.

Yet I had opened the door
to a world of possibilities and
had brought attention to running as a way of life.

The time was ripe.
Once the idea was made public,
other women began to filter in.
More and more women every year
until six years later, in 1972,
even the officials recognized women as 'official.'
I was to run two more years,
1967 and 1968,
my beloved Boston Marathon.

I sought the quiet places I'd left,
the mountain trails, the vast blue sky,
the nameless clouds,
forests, deserts and beaches.

I returned to reestablish
my bond with Nature,
with the Source of all Being.

Once again running
became a way to express joy.

I am glad those who followed me
have opened up competitive running to women.
I am even more pleased that people,
men and women, everywhere are
finding what they truly love in life.

Especially I appreciate the people
who quietly and privately
go about their lives and running
without the thought or possibility
of winning marathons,
but whose balance, courage, and
perseverance is heroic,
perhaps more so
for being unnoticed and unacclaimed.

People, ordinary people,
are extraordinary,
whether given credit or not.

Is the mountain flower
less beautiful
because it blooms unnoticed?
I think not.

Postscript

This poem is dedicated to the people of the

Boston Athletic Association, who have become
my second family.
Forty-two years later I am thankful that I continue to run.
I am constantly delighted
by meeting extraordinary and wonderful people, many of whom also celebrate
life by running.

Bobbi Gibb 1966

Chapter Four

Susan Lance

I've known Susan Lance almost six years.

Conservatively I've run 5,000 miles with her. Conservatively.

It seems odd using the word 'conservative' when talking about Susan, because when it comes to running, Susan is anything *but*.

I've seen the rise of many-a-runner over the past 30 years, but I have never seen one as dramatic—or *quick* as the one I've seen in Susan.

In the spring of 2004 Susan ran the farthest distance of her life: 41.2 miles. Six months later Susan was about to start a 24-hour run when a fellow runner asked her about her goal for the event. She replied that she would like to run 100 miles. The other runner (who knew her previous best was 41.2 miles) suggested she set her sights on a more realistic 50 miles.

Susan went on to run 50 miles that day. Not once, but twice...and then some. She finished with 107.4 miles and placed 5th among a deep and talented field of veteran women distance runners.

The defining characteristic in Susan the runner is her determination. Once she sets her sights on a goal, she'll do everything in her power to achieve it.

Don't dare suggest she settle for less.

Susan Lance

GOOD THING, SMALL PACKAGE

My good friend and running partner Al Barker is a volunteer coach for the Atlanta Track Club. Al has had many clients over the years, but none have been what you would call 'success stories.' Many corresponded with Al over the phone or via E-mail, but failed to show up for their scheduled initial run with him. For those who show up for their initial run, well…they didn't fare so well either. One runner with a goal of running a half marathon completed a six-mile run with Al, only to fade into oblivion--never to be heard from again. Another of Al's clients, after training with him for several months, entered his first 10K, only to be taken away by ambulance when he collapsed at the three-mile mark. That was the moment when I jokingly began referring to Al as the 'coach of death.'

And then there's Susan Lance. Susan is the exception. She is, without a doubt, a story of success.

Susan had run in high school as a means of getting in shape to enjoy her true passion (at the time) of riding horses. As a native of Ohio, it was inevitable that she would one day become a Buckeye. She got her B.S. from Ashland University and then graduated from the Ohio State University, earning a D.V.M (doctorate in veterinary medicine) in 1986 and later a PhD in epidemiology. She went to work for the Centers for Disease Control in both Colorado and Wyoming and later worked for the state health department in South Dakota. Throughout this time, her running regrettably became sporadic as her job kept her extremely busy and—ironically—*on the run* most of the time.

In 1998 she accepted a job in Atlanta with the Georgia Division of Public Health. In 1999 she resumed a regular running program and competed in the Peachtree Road Race and ran her first marathon (Atlanta) on Thanksgiving Day in 2001. Her passion for running grew stronger in the months to come, and in 2003 she inquired with the Atlanta Track Club about the possibility of getting a personal coach to lower her marathon PR to 3:30 or better.

Susan ran with Al and I and our regular Sunday morning group for the first time in the fall of 2003. Al introduced her as his 'client,' and I'll leave it to your imagination what immediately went through my mind. But over the course of that first 20-mile run with Susan, I could see that she was different. She was, indeed, the exception. I knew that I would be seeing Susan the following Sunday, and even the Sunday after that. I could tell Susan was willing to do whatever it took to be the best runner she could possibly be. You see, it was obvious that she *enjoyed* being out on the paths with our group for three hours or more every Sunday morning. In fact, the only negative aspect of the three-hour run from Susan's perspective was that it was *only* three hours.

'She's got legs that just won't quit' is a cliché not usually attributed to someone with a diminutive five foot one inch frame. But when it comes to Susan, it is definitely *not* a cliché. When it comes to running, she just doesn't seem to ever get enough. Conservatively, Susan figures that since 2001 she has run approximately 360 days out of each year. Her weekly mileage regularly hovers in the low 70's—the exceptions being taper and recovery weeks before and after an important ultra, respectively, and of course the week including the ultra itself. Trail runs of 100 miles are Susan's favorite, although she has soft spots in her heart for some of the 'shorter' events such as the Tallahassee Ultra Distance Classic 50 Mile Run and the Strolling Jim 40 Mile Run—in both events she was first woman master finisher in 2007. In 2008, she upped the ante at Strolling Jim and captured the overall women's championship.

Susan's progression in the ultra ranks has been nothing short of phenomenal. She ran her first ultra—a 50K—in November of 2003. Six months later she ran 41.2 miles at Strolling Jim in Wartrace, Tennessee. Six months after that she entered the San Diego One Day Run, which was hosting the American Ultra Association National 24-Hour Championship. Optimistically Susan was hoping to cover 100 miles, although a fellow running club member—who was also in the event—encouraged her to set her sights on a more realistic goal of 50 miles. After all, the longest distance she had ever run prior to the event was 41.2 miles. Imagine her—and everyone else's surprise when she ran an amazing 107.4 miles, realizing a 5th place finish among the women in a deep and experienced field of ultrarunners.

But 2004 was just the beginning of an amazing run of success and endurance.

In 2005 Susan finished third in her age group in the Olander Park 100 Mile National Championship (24th overall) in a time of 22:27:41, and returned to San Diego two months later and improved on her 24-hour performance from the year before by covering 109.5 miles (and again was the 5th place woman, only this time she was the National Champion in her age group as well).

In 2006 Susan completed the challenging Grand Teton 100 Mile Run (30:20:19, 4th place woman and 12th place overall) and was first woman at the Tallahassee Ultra Distance Classic 50K (4:43:14). She also was first woman (and tied for 3rd overall) at the annual Hot to Trot 8 Hour Run (Atlanta) completing 43.5 miles (a course record) after finishing second the two previous years.

In 2007 Susan ran 108 miles in a 'treadmill challenge' in Atlanta, finishing first among both the solo runners *and* the 'relay' teams. In the more traditional events, Susan won the women's masters title at the inaugural Sweetwater 50K

(6:23:58), the aforementioned Strolling Jim 40-Mile Run (6:27:55), the Twisted Ankle (trail) Marathon (4:49:17), and the aforementioned Tallahassee Ultra Distance Classic 50 Mile Run (7:53:13). Beyond her masters titles, she also completed the Western States Endurance Run (29:11:42), won the National Trail Marathon Age Group Championship in the DuPont Forest Trail Marathon (3:47:18), completed the Mountain Masochist 50 Mile Run (11:24:22), and won her age group in the Atlanta Marathon (3:43:58). Finally, Susan was the overall women's champion in the Lean Horse 100 Mile Run (20:42:00), and to put an exclamation point on her banner/breakout year, set a course record in the process!

It's hard to imagine anyone having as much success as Susan in her first four years of ultrarunning...or anyone with a brighter future in the sport.

Susan's intensity and commitment to running is matched only by her willingness to help and inspire other runners. Many times she has sacrificed personal goals to support a fellow runner in achieving his or her goals or to assist a fellow runner in need of help. Her unselfishness spills over into her personal life as well. It is virtually impossible for Susan to turn away from a stray dog, cat, or any other four-legged creature that happens to cross her path—which happens quite frequently, by the way.

It's hard to imagine that someone with a demanding position as the State Epidemiologist with the Georgia Division of Public Health—which requires a 2.5 hour daily round-trip commute to Atlanta from her small farm in Whitesburg, Georgia--can find time to squeeze in 70+ miles a week. Not to mention the time commitment for races of 50 and 100 miles on the weekend and the twice-a-day task of feeding her pets...which requires about an hour a day during the week and a couple of hours more each weekend. After all, she has over two dozen mouths to feed. Her normal stable consists of four dogs, eight cats, eight birds, seven chickens, three horses and a goat (Rupert) who *thinks* he's a horse. One of the cutest things I've ever seen was when Susan and I pulled up in her driveway after a race and she got out of the car, walked to the fence, and all three horses—*and Rupert*—came galloping across the pasture to see her. Absolutely priceless.

Susan has set her sights on returning to the Western States Endurance Run once she turns 50, as she would one day like to win her age group (50-59) at the most prestigious trail ultra in the world. With the intensity, focus, and determination Susan has on ultrarunning, I expect it will happen; sooner rather than later.

After all, Susan is the exception. Her talent and desire make her a formidable presence in the world of ultrarunning. I look forward to seeing her achieve a ranking as one of the finest long-distance runners in the country, if not the world. When she does, I'll think back to the first time she ran with

Al and I in the fall of 2003. I'll remember that I knew from that moment on what she was capable of accomplishing. And I know a subtle smile will cross my face when I realize I--before anyone else--knew the type of ultrarunning career Susan was going to have...a career that can be summed up in two words:

Absolutely priceless.

THE REAL ME

By Susan Lance

Writing this is a tough task for me knowing Scott's aversion to George Sheehan-ish writing. He asked me quite simply 'why do you run?' For me, the answer to that falls into several categories, and any of them could drift perilously close into that territory. So Scott, if I cross the (Sheehan) line, please forgive me.

In the most superficial sense, I run because it provides stress relief. I have a high pressure job, a long and hellish commute, and daily farm chores on top of all that. Running has raised my threshold for irritation and given me far more patience dealing with people, animals and machines! The miles I run reduce anxiety, anger and strangely sadness, too. The uninterrupted time allows me to 'rearrange my brain,' and helps me work through problems and keep them in perspective. The big picture returns as I run.

Another reason I run is because of the people I've met through running. My closest friends (ironically, those other than my boyfriend Ken!) are people I've met through running. The self selection of people who run long distances concentrates attributes I find important in friends. The ability to tolerate extreme discomfort seems to strip the 'veneer' from people. My running friends have seen me at my best, but also at my worst and/or my weakest, and yet still like me. I believe I've become closer to the people I've met during races than others I've known for years because when you're pushing yourself so hard, there's no energy to be anything other than exactly who you are. The other thing I've discovered recently is that I've met a much broader group of people than I've known in the past. This has uncovered stereotypes I held that were previously concealed from me, and has allowed me to free myself from them. Finally, the selflessness of race volunteers and the camaraderie of other runners continually expose me to the better side of people, which keeps cynicism at bay.

Finally, there's the self discovery thing. Running provides many opportunities to deal with adversity...like most things, the more practice the better the performance. I once thought that adversity training applied primarily to running, which is terrific; but in reality it applies to life as well. I now find it easier to do hard things at work (speak truth to power, take big risks, etc.) because I know I can deal with the consequences, regardless of what they may be. The confidence to face difficult situations relying on your own internal resources is a priceless gift, and I've found it through running.

Lame at Lean Horse 100

Lessons in patience, humility and pain management

By Susan Lance

I arrived in South Dakota on Wednesday August 20th, 2008 spooked by my trip the year before when my flight was supposed to leave Thursday morning but I didn't arrive at race headquarters until 7 p.m. Friday evening with a race start scheduled for 6 a.m. the next morning.   I visited some of my old haunts in the Rapid City area (I lived in South Dakota from 1994-1998) and stayed at the historic old hotel downtown, the Alex Johnson.   On Thursday morning, I attended a conference call at work (couldn't get away completely) and drove down to Hill City to walk part of the trail near the turn around. Both Wednesday and Thursday were HOT, with highs in the upper 90's.   I kept checking the weather which kept saying it was going to cool abruptly for Saturday, but it seemed hard to believe.   I picked Scott Ludwig up at the airport around 8:15 p.m. on Thursday and we met Jill Floyd and Ken (her husband) and Scott's friend Amy Yanni (he met her a couple years ago at the Museum of Aviation marathon at Warner Robins) and her husband Dan at an Italian restaurant, Botticelli's in downtown Rapid City.   We had a nice meal, but Scott was obviously exhausted and nearly silent (I later learned he'd been awake nearly 24 hours straight).   We left Rapid City after 10 p.m. and drove to Hot Springs.   I accidentally took the long route and it was quite late when we arrived at the Best Western, which was next door to race headquarters. It was especially late for Scott since Hot Springs is on Mountain Time, two hours behind the time zone Scott and I left behind in Georgia.

We got up early on Friday and I gave Scott the grand tour of the southern Black Hills--Custer State Park, Needles Highway and a view of Mount Rushmore.   We saw loads of wildlife--many bison and pronghorns, a coyote, a marmot, tiny chipmunks and a few 'wild' burros.   Two of the burros stuck their heads into Scott's open window to visit and beg for a treat.   We returned for our packet pick up and for the race briefing.   Scott gave a nice inspirational talk at the race briefing after being invited to speak by race director Jerry Dunn.   Scott, Jill and Ken, Gary and Peg Griffin and I then went to Pizza Hut (we were nervous about the cookout pre race meal) for dinner.   There we ran into my friends Dann and Shannon Fisher.   I ran part of the 2007 race with Dann and met Shannon and Bart, their adorable dog at various aid stations and at the post race meal.   We went back to the hotel and retired for an early night and a 4 a.m. wake up call.

We'd done much of our preparation the night before and after showers, a few last minute adjustments, and a little breakfast at the hotel, we headed next door for the pre race check in. We met Gary and Jill and waited a little nervously for the 6 a.m. start. It was past dawn at 6 a.m. and we left running through the lovely, historic town of Hot Springs. This year I tried to pay attention since the in town markings last year were very difficult to follow in the dark. Scott and I decided to run together as much as possible and were aiming for a 9:30 50-mile goal and a possible sub-20 hour finish. Last year I ran the course in 20:42 and this year the weather was predicted to be cooler, and I was hopeful I could break 20 hours.

The first 16.6 miles of the race are through Hot Springs, up through the Cold Brook recreational area and then out onto Argyle Road. Argyle Road is a nice gravel road, with many hills. Although it seems like it is mainly uphill going out (and according to the elevation charts it is), it seems mostly uphill returning also. Jerry kindly put small strips of plywood for the runners across the cattle guards this year, which was a nice touch; especially in the dark on the return trip.

Scott and I ran steadily and without much extraneous effort out to the Mickelson Trail. Both of us were feeling pretty good and not especially stressed by the pace. Once we hit the trail, I noticed my feet, which had been a bit sorer than normal, were getting increasingly worse, but nothing more than a mild annoyance. Scott's back issue was bothering him a little but didn't seem excessive. At the 25-mile mark all was well and he decided to continue on for the 100 mile race instead of opting for the 50 miler. We struggled a bit around 30 miles as the temperature started to rise and we headed uphill, but we hit a nice downhill section before Custer and arrived at the aid station in Custer (~35 miles) in good shape and good spirits and on pace. After this point the course markings seemed off, and we started to fret. The aid station at 40 miles seemed much farther than five miles from Custer, and the next aid station (Oreville) seemed much further than five miles past that. We were beginning to believe we'd fallen behind our pace, which was very demoralizing. Just past the 45 mile aid station, we met Dann on his way back--he was having a great day! Shortly after that, we encountered Gary, who'd run the first 50 in 8:21. He looked hot and exhausted and I was worried about him (though as it turned out, he did great!).

Eventually we found the mile markers *were* off and we reached the aid station that's just before the turnaround much quicker than we expected. We bypassed it to get to the turnaround in 9:28. Since our goal was 9:30 we were pleased, but thought that it seemed like we'd really run faster than this pace. Among the women I was in second place, far behind Jenny Capel, and we were probably among the top 15 runners at that point. We turned around to go back and decided to walk briefly. Unfortunately, that is when disaster struck!

Right after the turnaround it suddenly felt like someone put a knife through my foot an inch or so in front of my left heel. Walking was increasingly painful and running was impossible. Every step was agonizing. I was on the verge of tears several times because I didn't see how I could tolerate the pain, continue on for 50 miles and finish. I thought the pain I was feeling was consistent with plantar fasciitis, but I'd never had that in the past and couldn't figure out why/how it would appear out of the blue in the middle of a race. About the same time my foot began to hurt, Scott's pain began to increase substantially and move around in his legs. Neither of us could do much more than walk—our several attempts at running between miles 50 and 60 were very short and followed by enough pain to make us think hard about trying it again. The only respite from the misery was seeing dozens of mule deer as dusk set it in; they were lovely and graceful and looking for them kept us somewhat occupied.

The miles between the aid stations seemed to expand exponentially the further we went. By the time we hit Custer (about mile 65) both of us were miserable. I was basically done eating and drinking by then. I wasn't moving fast enough to require much intake. Scott was dying for a beer at Custer, but the aid station volunteers first thought he was kidding and then said they didn't have any, but as we left the aid station a man approached us and told Scott he'd have a beer for him at the next aid station, Carroll Creek. The distance to the next aid station seemed endless. In addition to the sheer tedium of walking, it began to get dark. Other runners began to pass us, first as sort of a trickle then as a torrent. This was really demoralizing! Scott spent much of the time between the three aid stations talking about how good the beer would taste….however, when we arrived at the aid station, the man who had promised the beer said he didn't have one. Scott was devastated. I don't think the man realized how much these sort of promises mean during an ultra.

The stretch before the Pringle aid station might have been my lowest time. It was dark, Scott was miserable and demoralized by the man's broken promise about the beer, and the distance seemed stretched all out of proportion. Although it was six miles, it easily felt like 15. When we reached Pringle (I was convinced that the aid station workers had packed up and gone home and the aid station was deserted), a beer appeared for Scott!!! He was delighted! The aid station workers seemed stunned when he chugged the whole thing! The next aid station at Lime Kiln was four miles away, but my foot had become exquisitely painful and I was again on the verge of tears wondering how I could finish. Ominously my right foot was beginning to hurt in the same place my left foot hurt before the devastating pain started and I was beginning to wonder how I could finish if both feet felt like I was walking on broken glass.

When we arrived at Lime Kiln, another beer was waiting for Scott! He chugged that one too, had some chicken soup (they insisted that I have some too and didn't seem to understand I am a vegetarian), and we left for the Argyle Road aid station at the end of the Mickelson Trail and the beginning of Argyle Road. This was another extremely long stretch that had substantial uphill sections. I thought we would never get to the aid station and Argyle Road. Scott's pain began to increase in this stretch and we staggered into the aid station where Scott was greeted with yet another beer! Both of us were having trouble standing without staggering around trying to keep our feet under us. I think the aid station volunteers wondered if Scott had guzzled too much beer, but it was the beginning of another developing problem.

We left the aid station somewhat relieved by the change in scenery on the road; however the downside became apparent almost immediately. Several more runners were passing us and their crew cars were forcing us to the edges of the road where running was much more difficult than in the middle. Probably in an attempt not to disturb us, they hung back and made us traverse the edge for much longer than if they had just driven directly past. The dust they generated even going slowly was choking. Scott began having trouble running at the sloped edge of the road and I was trying to figure out what was going on. About then a couple passed us, a woman runner and her pacer husband. We noticed that she was leaning to the left pretty significantly, and Scott commented about the lean. It was then I noticed that he too was leaning, only to the right. He couldn't tell he was leaning but before long he started veering off the edge of the road to the right. He went all the way off the road at one point and the husband of the other leaning runner retrieved him. He was mortified for people to see him this way. I told him it was nothing he had any control over and nothing to be embarrassed about, but I could see it really bothered him.

The two aid stations on Argyle Road last year were combined into one this year and the distance to it seemed almost insurmountable. What had seemed like mostly uphill going out also seemed mostly uphill coming back. For me, it didn't matter. Walking uphill and downhill were equally painful, although Scott initially seemed to suffer more on the uphills. He was beginning to need to stop regularly to stretch out his back, which slowed us down even more. When we finally arrived at the Argyle Road aid station, the very nice man there couldn't really tell us where we were mile wise. He gave us three different numbers and more than a mile and a half separated them. I realize this doesn't seem like a big discrepancy if you're in a car, but after you've run approximately 90 miles, knowing exactly how much remained was really important and he couldn't help us. The stretch between this aid station and the one at Cold Brook Recreational area was another miserable and demoralizing stretch with many runners passing us. I'd begun to regret that I told Scott the story of a runner last year who'd made it 96 miles before succumbing to back pain. I could see this story was beginning to have real meaning for him as the distance he could go before stopping to stretch his back was becoming exponentially shorter the further we went.

After we left Cold Brook, with about four miles remaining Scott was in tremendous pain. I felt helpless since there was nothing I could really do to help. We struggled on very slowly, with a stop for back stretching every 100 feet or so, and the distance between stretches was decreasing. I could see that he really doubted he could finish. After we got into Hot Springs, he could barely move. Even though I thought we had less than two miles to go, I couldn't imagine how he could go on. Finally we decided to see if he leaned on me if we could make better forward progress. This helped a little, and the distance between stretches actually increased for a short time, but soon the pain was limiting our forward progress again. We decided to switch sides so that I was supporting his leaning side and forcing him into a more upright position. This worked much better for him, but unfortunately it placed his weight on my left side and over my very, very painful left foot. I knew my pain was nothing compared to his though and I also knew we were less than a mile from the end so I knew I could tolerate it. We made much faster progress in this configuration and soon the finish line was in sight. I have been very, very happy to see the finish line at every 100 miler I've done, but I think this was the sweetest. We had both battled severe pain for 16 hours and against all odds finished in 25:24 (7:24 a.m.). As it turned out, this put us in the top half of all finishers. Jill's husband Ken was there and took our picture. Although Jill was not very far behind us and we were really excited to see her finish her first 100 miler, we knew we had to get some sleep before we needed to pack and check out of our room by noon. We both collapsed on the beds in our race clothes and slept until our wakeup call at 10:30 am.

We got up very gingerly. When I finally took my shoe and sock off before getting in the shower, I saw that I had a huge 'bruise' and a large amount of swelling on the bottom of my foot in the arch area. I realized then that I must have more than just inflammation of my plantar fascia. As I predicted, Scott's lean was gone. The post race ceremony was terrific: watching Dann (who set a 100 mile PR and finished 5th overall), Gary (at age 58 who finished in an astonishing 19 hours) and Jill get their awards was wonderful. I was somewhat embarrassed and disappointed (at the time anyway) about my finishing time, but in retrospect it's amazing we finished at all.

I learned much about persistence, tedium and pain management (Scott and I consumed a large amount of ibuprofen which had absolutely no impact for either of us) and humility. We must have been passed by more than 25 runners in the last 50 miles and at the time it might have been the most painful thing for me. In retrospect I am proud we finished. Having Scott there to share the pain, humiliation, tedium and misery was important. I am not sure I could've finished by myself.

Post script 9/20/08 - We got back to Atlanta on Monday evening. My foot was very, very sore. I wanted to see a podiatrist but needed to get a referral from my primary care doctor, so by the time I arrived at the podiatrist's office it was Thursday. He told me I'd ruptured my plantar fascia, and had basically done a nonsurgical 'surgical repair' of a too tight plantar fascia and that he was going to treat me like a post surgical patient. The prognosis was good, he said, as long as I cooperated and didn't try to run again too soon. For someone who has run an average of 70 miles a week for the last four years this was pretty hard to hear. I was in an air cast for three weeks: no running at all. After two weeks in the 'boot,' he cleared me to work out on equipment at the gym as long as I could keep my foot flat. I found the arc trainer most comfortable and spent at least an hour/day doing hill intervals on it. Four weeks after the race I ran my first steps. I did an hour on the arc trainer before I tried to run so I wouldn't be tempted to run too far, and ran four slow miles on the ½ mile track at Clinton Park. Other than a little tingling, my foot didn't feel too bad. Maybe I'll be back to the races sooner than I expected!

Chapter Five

Elizabeth Hurdman

I've always admired people that truly enjoy life. People that wake up in the morning and just *know* it's going to be a good day.

Elizabeth Hurdman truly enjoys life.

If you ever have the opportunity to meet Elizabeth and see the smile on her face and hear the excitement and optimism in her voice…well, let me just say that if you weren't having a good day up until then, expect things to get better.

Elizabeth has that affect on you.

She has that affect on a lot of people.

Of all the people I've known in my life, Elizabeth is near the top of the list of those who make the most of each and every day.

You would expect as much from someone who truly enjoys life.

Someone like Elizabeth Hurdman.

Elizabeth Hurdman

LIGHT AT THE END OF THE TUNNEL

I met Elizabeth Hurdman briefly, hours after she and I crossed the finish line of the 2008 Lean Horse Hundred (mile run).

I came to know *of* Elizabeth Hurdman courtesy of her husband Jeff after a most unusual encounter during the race.

It was somewhere around the 93 or 94 mile mark around 5:00 a.m. on a dark, lonely road in the Black Hills of South Dakota. I was having a hard time moving forward in a straight line, when suddenly I was passed by two runners—a man followed closely by a woman who I assumed were husband and wife, as the woman was literally on the heels of the man—only to find myself veering to the right side of the road and ultimately falling off the shoulder. I was having a hard time tackling the slight incline to get back on the road when the man walked towards me, offered me his hand and pulled me back into the middle of the road. I thanked him and he said 'no problem' and that he 'was used to pulling people out of the ditches in Canada.' As he and the woman pulled away, he asked me if I would write a book about him (he had heard me say at the pre-race meeting that I was writing a book about my personal running heroes). Kiddingly I told him I would.

Well, not exactly. The man, Jeff Hurdman, sent me an E-mail shortly after the race:

> We met around 5:00 a.m. last Sunday on the Argyle Road in South Dakota. I'm the Canadian guy that helped pull you up onto the road. What an experience: being between two runners, each of whom was severely bent in different directions and skittering like crabs to opposite sides of the road!
>
> The reason for my note is to follow-up on something you said in your pre-race address: you were writing a book about the amazing accomplishments of runners who are simply too humble to tell their own stories and I have one for you.
>
> The lady that I was running with (my wife), Elizabeth Hurdman, has an eye disease called retinitis pigmentosa. While she is unlikely to mention it, in the daytime this has left her with a 95 to 97% vision loss and at night she is completely blind. Just leaving the front door of the house is an act of courage and fortitude.
>
> With her time of 24:20 at Lean Horse, she placed first in her age group, and was 5ᵗʰ female and 30ᵗʰ overall. Elizabeth ran unaccompanied for

the first 50 miles and I paced her in for the second 50.

At the 2007 Umstead 100 Mile Run, Elizabeth quite probably became the first blind person to complete a 100 miler (in 25:23). She placed 3rd in the visually-impaired category at the 2004 Boston Marathon. Typically, not being content with her achievements to date, she is entering a triathlon training camp in a couple of weeks to push herself even farther 'out there.'

There's an enormous amount of quiet courage in the running community. As you can tell, she's certainly my running hero.

After reading that, she became one of *my* running heroes as well. It is my privilege to tell the story of Elizabeth Alexandra Hurdman.

Elizabeth was born in Heywood, Lancashire, England and immigrated to Brantford, Ontario, Canada in March of 1957 when she was barely a month old.

She met her future husband Jeff during graduate school at the University of Guelph (Elizabeth earned an M.A. in English Education) in Ontario. They were married in 1984 and now live in Toronto with (in her own words) 'our Harley-Davidson.'

As for her eye disease, Elizabeth was diagnosed in 1982. Retinitis Pigmentosa is an inherited eye disease that causes degeneration of the retina and progressive, relentless loss of sight. The first symptom is night blindness, followed by loss of peripheral vision and eventual tunnel vision. There is no treatment or cure.

To truly understand the effects of the disease, it's best to hear it described in Elizabeth's own words:

Although my initial symptoms were evident by the time I was a teenager, the impact was subtle, and as no one else in the family seemed to be affected, I banged around believing I was just a natural klutz. I felt liberated when I learned it was an eye disease causing the trouble. I currently have less than 10 degrees of peripheral sight in my right eye. The left eye has macular damage, causing considerable blurring in the restricted vision of that eye. For me, the world is flat. I have virtually no depth perception and use shadows and other cues to estimate distance and ground texture.

That puts the occasional blister or shin splint in perspective, doesn't it?

Elizabeth has quite an impressive resume following graduate school, including:

- High school English teacher for special needs students with the Etobicoke Board of Education.
- Volunteer patient education coordinator with the Toronto Congenital Cardiac Centre for adults, where she developed medical information materials and served as an advocate for the patients.
- Member of the Canadian Adult Congenital Heart (CACH) Network.
- Manager of Research and Information Programs with the RP Eye Research Institute (later to become The Foundation Fighting Blindness).
- Chairman of the Community Disability Steering Committee with the Division of Parks, Forestry and Recreation for the City of Toronto.

Elizabeth has quite an impressive *running* resume as well. She began what she refers to as 'real' running when she met Amie Chong through the Achilles Track Club (ATC). The ATC was established to encourage disabled people to participate in long-distance running with the general public. Her first marathon began as a training run with Amie in March of 2001 in New Jersey. The two of them met for a training run in Prospect Park and they found themselves finishing the Achilles Marathon in just over four-and-a-half hours. Elizabeth refers to Amie as her greatest running mentor, who showed her the ropes and guided her in her early races and taught her about shoes, clothes, hydrating and most importantly having fun. Amie encouraged her to go, and since then Elizabeth hasn't stopped.

Elizabeth is grateful to the many great people she's had the privilege of running with, especially the giving souls who have been willing to take the time to guide her, both in training and in races. 'Guiding' means the runner serves as Elizabeth's eyes: they tell her what lies ahead and what to expect. When the running is congested, the guide and Elizabeth tether together with a mountaineering rope or small lanyard. In the larger races, like the New York City Marathon, Elizabeth has had up to three people helping her out: one running ahead to clear the way, and one on either side of her. As Elizabeth's vision is on the decline, she opts for smaller races she can run independently. Ultras, as you can imagine, work well for her.

Elizabeth opened up her running journals to me, and it was a delight reading some of her comments:

New York City Marathon, November 2001, 4:05

An amazing experience to be in New York so soon after 9/11. I develop a stress fracture during the race, but have the best of people, Jackie Dupuis and Steve Ferracuti to help me complete a rather painful but exhilarating day.

New York City Marathon, November 2002, 4:31
This is Jeff's very first marathon. I run with JJ Johnson and Larry Bock picks me up at the halfway point.

National Capital Marathon, May 2003, 3:56
A Boston qualifier for me. Guides were Rudy Hollywood, Michael Dawson and Jackie Dupuis.

Boston Marathon, April 2004, 4:29
82 degrees at the start! Guides were Jeff, Larry Bock and Jackie Dupuis.

Self Transcendence (42 miles completed), June 2005, 6:00
I think I am following Jeff, but I end up sprawled in a giant sand pile. I have to stop, shower and change my clothes. I looked like a giant sugar donut.

Canandaigua Ultra 50-Mile Run, October 2005, 9:12
I follow the white line on the shoulder of the road. Jeff starts with me in the morning dark for three miles, and then paces me in for the last six so I don't get lost.

New York City Marathon, November 2006, 4:16
Very pretty 1K loop course; cinch to navigate and I only fall once.

Umstead 100 Mile Race, April 2007, 25:23
More fun than a barrel of monkeys. Helen Malmberg runs first loop with me while it is dark; at night I take turns with Larry Bock, Jackie Dupuis and Duff McLaren.

Friendly Massey Marathon, July 2007, 4:12
Only a couple hundred runners, so I go it alone. I get a bit lost once but am retrieved by other runners!

Death Valley Marathon, December 2007, 4:17
I had planned to run with Jeff who was doing the half, but found out at the start line that the half starts 10 minutes later. I follow a bunch of guys who claim to be targeting 4 hours. They were running 8 minute miles and I cramp up. I wish I could read my own watch!

Tampa Bay Gasparilla Marathon, February 2008, 4:12

This is Jeff's debut after having ACL reconstructive surgery the previous May (Yes! Be impressed.). We run together and Larry Bock helps out for the first 6 miles when it is pitch dark (to me, anyway).

Toronto Ultra 100K, May 2008, 11:17
This is a 5K out and back course on a bike path that I know. I manage, but get really, really bored and am happy when the monsoon rains and wind begin.

Badwater Ultramarathon, July 2008, Crew Member
One of the best experiences of my running life! Mike Whelan was my runner and he was awesome!

Lean Horse 100 Mile Run, August 2008, 24:20
Jeff starts out with me in the morning dimness and helps me navigate the first part of the course; he picks me up at the 50 mile turnaround. I have never had so much fun than I did running back with my sweetheart in the dark. Jeff retrieves Scott Ludwig from a ditch before the night is over.

As I mentioned earlier, I met Elizabeth Hurdman briefly, hours after she and I crossed the finish line of the Lean Horse Hundred. Yet it seems like I've known her all my life.

You're a lucky man, Jeff Hurdman. I completely understand why she's your hero.

I hope you don't mind sharing.

A CLEAR VISION

By Elizabeth Hurdman

Running

Whether I am trotting about in the shade of the forest or racing headlong around a track, I am mindful of my good fortune. I am grateful for the kindness of the runners who guide me when I need a watchful eye. I am overwhelmed by the general goodness of people who volunteer time, advice and interest.

I love to go for rambles, and I am grateful for having a body that lets me explore roads and paths, hidden and public spaces. It feels equally as good when I inhale the sweet fragrance of milkweed or the mouth-watering aroma of fresh chocolate chip cookies from the Christie's giant bakery.

Losing Myself

Getting ready for a long race is a wonderful thing. It provides the incentive for time-consuming, leisurely explorations. One of the advantages of poor vision is the ease of getting lost. That is how I became a long-distance runner – I kept missing my landmarks. I soon quit worrying about reaching location X in Y minutes, and brought my focus to what I wanted to accomplish during the run. Sometimes I look for hills to climb, sometimes I want flat and fast and sometimes I just want to traipse around in pretty places.

By being lost much of the time, I have learned the benefits of being prepared: I carry fluids, food, money, and a cell phone … lots of stuff (sometimes I wear a backpack with a change of clothes). By not knowing what to expect, I have learned to keep my wits about me, and to be sensitive to the environment: the road beneath my feet, the changing weather, leaves falling from the sky, cars idling at intersections, a moose trotting up the road towards me, the Haliburton heavy foot squirrel digging for acorns. *(Did you know it is good luck to catch a falling leaf?)*

I am frequently awed by the commitment to training displayed by many of my friends, mentors and role models. I am undisciplined in my approach, and this may be a bit due to the limitations I have as a visually impaired runner. I simply cannot train the way other runners do. However, my adaptations have evolved into a self-indulgent, do-as-you-feel approach to training. My undiscovered country is the hard breathing, fast-as-you-can kind of running. I look forward to exploring it, too.

What I have found to be True

I am not a well-qualified or successful runner, but running has opened the doors for me, and I suspect that it has for many of us who tie our shoelaces and are transformed.

I know that many runners with normal vision are perplexed at my enthusiasm for being out on the road. They wonder 'Isn't it boring if you can't see the view?' and 'Is it worth the hassle if you have to run with a guide?' And I think, 'Guys, you should try running with a blindfold, it's like running on clouds' and 'The world really comes alive if you're not bogged down with images.' So, with that in mind, here are some thoughts about running:

Be physically ready (aka 'Do your homework') so you can let yourself go. A prepared body will have a seamless connection with the mind. Working in harmony, this team will take you places!

Honor your body. Really. Treat it nicely and with respect. Massage those tired muscles, rub cream into those cracked feet, and stretch out those tight hamstrings! Patience and gentle persistence will take you further distances in a happier way.

Be in your moment. Each footfall and each breath are like snowflakes, unique and transient. Step back and be a calm observer. Feel the world in you. Skim over the earth.

Be grateful. Running is a natural tonic. It soothes and invigorates, engages your mind and body, and can make you happy, healthy and strong. Feel lucky you can run.

Be humble. With respect to other runners. With respect to what your body will do for you. Our bodies are amazing machines!

The view is always the best from the top of a hill.

THE LONG, HOT RUN FROM
HOPKINTON TO BOSTON

By Elizabeth Hurdman

The timing mats laid out for the 108th running of the Boston Marathon were far in the distance, but ready to receive the starting signal from the Champion Chips laced securely to the shoes on our impatient, shuffling feet as we began our 26.2 mile odyssey towards Boston. Golly, the sun beating down on our shoulders felt great! Gee, was that a sunburn beginning before the starting gun fired? Thank goodness for SPF 30!

Beads of sweat are trickling down the neck of the runner in front of me. A sea of white hats stretches in all directions. We listlessly look for people we know, or other Canadians standing the same vigil. An announcer lets us know that the race has started, but we don't do anything but shift our weight from one foot to the other.

Finally, a ripple of movement passes through the pack and we slowly surge forward.

Jackie moves in front to take the lead, a little Canadian flag bobbing in her hair. Jeff falls to the right with tether in hand, already sighing at the thought of the unseasonable heat. Together we trot down the long, undulating road that stretches from Hopkinton to Boston. All those training runs in subzero temperatures seem very long ago. The tether, usually light as a feather, soon becomes a sodden anaconda in our hands. How is it possible that we are expending so much effort when we are moving so slowly? We've got twenty miles to go and we're ready for a break, if not a nap!

Jackie slices a path through the crowd with Jeff and me trailing along in her wake. It gets tougher as time goes by: some runners are starting to weave, while others dart from one side of the road to the other, desperately seeking the fountains of water spewing from lawn hoses held by leering middle-aged men. We welcome water from everywhere and anywhere… from the friendly aid stations, from kids wielding super soakers, from sprinklers and even hastily rigged shower heads.

And we're only half way! We pass the screaming Valkyries of Wellesley. No, I don't want to kiss any of you! Larry is waiting for us just past the 21K mats. Jackie and Jeff are relieved to see him. By now they remind me of a pot of mussels – tough, sweet, and well, kind of steamy. Larry picks up the tether, and to my relief he doesn't say 'mush.' He can tell by looking at us that we're in no mood to hurry things along.

Overheated bodies are strewn along the roadways and we check each other to make sure that we're taking in fluids. We pass and re-pass 'Bobby,' which was entertaining at first but eventually became somewhat annoying (*can't the fans see the rest of us?*). Are we moving forward or is this some kind of crazy re-wind? My legs weigh a lot more than I thought they did. So much for months of doing squats.

Jackie relentlessly beats a path through the steaming jungle of runners. Many are swaying to and fro. Some have developed a greenish tint and look ready to topple.

Suddenly, around mile 23 we see another couple using a tether. Wait a minute! A surge of adrenaline galvanizes my cramping calves and I'm off with the grace of a stiff-legged hippo. Larry, Jackie and Jeff simultaneously curse and encourage me…which I didn't think possible but now know better. It may not look like it if you check the facts, but we flew the last three miles (*well, at least it felt like it*). All concerns about the 85 degree temperatures evaporated. Honestly, when we hit the finish line we were still picking up speed.

Our final dash guaranteed my place on the podium as the third place female visually impaired runner. You can't judge success by the clock (*4:29:09 – yikes!*). Truth to tell, the triumph belongs to the people who led me safely through the seven rings of hell on April 19, 2004: Jackie Dupuis, Larry Bock and Jeff Hurdman.

Chapter Six

Amy Costa

After my parents passed away in the fall of 2007, I went to Tallahassee in December to compete in an ultra. I wanted to make the trip to reunite with old friends and try to take my mind off things for a while by running for a very long time.

The Race Director provided everyone some last-minute instructions before directing the runners to the starting line. He also dedicated the race to my parents, as he knew I was running and that both my parents had recently passed away.

Amy Costa ran with me for a little while once the race began. She said she had lost her father and during the first marathon she ran after he passed she was certain he was riding on her shoulder that day. *(Coincidentally I ran that race as well, the 1997 Shamrock Marathon. Small world.)*

Her words were an inspiration, and for 31 miles I could feel my dad on one shoulder and my mom on the other.

Amy, if I haven't said it before, I'm saying it now.

Thank you.

Amy Costa

ULTRARUNNING'S BEST KEPT SECRET

In 2006 she ran the 7th fastest 50 miler in the United States. In 2007 she improved on her 50 mile time and improved her national ranking to 6th. What to do for an encore? How about win a 100-mile race in 2008? And not just win the women's division, mind you, but win the race outright, leaving all the men in the field in her wake. Well, that's exactly what happened, as she ran an impressive 100-mile race at the Iron Horse 100 in Jacksonville, Florida. Her time? An outstanding 17:46.

I can hear what you're thinking. 'It must be Pam Reed.' Sorry, but you would be wrong.

'In that case, how about Monica Scholz?' Wrong again.

If I were to tell you she lives and predominately runs in the southeast, would that help?

'How about Anne Lundblad?' Sorry.

'Jamie Donaldson? But doesn't she live out west?' You're getting colder.

What if I were to tell you she ran her amazing 100-miler in her hometown? Would that help?

'Errrrrrrrrrrrr...'

OK, enough with the suspense. This amazing woman is none other than Jacksonville's own Amy Costa.

I can see your pursed lips silently asking 'who?' Allow me to introduce you to Amy Stratton Costa, who may indeed be ultrarunning's best kept secret.

Amy was born on October 21, 1964 in Bel Air, Maryland. Growing up, she led a very active life. She played tennis and field hockey, swam, and rode horses. Ultimately her play in high school led to a joint field hockey/tennis scholarship at West Chester University in Pennsylvania. While enrolled in college she began running for fun, although she refers to those runs as her 'study breaks.' Although her tennis coach advised her to 'stop running so much' as it could possibly detract from her speed on the tennis court, Amy retaliated by saying she wanted to run a marathon. The coach asked Amy to put her 26.2 mile aspiration on hold until after college.

Following her coach's advice, Amy waited to run her first marathon. Amy had competed in a few triathlons in college, but her first true *running* race was the Baltimore Zoo Zoom 5K. She was hooked, and several months later— with her mother giving her the courage to give it a try, Amy decided to try her first marathon, the Marine Corp Marathon at the age of 22. Amy didn't know if she could finish since she 'never really ran much, but it sounded like a good challenge.' Admittedly she was scared, but Amy took the challenge to heart and made it to the finish line. Tragically, her mother had passed away several months prior and wasn't there to see her courageous daughter cross the finish line. Not in person, anyway, but most certainly her mother was watching from above.

Amy began working for Outward Bound, a non-profit organization consisting of wilderness schools and urban centers in the United States as well as 40 schools internationally for adults, teens, corporations and health services. This allowed her the opportunity to run on trails every day before the rest of her crew woke up. Amy was also an avid rock climber and mountaineer, which is how she met her future husband Joe: climbing in Joshua Tree National Monument in California. Amy and Joe shared their passion for the great outdoors by climbing mountains all over North and South America. In the late 1980's Joe was doing a medical rotation in the jungles of Peru, which allowed him and Amy to climb the volcanoes before and after the medical mission work. Of course, Amy managed to squeeze in a couple of marathons between her courses. To this day Amy remains involved with Outward Bound, serving on its Discover Board. She is also trying to start an urban center in Jacksonville which she hopes one day will work with people of all races, ages and backgrounds.

Joe was in the US Navy for 13+ years as a medical student, resident, flight surgeon and urologist. As a military family, Amy and Joe moved frequently, living in Florida, California, Virginia, Iceland, Iowa and Maryland. For the past five years they have made their home in Jacksonville. The Costa's finished their Naval service in 2003. Joe is currently employed by the University of Florida's Shands Hospital in Jacksonville.

Rounding out the Costa family are their children: Micayla (age 15), Jordyn (13), Josh (12) and the family dog, Ziggy, a beautiful yellow lab.

Amy says she has run about 40 marathons, but her true passion is running ultras. She has run four or five ultras every year since 2000. Her first ultra, the Hat Run 50K in Susquehanna, Maryland is where she fell in love with the trails...and she's never looked back. Being the proud mother of three children occupies much of her time, since she is 'a full time mom and chauffeur.' In her free time she runs on the trails in the Guana Preserve, a beautiful area between St. Augustine and Jacksonville along the coast of the Atlantic Ocean. Amy also swims—more so when she is injured—and tends to be obsessive about her yardage (and following suit, with her running she can be obsessive about her mileage).

Running. Swimming. Climbing. Tennis. Field hockey. Horses. Mountains. Volcanoes. Trails. Children. Dog. Husband. Career. Anything else?

Of course!   There's her *other* interests, including kayaking, skiing, gardening, and even two that don't require a lot of energy: reading a good book and going to the beach.

Amy offers the following as her proudest moments in running:

1987 Marine Corp Marathon. Amy's first marathon was memorable as her dad, brother Bill and sister Stacy were all there to support her as she made her debut a successful one, running a solid 3:41 several months after she lost her mom in a car accident.

1996 Marine Corp Marathon. Amy's time (4:45) was insignificant. What *was* significant was that she ran the marathon a mere six weeks after giving birth to Josh (her third child in four years, a time when she wasn't able to run any marathons), and her dad and husband Joe were waiting for her at the finish line, holding her two daughters and newborn son. She remembers her dad being so proud of her, and will forever remember the smile on his face. It was then that she knew that she was, in her words 'going to be me,' running and being a good mom.

1997 Shamrock Marathon. After losing her dad to cancer, Amy's friends encouraged her to run the marathon. Amy is certain her dad was riding on her shoulder that day. She qualified for the Boston Marathon, and didn't even realize it until someone told her afterwards.

2000 Hat Run 50K. Amy completed her first ultra, fell in love with the trails and never looked back. I know you've heard that before, but it bears repeating. In fact, I'll say it one more time: She's never looked back; she simply doesn't have time.

2007 Rocky Raccoon 100 Mile Run. Amy ran 22:15 in her first 100-miler, which was good enough for the 21st fastest time in the country that year.

And let's not forgot those two quick 50-milers Amy ran in December of 2006 and 2007 (at the Tallahassee Ultra Distance Classic in Wakulla Springs) in outstanding times of 7:30 and 7:21, respectively, which served as stepping stones leading to her triumph at the Iron Horse 100 in 2008.

In time it's inevitable that the name of Amy Costa will no longer cause people in the ultra community to purse their lips and silently ask 'who?' Rather, they will be pursing their lips and silently saying 'wow!'

Amy Costa, ultrarunning's best kept secret.

For now.

FAMILY AFFAIR

By Amy Costa

I have learned that a big part of running ultra races is not the time I run, or even my place of finish. For me, the folks I meet and the adventures I experience along the way are what matter most. I try and enjoy the little things, and treasure the camaraderie that is the signature of the ultra community.

Regardless of where my running travels take me, I can go to a race and chat for hours with a fellow runner (at first a total stranger) about different races, the people we have met, and the similarities of our adventures and lifestyles (at this point it's as if we have been lifelong friends).

I think it is so cool that we are all so different. We all have different occupations, different families, and different backgrounds. Yet when we get together at a race and the gun goes off, we are all the same in so many ways. Your friends think you are a little weird for running the miles you do and the commitment you give it in your life. Your own family has long since given up trying to figure out how this happened to you and realize now they have no choice but to accept one distinct, crystal-clear fact: *it is simply who you are!*

Only a fellow ultra runner truly understands.

It is the ultimate unspoken bond shared by ultrarunners around the world. Sometimes if I am in a race and running hard I do not talk to a single person, but my strength is just being out there with the other runners. Sometimes they are laps/miles ahead of me or I am laps/miles ahead of them, or we are quietly passing each other throughout the race. If I am hurting or concentrating I may not say a single word, but being out there with everyone is my strength. Just being there that day—and occasionally night doing what I love with folks who love it as much as I is my motivation to keep moving!

We are all there together. It doesn't matter if one does the race five hours faster then the other; it is the strength I get from being on the course with everyone! We all have our own story and uniqueness that puts us in this situation. I can't help but smile when I see the 70+ year old runners pass me by. *I love it!* Our sport has so many older runners, and they are my true motivation. They give me so much inspiration…the ones that are running/walking 100 miles in 20 degree temperatures at 2:00 in the morning and will be out there until the sun comes up…….they are my heroes!

I can only hope I am still running races when I reach 70. I love hearing their stories about the races they've run. When I am hurting out on a course and I see them still out there plugging away I feel it is my duty to the sport to keep going. If they are still out there pushing their limits, then so should I!

Ultrarunning has given me so much! I love that the races are low key, frequently held in the remote wilderness, and the hype is not so much on winning but rather on finishing. And of course meeting new friends, catching up with old ones and sharing experiences. It has enriched my life and I thank my family foremost for putting up with my passion and the unbelievable support they offer.

If it was not for my husband Joe--who encourages and supports and appreciates my love of the sport, I would never be doing this! He has never objected to any race I wanted to run and he does anything in his power to help me work out logistics for our family affairs so I can train and race! I love him dearly and there is not a day I run that I don't realize how much he has given me in love and support! I am blessed to have him! Thank goodness he likes running and is such a good sport, as I am notorious for signing him up for races without him knowing it! *(Joe, I promise I will always sign you up for half the distance I run).*

My children Micayla, Jordyn and Josh are the bomb! Ever since they were babies they have been pulled to races. I have thrown them in joggers when they were two weeks old (in Iceland) to 'compete' in their first races. They grew up in joggers eating breakfast on the road, counting dogs and playing 'I spy' with me as I did my morning run. They have done a zillion family fun runs held before longer races and have spent hours in woods and trails waiting for their mother to come by, all dirty and smiling and I reciprocate by telling them how much I love them for being there! They always support me and ask about my running and training and genuinely care about my performances! They have been my crew at Western States and have experienced many all-nighters. They know how to fill bottles of electrolyte fluids and jog beside runners and cheer them on while handing them anything they may need to keep running. They have seen me win and they have seen me fail! They have seen me happy and they have seen me cry!

I hope what they remember most is what ultrarunners do: we just keep running. Not for fame, not for recognition, but simply because it is something we love to do!

All three of my children are competitive swimmers and runners and play soccer and run high school cross country. So naturally most days you will find me happily driving them to the athletic event of the day and cheering them on. I could not be prouder of them, and I always try my absolute best not to miss any event they are in. I love to watch them more then anything, and I always put them first.

How do I find time for my running? Well, I figure out my race schedule after I see the year's calendar and search for races (anywhere in the country) that are held over a weekend when they are not competing. As much as I love running I know I will always have it. However, I never want to regret missing this time with the kids and missing out on any of the events in their lives! Later in life there will be more time for more races (and believe me--there are *a lot* on my 'to do' list).   I may not be as fast in the years to come, but who cares! It is raising my children, being a mother and wife, and sharing our lives together as a family that matter most to me. What I have learned from being a parent always keeps my running in perspective.

I can only hope they have learned from being around the ultra community. You will have bad days and you will have good days. But the one thing you learn is you just keep going. You learn to get over your bad races and keep training and keep trying, because after all the important thing is that you are out there running.

In the end you realize it is not whether you win or lose or if you run a personal best. Ultimately, it boils down to the person you become along the way.

Your actions, your lifestyle and your dedication to something you are passionate about are what make you a success in life!

I remember my parents always telling me to have a goal and push yourself to try hard things that scare you.   It is okay to fail, as it means it was a challenging and difficult goal. Just keep working on it until you get it. If you hit your goal on the first try, it was probably too easy for you, so set a harder goal! I think most people would be surprised at the goals they can accomplish if they put their minds—and hearts to it.

I relate this so much to both life and running! Running for me puts my life in order! I am not sure how I got into running 50 and 100 mile races … I am not even sure why I do it?   But I do know I'm in it for the long run.

I thank all the fellow runners who I have met along the way who have encouraged me and given me the courage to keep striving and pushing my limits!   I will always try and do the same for you!

BLAME IT ON THE MOON

By Amy Costa

This is my twilight zone!

The Bethel Hill Midnight Boogie is a hilly 50 mile road race in Ellerbe, North Carolina. As the race begins at 6:00 p.m., you run in the moonlight.

But for me, the real adventure was getting to the starting line.

It started on a very hot and muggy morning in Jacksonville, Florida in June. My husband Joe was taking our three children Micayla, Jordyn and Josh to a summer swim meet. I was getting one of my 'Mom's Day Off' doing one of my favorite things in the world: heading out to run in an ultra. I decided to drive up on the day of the race, leaving Jacksonville early in the morning as it would take me seven hours to make the drive to the small town of Ellerbe.

I left feeling pretty sick, with a slight fever and aches in several spots on my body. But I had done so many logistical manipulations with our family schedule (which believe me is a huge feat in and of itself) just to get away for 24 hours that there was no way I was not going. Even if I felt horrible, which I most certainly did.

I headed north on I-95 for several hours, finally reaching my exit near a very small town in South Carolina. I filled up my car with gas and looked inside the station for any decent, somewhat healthy food for lunch. All I found was trail mix and Gatorade.

About two minutes down the road I was pulled over by the local law enforcement. Two more minutes and I was slapped with a $300 fine for driving too fast through this small rural town. I was pretty shaken up after that, furious that the officer didn't show any sympathy or care that a female was making such a long drive alone just to run 50 miles through the night. (I threw that last part in, just in case he might be a runner. Obviously he wasn't.)

I continued on and within a half hour my wheel seemed to be falling off, which could only mean one thing. The dreaded flat tire! I pulled into an old gas station, and with the help from an almost-capable 100-year old man I changed my tire! It was around 2:00 or 3:00 p.m. at this point, and I still had several hours to drive (remember, the race starts at 6:00 p.m.—*tonight!*).

Now I was really feeling stressed and sick and wondering if these signs are telling me something! I was beginning to wonder if running 50 miles tonight in the middle of nowhere was really worth it.

As all ultra runners do, I pushed on--driving the back roads of South Carolina following some inane map quest directions leading me in a few circles before I made it to North Carolina. I drove on, and on and on.....and finally found the small town of Ellerbe.

Actually, 'small' may be an exaggeration.

If you've ever been there you know what I mean: very small, not much new and not much going on. It consisted all of two blocks. I didn't notice anything open or even any people, for that matter.   I was in desperate need of something good to eat.

A small panic set in, the kind I get when I know I need some nourishment before beginning an ultra. After all, it was going to be a really long night. The only place that I found open was an old gas station with a food mart of sorts inside. I went in and could not find much of anything to eat. The shelves were quite bare and what food was there had obviously been there for quite some time.   The only thing I could find was bread and, thank goodness, some peanut butter (but no honey). I was slightly relieved when I found water and Gatorade. I was literally starving at this point! I thought I deserved a candy bar before the race.

I then went and stood in a long line forming at the cash register. There had to be at least 10 or 12 people *(could this be the entire town?)* in line. Have I mentioned that I was starving?...had a fever?...had to run 50 miles soon?

I couldn't wait to get out of there and into my car. It would only take me five minutes to drive to the start. In my wildest imagination I couldn't imagine running well, considering the way I felt and what I had been through.

When it was finally my turn I went to the counter and put down my food, the man behind the counter looked worse then I did. He was white as a ghost (actually, a shade of pale gray) and just stared at me. He didn't move or speak; he simply stared and ultimately scared the daylights out of me. The next thing I knew he just fell sideways on the ground behind the counter, striking the ground with a considerable 'thud.' Not a soul in the tiny store moved or reacted. I ran around the counter only to find out he was unconscious. I called for help and no one seemed to care...and they all just looked at me. I turned him over, tried to open his airway and take his pulse, at the same time pleading with everyone, *someone* to call 911 and get some help.

Finally a man from the back room came out and said 'Oh, there he goes again' and he went up to the man on the ground and gave him a hard kick on his shoe--as hard as he could, while swearing at him the entire time.

The man started to come to. I was trying to ask him what happened and ignore the anger of this other man. He told me he was diabetic, so I gave him my candy bar which was still on the counter...and still not paid for. I helped him up and he proceeded to walk directly into the back room. The other man, who was still noticeably angry, began to wait on the customers in line (which had grown even longer during the excitement).   I noticed everyone was looking at me like I was crazy for being behind the counter. I then had to wait at the end of the line again to pay for my bread and drinks (but no candy bar), and not the first person said a word about what has just happened. How incredibly odd.

I got back in my car and drove out of there thinking this had to be the strangest day of my life. All I wanted to do was find the start of the race and be around normal people! You know, like a group of ultra runners who were gathering in 90 degree temperatures with 100% humidity to run 50 miles starting at 6:00 p.m. on a Friday night and run through the night in the middle of nowhere. You know, normal people like you and me!

Luckily I found the start of the race and let out a sigh of relief. After the day I had been through, it was the most amazing thing I'd ever seen. I made it!

I found this beautiful little church at the peak of a hill along a country road. I pulled into the church lot where runners were gathered and getting their gear together for the race. The time now was about 4:30 p.m. I had about 90 minutes before the start of the race, and I desperately needed to lie down. I was shaking, I was tired, and my nerves were literally shot!

After I checked in with a volunteer I grabbed a blanket—and of course my food and drink from my car and searched for a place to nap. I saw some trees behind the church so I walked around behind the building and found a quaint old cemetery with a beautiful oak tree which was swaying ever-so-slightly, creating what I'm sure was the only breeze in the state. I found a perfect patch of grass under the tree between Gertude and Nathan, who didn't seem to mind my company. I set the alarm on my watch to wake me up in 40 minutes. I called my husband and checked in with the kids and got updates on the day's swimming exploits.

I briefly told my husband of my adventure and assured him I was in one piece, although a little worse for the wear. I told him I was lying between Gertrude and Nathan. He asked me if they were two of my ultra buddies who I run into at races. I told him I didn't think I had ever met them before… since they had died in the 19th century. He was wise to say he didn't want to ask, told me to be safe and he'd call me in 40 minutes to wake me up.

Surprisingly, I felt so at peace and relaxed lying there, I fell fast asleep.

Forty minutes later my phone rang and as he always does, my husband wished me luck and support and told me to just have fun and enjoy myself. He is good about reminding me not to stress about my performance and to simply have fun. God bless him: he probably wishes he had a normal wife, not one who will lie in a cemetery in the middle of North Carolina moments before running through the night!

I had a quick picnic with my bread, peanut butter and drink and headed to the starting line. I wondered what kind of run I would have, especially since I still wasn't feeling well.

As I approached the start I saw my dear friend Gary Griffin from Tallahassee. As always, he greeted me with his huge smile, welcomed me and immediately got me excited about being there! He introduced me to Helen Cox and I began seeing other runners I recognized from other races. After a quick briefing from the race director, a loud shotgun blast signaled the start of the race and we were off.

I wasn't sure what my strategy for the race was going to be. After all, I hadn't had a lot of time to think about it throughout the day. I was just so relieved to make it to the starting line. After that, running 50 miles through the night in miserable conditions was going to be a walk in the park. It was literally going to be the easiest part of my day.

Miraculously, I felt good from the start. I enjoyed chatting with Gary and Helen for a while. As it began to get dark, I just put it in 'cruise control' and really enjoyed being out there. The stars illuminated the clear summer sky and the fireflies in the valleys were amazing! It was a great little show. It was one of those 'Zen runs' that you occasionally have but always remember. Everything you see and experience seems to be 'just right.' The fellow runners, the cows in the fields at midnight and the lights flickering in the windows of the few houses you pass. I didn't really think about running, but more about how weird the day had been.

And yet how here I was, all alone running in the dark in the wee hours of the morning in the middle of nowhere…and I couldn't have been happier or more content.

I ended up having a good run: first woman and second overall, finishing in seven hours and 44 minutes. It was not a personal best, but on this challenging course, I was very satisfied. I finished in a big electrical storm which, after the events of the previous day wasn't such a big deal.

Race Director Doug Dawkins gave me a huge 'Moon' as my award and I finally—*finally* got to enjoy some delicious food. The rain was so hard at the finish that I considered my wisest move was to get back in my car (after all, it was now almost 2:00 a.m. at this point). I really didn't have anywhere to go or be, so I just started driving out of Ellerbe. I got a cup of hot coffee along the road and headed south for Jacksonville. When I got home, I shared my Ellerbe adventure with my family and friends.

Rod Serling would have loved it.

Chapter Seven

Kelly Murzynsky

Kelly Murzynsky is an amazing and talented runner.

She has the potential to be one of the finest short-distance (10K) runners in the nation in the Masters Division.

She also has the potential to be one of the finest marathon runners in the nation in the Masters Division.

Finally, she has the potential to be one of the finest ultra distance runners in the nation...in *any* division.

It all depends on what distance she sets her sights on and what she wants to achieve.

Just know that whatever she decides, well...*look out world!*

Kelly Murzynsky

BATTING A THOUSAND

If running ultras was measured in baseball terminology, Kelly Murzynsky would be batting a thousand.

Having placed first in all four ultras she has competed in at this point in her running career, her 'batting average' is a perfect four for four.

Over four consecutive years (2001 through 2004) Kelly was the first female finisher in the 2001 Tallahassee Ultra Distance Classic (TUDC) 50K with a 3:57:03 (which also placed her 2nd overall); the 2002 (and inaugural) Peachtree City (PTC) 50K with a 3:57:09 (5th overall); the 2003 PTC 50K with a 3:59:40 (6th overall); and the 2004 TUDC 50K with a 4:03:10 (3rd overall).

Not a bad track record for an ultra novice.

Kelly has been running for the better part of three decades, falling in love with the sport (and the opposite sex as well) in the first grade. She enjoyed running on 'field days' growing up, and when she attended high school at the Berry Academy (Rome, Georgia) she competed in cross country and track, specializing in the distance events: the mile, the two-mile and the mile relay. She tried out for the hurdles but was too short (or quite possibly because she couldn't jump high enough) to generate enough speed to compete in this event.

Kelly attended Emory at Oxford only to find that neither cross country or track were offered as an intercollegiate sport for women; only tennis and swimming were available. She subsequently gained 15 pounds as a freshman.

In 1992 a colleague at work who Kelly didn't consider to be particularly 'fit' successfully completed the Peachtree Road Race. Kelly figured if *she* could do it, she could too.

Kelly did, and before long she was running lots of local 10K's while building quite an impressive running resume in the process. After running the Atlanta Half-Marathon in 1993 she met Joe Murzynsky and 'fell madly in love.' Running took a backseat to her newfound romance; she wouldn't run another race for three years.

During this period Kelly's professional career occupied most of her time, as she complemented her full-time job as a dental hygienist with a part-time job as a personal trainer. Joe kept busy with a full-time job with Delta airlines, a regular and diligent workout regimen (at the gym where Kelly worked), duties as a father to daughters Sara and Danielle (from a previous marriage) and, of course his marriage to Kelly.

Kelly's passion for the sport returned in 1996. She trained diligently with Team in Training and ran a 3:39 Chicago Marathon—quite an impressive debut for 26.2 miles. In fact, it qualified her for the prestigious Boston Marathon. Although she wouldn't actually run on Patriot's Day in Massachusetts until 2000, the foundation for a promising long-distance running career had been established.

In 1999, Kelly ran 15 miles on a treadmill and decided she would give the marathon another shot. She counted 18 weeks out, which she felt was an adequate amount of time to prepare for 26.2 miles and targeted the 2000 Mardi Gras Marathon. Eighteen weeks later, Kelly lowered her personal best by 15 minutes with a 3:24 finish.

But her success in New Orleans was only the beginning. Over the next four years Kelly would:

- Lower her personal best by another seven minutes (by running 3:17 in the 2000 Shamrock Marathon)
- Match her newly-established personal best one month later at the Boston Marathon
- Finish her first trail marathon (3:40 at the 2000 Napa Valley Marathon)
- Lower her personal best by over 10 minutes by running 3:06:04 in the 2001 Steamtown Marathon (and finishing as the 8th place woman in a rather competitive field)
- Win the 2002 Cleveland Marathon (3:13:48)
- Win the 2003 Pensacola Blue Angel Marathon (3:15:45)

Kelly's four ultra championships put an exclamation point on her impressive four-year run in long distance running. Kelly could have been content to become one of the dominant female 10K runners in the southeast; instead she opted to make her mark at the national level at the marathon distance and beyond. Kelly's four ultra victories and two marathon wins secured her spot as one of the best long-distance road runners in the country.

When Joe's career with Delta ended in 2005 Kelly, Joe and their faithful black lab Buster moved to sunny Santa Rosa Beach, Florida. Joe now works with the South Walton Fire District and Kelly is now employed with It's a 'Shore' Thing Wedding and Event Planners. Buster enjoys running on the beach, lounging around the house and playing with his new little brother Tango (also a black lab).

Kelly is eager to return to the running prominence she reached just after the turn of the century and admits that training in the heat and humidity of Florida is tough. Her best training buddy is friend Lisa, a veteran of several full Ironman competitions who Kelly admiringly refers to as *'the pacer from hell.'*

Seeing as Kelly is *hell-bent* on getting back in tip-top running shape, she couldn't have selected a better training partner.

In time Kelly will return to running ultras. After all, *running like hell* after taking short sabbaticals from competitive running has become her modus operandi.

Before long Kelly will be returning to the starting line of an ultra with every intention of maintaining her perfect batting average.

Five for five. Count on it.

KISS THE BOYS

By Kelly Murzynsky

I began running in first grade.

We played a game called 'catch 'em and kiss 'em.' The rules were simple: the boys chased the girls, and whoever they caught they could kiss.

However, the boys could never catch me. So we decided to change the game around and let the girls chase the boys. Since I was the fastest runner in the class, I pretty much had my choice of any boy in class I wanted to kiss.

I've loved running ever since.

I've learned to love it even more in the past 30 years.

I feel it's my duty to share some of the subtleties of the sport I've learned which may enrich your perspective and/or relationship with running:

- Runners—for the most part are really, really good people. Dedicated. Committed. Determined. Honest. Disciplined. Their approach to running mirrors their approach to life (or perhaps their approach to life mirrors their approach to running).
- Run for long distances and you are prone to lose a toenail or two. However, trust me when I tell you that four coats of nail polish can effectively replace any missing toenail. Just be sure to 'color between the lines.'
- If you surround yourself with good running friends, you will never need a chronograph or GPS; someone will certainly take up your slack and advise the group of the distance covered, distance remaining, pace per mile, etc. during your runs together.
- The world is your bathroom. Don't believe me? Then try this little experiment:

The next time you have a long run planned for early in the morning, indulge in a hearty Thai dinner the night before—the spicier the better.

- You don't have to be a licensed medical doctor to perform minor foot surgery.
- A few cocktails the night before a race never truly hurt anyone (no matter *what* they may say).
- A spouse who supports your running habit is one of God's greatest gifts. *(Joe, I love you—and if I had known you when we were both six years old, you're a** would have so been mine!).*

GUARDIAN ANGEL

By Kelly Murzynsky

Sami was my grandmother. She is the smartest person I've ever known.

She did the crossword puzzle in the *Chicago Tribune* everyday. In pen.

She was confident and independent. Single most of her life, she lived alone in the city, never owned a car and knew her way around town better than anyone else in the family.

Even when the weather was atrocious she walked or used public transportation.

She taught aerobics at the senior center.

She took Tai Chi, spoke Greek and Portuguese and hated pigeons.

I loved her.

She began a fierce battle with cancer in 1995. Sami wore a tiny guardian angel pin to protect her during her journey.

She gave me one too. From that day on, I've worn that pin on my shorts in every race I've run.

The angel reminds me of her strength and courage. It puts my running into perspective. Running marathons is tough but racing an opponent that you can't see must be unimaginable. I ran hard.

Sami ran even harder in her race against the odds.

In 2001 (six years after Sami was diagnosed with cancer) I ran my first ultra, the Tallahassee Ultra Distance Classic 50K. I pinned the angel to my shorts, thought of Sami and had an amazing race that day.

That very same night I received word that it was 'time' to come to Chicago as Sami's race was coming to an end. I left the next morning.

When I arrived at Sami's home she looked as if she was sleeping. I'm not sure whether or not she could hear me, but just the same I held her hand and began to tell her about my race. I told her that I pinned on my angel that morning--just for her, and not only did I run well, I won the race!

At that moment she opened her eyes, smiled and said 'Yea, Kelly.'

That race will forever hold a place in my heart. In Sami's final hours--at the end of her race, she was cheering for me.

Chapter Eight

Janice Anderson

Janice Anderson is the most *committed* person to the sport of running I personally know.

She supports and promotes running on many levels as she has been:

- a competitor on the national level;
- a competitor representing our country on the *inter*national level;
- a course record holder;
- a champion;
- a race director;
- a running organization executive;
- a running club president;
- a running club *founder.*

In most cases, Janice has filled the bill not once or twice, but *several* times.

That, my friends, is commitment.

That…is Janice Anderson.

Janice Anderson

HAPPY TRAILS

In 2003 Janice Anderson and her husband Craig bought a home at the base of Kennesaw Mountain in Marietta, Georgia for one reason and one reason alone: it allowed Janice easy access to the trails.

Whether the trails are composed of rocks, roots, mud, water, dirt, cinder, mulch, pine needles, leaves or any combination whatsoever, you can be sure of one thing: Janice will *love* them!

Although she insists she is not part mountain goat, having seen her run on many different surfaces over the years I would beg to differ. This lady is more at home running up and down steep mountain trails during a hailstorm—*at night*--than you or I sitting at home on the sofa next to a warm and cozy fireplace on a cold winter day.

Janice began running in Huntsville, Alabama at the age of 11. Although she liked all sports, she preferred running as it didn't require any hand-eye coordination. Also it didn't hurt that her dad was very supportive of her running career from the very beginning. Looking through Janice's running logs—which she has maintained vigilantly since the 6th grade—there are many 'commentary' entries made by dad regarding how she felt, how she acted, and anything else Janice may have overlooked that he felt was relevant to her aspirations as a runner. Janice estimates that her lifetime mileage exceeds 75,000 miles, each step meticulously documented in the annals of her running logs.

Success came quickly for Janice. While attending Catholic elementary school, Janice began running competitively (not for the school however, as it didn't have a running team) at road races across the southeast. She ran her first Peachtree Road Race as an 8th grader in 1979, and completed the challenging 6.2 mile course in a respectable 50 minutes. Later that same year she ran her first marathon in Huntsville in a formidable time for a 13-year old: 3 hours and 41 minutes.

Ten years later Janice got her feet wet in the world of ultrarunning at the Strolling Jim 40-Mile Run in Wartrace, Tennessee where she missed setting the course record by one minute. Six years later (1995) she would set the course record by running the hilly 41.2 miles in 5 hours and 13 minutes, a pace of less than 8 minutes per mile. There would be more course records in Janice's future.

Janice trained with ultra pal Joe Schroeder throughout 1994 in the north Georgia mountains to prepare Joe for his first Western States Endurance Run. Janice became so enamored with running through the mountains that one year later she would toe the starting line of Western States in Squaw Valley, California, and complete her first official 100 mile ultra. She was hooked.

But Western States was just the beginning. By the turn of the century, Janice established course records in no less than 14 different ultra events while winning the majority of the 53 ultramarathon titles she has collected in her brilliant career.

Janice's course records (event, date, and time) include:

- Atlanta Track Club 50 Mile Run, January 1993, 6:43
- Pine Mountain 46 Mile Trail Run, November 1993, 8:29
- Mountain Masochist 50 Mile Trail Run, March 1994, 8:27
- Mississippi 50 Mile, March 1994, 7:40
- Raccoon Valley 50 Mile Run, July 1994, 7:15
- Cherokee Foothills 50K Trail Run, March 1995, 4:52
- Strolling Jim 40 Mile Run, May 1995, 5:13
- Old Dominion 100 Mile Run, May 1997, 18:25
- Mountain Mist 50K Trail Run, January 1998, 5:02
- Atlanta Fat Ass 50K, January 1999, 3:56
- Rocky Raccoon 100 Mile Run, February 2000, 16:03
- Umstead 100 Mile Run, April 2000, 18:02
- Mohican 100 Mile Run, June 2000, 18:53
- Arkansas Traveler 100 Mile Run, October 2000, 17:47

What's even more amazing is that some of these course records were 'multi' records, which is to say that Janice was bettering the course record *she had established earlier*.

To complement these course records, her resume includes six wins at Strolling Jim, four wins at Mountain Masochist, and three wins at Mountain Mist...not to mention her seven-year winning streak at the Atlanta Fat Ass 50K (1994 – 2000).

Janice has some other notable performances as well:

- 2nd place Female (21:07) in the 1997 Western States Endurance Run
- Member of the Trailwalker Team that established a team course record for 100K (15:12) in October 2002
- 1st place Female (7:40) in the 1995 JFK 50 Mile Run
- 1st place Female (8:19) in the 2003 Leone Divide 50 Mile Run
- 1st place Female (8:42) in the 1993 Del Passatore 100K

Her proudest victory was in the 2000 Rocky Raccoon 100 Mile Run, as her personal best of 16:03 was not only a course record but at the time *a world record on trails,* and was in fact *the first time a woman had run better than 17 hours for 100 miles!* This amazing performance contributed to her being named the 2000 United States Track and Field's Ultra Runner of the Year. In addition, Janice ran five other 100 mile events, and in five of her six 100-milers she finished in less than 19 hours. Four of those events she won and set course records; in the other two she finished in second place (Vermont, finishing behind Ann Trason; and Massanutten, finishing behind Sue Johnson).

Janice's propensity for trails hides the fact that she had some speed on the roads as well. Her personal bests include:

- 17:21 for 5K
- 36:15 for 10K
- 2:54 for the marathon
- 3:43 for 50K (which was actually a split in a 100K race!)

Her prowess for ultras did not go unnoticed. Janice was a member of the Nike South Team from 1987 through 1992, a member of the Power Bar team from 1997 through 2000, a member of the USA 100K team in 1991 and 1996 through 1999 and a member of the Montrail Competitive Team from 2000 until 2006. She is currently a member of the competitive team for Phidippides. She was also an active member of the Atlanta Track Club from 1994 through 2006, which included a two-year stint as President. In 2004, Janice, Sally Brooking, Sarah Tynes and Meg Crawford formed the Georgia Ultrarunning and Trailrunning Society (GUTS) which has already grown to a membership of 250 and hosts six annual trail events in various areas in the northern half of Georgia.

Her favorite race is the Vermont 100, which she describes as 'low key and held on a beautiful course.' Her biggest regrets? Dropping out at Western States and Leadville, two of the most challenging 100 mile trail runs in the country. The course she finds the most difficult? Massanutten, another 100 mile trail run, which leads to a story that is a testament to the fire that burns inside of Janice.

At the 2000 Massanutten, Janice 'thinks she fell asleep' around midnight at approximately the 75-mile mark and fell to the ground. She woke up when she struck the ground and realized an excruciating pain in her arm (later it was determined that she had in fact broken it). She ran the final 25 miles holding her arm against her chest and finished in 2nd place (behind Sue

Johnson, as mentioned earlier), a feat that she considered a disappointment. She returned the next year to make amends and did just that…by winning the event!

Rocks…roots…sticks…stones…Janice loves everything about trails. In fact, she has her own version of the old children's' saying:

Sticks and stones may break my bones, but they won't ever keep me from finishing…

OLD HABITS DIE HARD

By Janice Anderson

Old habits die hard, and I can't seem to get rid of one in particular: running. I'm unable to recall the first time I actually hit the streets running, flying along in my K-mart 3-stripers, but I know that day changed my life forever. I started running in the late 1970's at the beginning of the running boom. Fixx, Shorter, Decker and of course 'Boston Billy' were the names of the day. As an eleven-year old, however, I had never heard of any of them. But when my dad took up 'jogging' I followed in his footsteps and soon became an expert, knowing everything there was to know about all of the popular running stars.

Athletics had already been a way for my parents to occupy my time, but more importantly to wear me out. I was a 'busy' child and constant, structured activity was a calming agent for me. I tried everything: swimming, ballet, basketball, softball, tennis and a few sports I barely even remember. I found most of the activities fun, but I did not really excel; my general lack of coordination being the general issue. Some might even say I was a klutz (which I still am to this day). Running was the first sport I had attempted that required little skill; just the willingness to train and put up with some pain. I had found my calling.

I eventually upgraded my K-mart shoes by placing first in my age group in a 10K (in 43:30) and winning my beloved first pair of Nikes. They were bright yellow with a light blue swoosh, very square in shape and with the original trademark waffle sole. They were then called the classic LDV's, and I proudly sported them daily and they immediately identified me with a group: runners! I wore them proudly for years.

By the time I was in 8th grade I was bored with running the average, run-of-the-mill road races. There had to be something more out there for me. My catholic school didn't have a competitive running team and I had already run the Peachtree Road Race and dozens of other races. So in late 1979 I decided to run a marathon in my hometown of Huntsville, Alabama: the Rocket City Marathon. I don't recall anyone protesting (not even my mother) over the idea.

My parents and I joined the local running group on their training runs and soon became a regular part of the group. I took their training plans and listened to all their tips on carbo-loading and avoiding 'the wall.' I even learned to spit! I never felt like a dorky little girl; I was just another runner. Sundays were long run days, and after church I would head out for 16-20 miles and return late in the afternoon, which would cause me to fall asleep through my favorite Sunday night television show, the *Wonderful World of Disney*.

To prepare for the impending marathon, our running group set out together for a string of races to build up for 'the big one.' We even took an exciting overnight road tip to Tennessee (OK, it seemed far away to me). At the time this was a huge deal to me as we rarely went on trips other than to grandmas or the beach. We didn't necessarily run together as a group, as we encompassed a wide array of age and speed, but our Huntsville squad made for a large cheering section during the awards ceremony.

Since the marathon was in my home town we participated in race preparations: stuffing packets, sorting shirts, making race signs and preparing the finish line (mom was a timer). The night before the marathon the race sponsored a spaghetti dinner at one of the local runner's homes. I remember it was packed and there was an actual buzz in the air as everyone made new friends and talked endlessly of training mileage, race strategy and injuries. Sadly I don't remember much of anything about the race itself. I recall my dad dropping me off at the start and later seeing him and other family members along the route. But I do recall 'hitting the wall' and struggling the last few miles. The finish was just a blur, but I got there in three hours and 41 minutes, a decent effort for my first marathon.

My early days as a runner have left me with a sense of community I don't think I will ever be without. I cherish running as much for the challenges it provides. Running is the perfect compliment to life, and affords me the opportunity to do something for myself to relieve the pressures and anxieties of the world around me.

The camaraderie, the friendships, and the lasting memories? Well, they're just the icing on the cake I know as running.

STARTING AT THE TOP

(After all, you've got to start somewhere!)

By Janice Anderson

The 1995 Western States Endurance Run really starts the day prior to the actual beginning of the race. Everyone must appear in Squaw Valley, California for the mandatory medical check-in and race briefing. First you receive your soon-to-be-cherished (or possibly despised) race number, then a giant bag stuffed full with goodies and enough Power Bars to actually last 100 miles. Next you join the queue for the medical check. My pulse and blood pressure seemed to be elevated, probably because of the altitude, and my weight was up as well, hopefully because of hydrating. A race official then attaches a medical ID bracelet to your wrist with all your vital information for the running world to see. What a great way to check out your competition with sly glances to check out the vital information on their ID tag!

Then all the runners and their crews gather on the lawn for the pre-race briefing. This year because of the snow there was a lot of lecturing about the possible dangers of frostbite, sunburn, falling into snow bowls, retina damage from bright sunlight, and the exorbitant cost of helicopter rescues. The race director offered all runners the opportunity to 'drop out now' and he would guarantee them entry into next year's race, and a good number of people took him up on the offer. After the pep talk runners milled about discussing various snow strategies using words foreign to most southerners: telemarking, crampons, ice bridges, tree wells and post holing. It all sounded very slow and painful, so I realistically set my goal for the first 24 miles at eight hours.

Still being on Eastern Standard Time, I was able to fall asleep by 9 p.m., which was a good thing since my wake up call was scheduled for 3:30 a.m. I slept like a rock, barely waking when my husband brought my pacer, Joe Schroeder in from the airport around midnight. By 4:30 a.m. we arrived at the starting line for check-in and last minute carbohydrate loading. The start is actually on a wide stretch of sidewalk and hundreds of people were crammed into the small area which made it feel much warmer than the actual 40 degrees. The 5 a.m. start crept closer and after three trips to the restroom I finally made my way into the pack of runners assembled on the starting line. Within a few moments we were off.

A mile later we were trekking into the snow and began our first climb straight up the ski slope. It was basically impossible to run so I just hiked directly behind another runner, using his footsteps to make my way up. As we came close to the top, an icy patch sent almost everyone sliding until they could dig their hands, feet, or other body part into the snow to stop their descent back to the bottom. The summit yielded a wonderful view of the valley and Lake Tahoe, snow-tipped mountains and a slowly snaking ribbon of runners winding upward.

The course was marked with small yellow and red flags plunged into the snow. No trail was visible. Trudging through the snow was difficult, changing constantly from crunchy and deep to slippery and steep, soft and powdery to hard packed. I made my way slow and steady, trying to stay with a small group of non-snow runners. Others went past us, flying through the snow like cats, passing on the left, on the right, and occasionally over the top of another runner who did a face plant in the snow. At a place called the elephant's trunk the normal switch backs were completely hidden so the course went straight up the side of the mountain. Traveling up the edge of the 60 degree hill which angled off sharply on both sides, I felt as if I was in some kind of arctic expedition, only without the safety ropes. On and on we went, taking almost two hours to travel five miles until we finally reached our next aid station. The supply helicopter came in for a landing just as I started to fill my empty water bottles. We all had to crouch down and literally hold on to our hats as paper cups went flying about. The chopper landed, dropping off a much-needed container of water.

The next section was even more difficult with snow drifts rising and falling over. The drifts were extremely deep, so much that the tops of tall pines poked out from the top of the snow. I found it impossible to run or even walk down the slopes because of the steepness. Some people were able to 'ski' down on both feet but I preferred the 'butt-slide' method. After 'running' for more than six hours, the first pieces of trail began to appear. However, we certainly weren't out of the woods yet. Markings suddenly became harder to follow. The snow melt had caused many flags to disappear and we were running straight across sage brush and through mud pits. At the top of one hill the markings led us to a large clearing where I saw footprints leading in several directions. It took a group of 30 of us more than five minutes to finally locate more markings and begin our way down the mountain. Minutes later we were on the trail and descending rapidly. Before I knew it we were totally out of the snow and had arrived at the 24 mile aid station. It was just before noon, and I was an hour ahead of my original game plan.

There was a mad rush to strip off all the extra clothing worn for the cold snow and change shoes and socks. I took my time, but it felt wonderful and finally I really began running. From there we ran on asphalt and dirt roads that led up to the 40-mile aid station. This was the first place I saw my crew. I was just so excited to see someone I knew, I had to blurt out one or two tales of the snow and tried not to dawdle at the station. From there the race continued on the official trail. Michigan Bluff was 15 miles away, but first I had to face two descents and two long climbs. The temperature was rising rapidly (it would eventually reach 115 degrees) and every time the shade yielded to an open area it was like running past a hot furnace blast. For the most part the heat was tolerable; it was, after all, a dry heat.

At one of the aid stations I was offered a 'shower.' I stood on a wooden box and was sprayed off as a volunteer held plastic over my shoes. I felt good as I neared the Michigan Bluff aid station; a favorite tune came on my headphones and I ran up the last portion of the climb. I again met my crew and really was having fun chatting, but they hurried me off. It was only six more miles to Foresthill station (62 miles). This is where I would begin to run with my pacer. This section went very quickly, as I was suddenly up the final hill to the Foresthill School. A huge crowd was gathered to watch, crew, pace but most definitely *support* the runners. I quickly did my mandatory weigh-in (still up four pounds!), grabbed a few things to eat--the peanut butter and jelly sandwiches and the boiled potatoes were excellent--took a few photos and then Joe and I were off. It was just after 8 p.m.

Nightfall came just after 9 p.m. and with almost no moon the trail was dark and foreign. It seemed much more closed in with branches and other brush hanging over the trail. The shadows my flashlight made against the hanging foliage looked like small animals that moved forward and grew bigger as we approached. I squealed just a few times and asked Joe to check out a few suspicious looking logs and limbs. The bright lights of the river aid station were visible from over a mile away. We reached the Rucky Chucky River crossing intact and boarded a rubber boat, dressed in life jackets for a quick midnight ride. Once across it was a two-mile climb up to Green Gate, the 80 mile point and the next spot to meet my crew. I started to jog up the climb and soon began to see signs of the station which had posted warnings of 'No Running' and 'Speed Zone Ahead.' At the top my crew greeted us with claps and cheers. It would be a long night for them too, but we were all in good spirits and joked around, taking a few group photos before Joe and I headed off into the night again.

The next section was the hardest for me. Each station was a full five miles apart. It seemed like an eternity before reaching the first one. Then it was more of the same to the next. Looking out into the valley we could see the lights of other runners moving slowly through the trees and far below we could see the lights of our next station. Not many of the glow lights that marked the trail were working and I constantly fretted over getting lost. Finally, the dim strains of music became audible and after a few more switch backs we were at the next aid station. Now it was only three miles to the next station. The sky began to lighten and soon a flashlight was not needed. I was able to pick up the pace, after having run slowly and tentatively for the last seven or eight hours, I was feeling rejuvenated by the daylight.

We came into the Highway 49 station (about 93 miles done!), the last spot to see my crew before the finish line. Also this would be the last weigh-in, where I was still up four pounds and feeling fine, although I was wobbly stepping up on the scale this time. My feet were wet and covered in mud so I opted to change into fresh shoes. I was afraid to look at my feet, but my husband announced there were no blisters...or blood, so I put on clean socks and shoes (all by myself!) and cleaned the mud off my legs. After having no other runners near us for hours, suddenly there were half a dozen at the aid station with me, including the first woman I had seen since Foresthill. I quickly got my things together and started off again. I promised to try and run the rest of the way. There were 6 ½ miles to go and it was 6 a.m.

Most of the terrain after Highway 49 was smooth and virtually flat, but as we approached the road that would lead us on the last mile to the stadium a hill could be seen rising ahead of us. Joe, who had run the year before told me the hill was really not too long. I passed the woman I had seen and then I passed a man, and then another and another and another. I reached the road still moving at a slight jog, but here a very steep hill loomed ahead, but I plowed on. There were at least three more men just ahead, each walking up the hill. I caught each one and then two more just after the hill's crest. We ran briskly down the other side toward the finish. I was really starting to feel like I was actually going to finish, so I picked up the pace. We passed one more runner just before we stepped onto the track at Auburn High School. I dropped my bottles and tried to garner up some speed for the final 300 meters, I felt like I was flying but it was hard to breathe because I thought I might cry.

I crossed the finish line, too happy to speak and grinning like crazy. It was now 7:36 a.m.--26 hours and 36 minutes since I began running. I got my finisher's medal and took my final medical check. Then I was treated to a podiatry exam (for blisters), a complementary blood test (screening for kidney failure) and a wonderful 30 minute massage. For the first time since the start of the race I felt a bit queasy and found it difficult to stand, not to mention move in a forward direction. It took me five minutes to complete the 200 meter walk to the car.

My husband drove us all back to our hotel for a quick nap. The race officially ended at 1 p.m. The cutoff had been extended two hours because of the snow, so the awards were not until 3 p.m. We had to take Joe to the airport for his flight home so I slept some more, easily drifting off in the car with the air conditioner blasting. The heat at the awards ceremony was worse than it had been during the race. Those who finished last were recognized first, and so it went. Each hour was grouped together and it wasn't long before my turn arrived. I placed 61st overall and 9th woman, as well as first in my age group (yes they do have age groups!). Then we loaded back into the car and once again I was fast asleep with happy memories of my first Western States.

Chapter Nine

Sarah Lowell

Sarah Lowell lives and breathes ultrarunning.

She is in her element when she is running free on an isolated trail, dodging roots and rocks and soaking in the fresh mountain air.

I spent time with Sarah the day before the 2006 Western States Endurance Run, an event in which she and I were both competing. It was obvious that she couldn't wait to get started, as she was a bundle of nervousness and excitement in the pre-race festivities in Squaw Valley, California.

Sarah suffered from dehydration during the race and unfortunately was forced to stop. When a friend told me of Sarah's situation as I approached one of the aid stations, I could sense her disappointment from afar as I knew how much the race meant to her.

Hours later as I was officially recognized as the last person to cross the finish line, Sarah greeted me with a big smile and a kiss on the cheek as she knew how much finishing the race meant to *me*.

Right then and there I knew without a doubt that Sarah Lowell not only lives and breathes ultrarunning, she *understands* it as well.

Sarah Lowell

THE POLAR PRINCESS

'I would love to be an arctic explorer.'

-Sarah Lowell

If anyone has the credentials to be an arctic explorer, it would be Sarah Lowell. A native of Clearwater, Florida, Sarah has been an Elementary Physical Education Specialist at the Cartoogechaye School in Franklin, North Carolina for the past 24 years. Sarah studied at Western Carolina University—where she earned her Bachelors and Masters Degrees in Education. Currently she is on the university's Adjunct Faculty as the instructor of the Physical Education seminar class. Sarah is a source of inspiration beyond the classroom as well. After hearing Sarah speak to the Asheville Track Club in 1999, Anne Riddle (now Lundblad)—who had been sitting in the front row of the room listening diligently, began running ultras. Today Anne is arguably the finest female trail ultrarunner in the nation.

Sarah however may be the finest female *extreme* trail ultrarunner in the nation. In 2007 she competed in the Arrowhead 135 Mile Ultramarathon which is held on snowmobile trails in northern Minnesota and featured temperatures reaching 40 degrees below zero—*without* factoring in the wind chill. Not only did Sarah finish the event in two days, seven hours and seven minutes; she was also the first woman to *ever* finish the race on foot and the *only person* to finish the event that year in what was called 'the ugliest trail conditions' the race has ever seen.

Over a running career spanning 31 years, Sarah cites the Arrowhead 135, the Coldfoot 100 and the Susitna 100 (the latter two in Alaska) as her favorite races. Her favorite training run was running Rim to Rim to Rim in the Grand Canyon with Janice Anderson in 2006. Sarah and Janice enjoyed each other's company for 13 hours as they completed the challenging 52+ mile run. While she doesn't have detailed records of her running accomplishments, she admits she's run 'at least 22 100-mile races and ten of them can be classified as arctic.' It is no wonder that she is admiringly referred to as 'the Polar Princess' in the, well, more *frigid* ultrarunning community. Additionally, she's run numerous 50-milers and 50K's and even competed in a triathlon or two. In what she refers to as the 'triathlon chapter' of her life, Sarah qualified for the famous Hawaii Ironman. However, as a young teacher she couldn't afford to go, so she opted to compete in an Ironman-distance event in Tampa, Florida instead.

Endurance was not always Sarah's forte. Her personal bests in a variety of distances are indicative of her ability to not only run far, but *fast* as well:

- 5K – 17:45
- 10K – 38:56
- Marathon – 2:59
- 50K – 3:55
- 50 Mile – 7:40
- 100 Mile – 19:23

Her 100 mile time of 19:23 just happens to be the Arctic Women's Record, by the way. Reflecting on her past personal bests, Sarah says 'it seems like it had to be in another lifetime, as it is so different from the runner that I am *now*.'

Growing up, Sarah had the support of her parents, Karen and John in her running endeavors through the years. Her sister Karen, whom Sarah calls 'the greatest sister in the world' was always in her corner as well. Sarah would be remiss if she failed to mention the importance of her *very* significant other family, most notably Emmi, the champion trail running Schnoodle.

Grete Waitz and Joan Benoit Samuelson provided the early inspiration for Sarah the runner. In fact, Sarah was trackside in Los Angeles when Benoit won the first women's Olympic gold medal in the marathon in 1984. Sarah was a mere 22 years old on that historic day, but her mind snapped a visual photograph that is still as brilliant and vivid as it was a quarter of a century ago. Today Sarah cites 'all the people who keep moving when the going gets tough' as her personal heroes; Grete and Joan just so happen to be the first two on her list.

Sarah is very active and involved in her community. In fact, once you see the list of her volunteer activities you'll be wondering how she finds time to teach five days a week, let alone run 40-60 miles every week:

- Fundraising for critically ill children and their families.
- Fundraising for the Special Olympics.
- Coordinating food drives for people in the community.
- Volunteering at food drives for the local animal shelter.
- Performing trail maintenance on the Bartram and Appalachian Trails.
- Volunteering at the events of the Special Olympics.

Teaching, running and volunteering. What else? I'm glad you asked.

Sarah lists her hobbies as high pointing, backpacking, travel, mountaineering, mountain biking, rock climbing, skiing, assorted snow sports and searching for new ultra challenges. 'High pointing,' by the way means reaching the highest summit in all 50 states.

(Please mention Sarah to the next person you hear say they'd like to run but they 'can't find the time')

Admittedly, Sarah's training method is 'always flying by the seat of my pants.' But for her it's worked. One would question how much thought went into what Sarah did in 2008.

After competing in the inaugural Arctic Grand Slam during the winter of 2008, which consisted of four races in 12 weeks totaling 455 *frozen* miles, Sarah ventured out to Death Valley in July to compete in the Badwater Ultramarathon, a 135 mile race through the desert which she finished in 45:34. In a period of four months, Sarah completed both the coldest and the hottest races on the planet. Talk about flying by the seat of your pants...

This helps explain why Sarah tried running the Barkley 100, reputed to be the toughest *trail* ultra on the planet (so tough that only seven runners have completed all 100 miles since the inaugural race in 1986). Surprisingly, Sarah isn't one of 'the seven.' Yet.

As for future goals, one day Sarah would like to hike the Appalachian Trail. Or better yet, *run* it.

Sarah also would like to run the Iditarod Trail Invitational Race (a race to Nome on the Idatarod Trail). The distance? 1,100 miles. It sounds impossible, doesn't it?

Not to the Polar Princess.

LESSON OF A LIFETIME

By Sarah Lowell

How well I remember the person who influenced me to become a competitive runner. One day I walked into my 11th grade English class and said hello to my teacher, Scott Trees. Scott was a first year teacher who had been asked (forced) to coach cross county and he needed two girls to fill the team. After a month in his class, he realized I was a good student academically, but that keeping me in my seat was going to be a challenge. I think I had pushed his patience to the edge one day. He called me to his desk and said 'I would like for you to consider running on the cross country team--it might be a good outlet for all that energy you have.' I was expecting to get yelled at and instead he asked me to do something that would help define who I was as a person and positively influence every day for the rest of my life.

As I reflect on this, I realize that Scott was even more extraordinary than I first realized back in 1978. He was a Notre Dame graduate, swam in college and had a perfect score on his SAT test. He was also born with a birth defect that left him with no hands or feet. He had eye glasses that were so thick, we all thought he was nearly blind. Yet he had perfect penmanship and a keen sense about people. Many of the other teachers in my life said my excess energy would certainly lead to problems in school and in my life. Scott wasn't one of them.

This teacher recognized the good in me. I ran my first two mile cross country race in 16:25 and I thought I was going to die. I remember that it hurt so much I told him there was no way I was doing it again. Of course all runners have a funny way of forgetting the discomfort and remembering the feeling of achievement, so I became a member of the team. When the season was over, I had lowered my personal best for two miles to 13:15. I couldn't wait until track season!

In January of 1979 Scott told me the boys' team was running the Orange Bowl Marathon in Miami. He asked me if I wanted to run...with him! Four months after I ran my first two mile race, Scott and I were running a marathon. The sound of Converse Chuck Taylors slapping the pavement (he wore the high tops and tied the laces around his ankles) is one of my fondest memories. I don't remember anything negative about that day. In fact, we finished in just under five hours and I actually liked the way I felt! Little did I know this was what I had been searching for--the runners high was amazing.

During track season my senior year I had a new coach since Scott decided to go back to school for a masters degree. I dedicated my season to him and lowered my two mile track time to 11:44. I was now *warming up* at a faster pace than I was *racing* at just twelve months earlier.

I have been a teacher for 24 years now, and was a coach for the first 12. Many of my students have become runners and moved on to run in college, several becoming All-Americans and qualifying for the Olympic Trials. Some run races for fitness, and some run just for fun.

I have a special place in my heart for the kids that can't sit still and I have devoted my life to helping them find 'their' outlet.

Scott Trees graduation from Princeton summa cum lauda in Economics. He received a Masters and PhD in Economics from Notre Dame after he left teaching. Currently he is a Professor of Economics at Siena College in New York.

Scott only taught at my school for one year. I was lucky.

THE BIG CHILL

Daniel's Polar Express

By Sarah Lowell

It was December 14th, 2006. I had just been accepted to run the Arrowhead 135 mile race in International Falls Minnesota, a mere two months away. It was also the day a sad announcement was made at our school: one of our kindergarten children, Daniel, had just been diagnosed with neuroblastoma, a very ugly childhood cancer. Just as the race would soon prove to be a pivotal moment in my life, the announcement led to a pivotal day in my life as it changed the way I thought about running in a race. I had taken a seven year sabbatical from arctic racing, one of my true passions in life. I'm not sure what led me to apply for Arrowhead, a 135-mile race through the icy, barren wilderness of the coldest parts of Minneosta, but it was absolutely one of those things you look back on and say that without a doubt, it was just meant to be. I never realized how isolating and devastating having a child with a serious illness could be. Most of the community didn't understand Daniel's illness and couldn't comprehend the fact he and his mother would spend the next 16 months living at St. Jude's Hospital in Memphis, Tennessee—ten hours away. I saw a need to raise awareness about the disease, drum up moral support for the family and raise money to help them get started on their incomprehensibly difficult journey. Daniel loved the movie *The Polar Express.* Thus, the sled I would be using at Arrowhead was to be called Daniel's Polar Express. It had a laminated picture of Daniel on the back of it. Any time during the race I was feeling low or tired, I would look at Daniel's smiling face. It would a constant reminder of how temporary my discomfort was and how I wanted to be as brave as Daniel.

Because the Arrowhead 135 is almost a completely self-supported race, runners are required to have mandatory survival gear that must be pulled behind them on a sled. Among the items necessary for competing (if not surviving!) are insulated water containers with water, 5,000 calories of food, a -20 rated sleeping bag, a stove, pot and fuel for melting snow and fixing meals, a bivy sack, a flashing red light for visibility, a headlamp, fire starter, and other optional items such as extra clothing, a tool kit, etc. The sled has to weigh at least 15 pounds at all times. You can be stopped on the course at any time and checked to see if you pass inspection. You must also pass inspection before the race starts. To get into the race, a runner must have a strong background in arctic racing and winter camping/mountaineering. Little did I know that my mountaineering skills would play an integral part in the successful completion of the race.

I missed my original flight from Minneapolis/Saint Paul to International Falls and had to wait four hours for the next one. I went to the book store to get something to read, and there was a copy of a brand new book by Ed Viesturs called *NO Shortcuts to the Top*. Reading this book for the next four hours reminded me of everything I had ever learned about extreme mountaineering, and how to take care of yourself and be smart. Ed's motto is 'getting to the top is optional; getting down is mandatory.' Sarah's motto is 'getting to the finish line is mandatory unless it becomes a life or death situation.' It proved to be the perfect time for a refresher course.

When I arrived in International Falls and stepped off the prop plane to walk into the airport, I felt the coldest air I had ever experienced. It was -33 and the wind was blowing. It was so cold that when they unloaded the luggage from the plane to the pick up area an old Samsonite plastic hard cover suitcase exploded, belongings going everywhere. When I arrived at the hotel/race headquarters I overheard employees talking about plugging in their car batteries and how cold it was *going* to get. When people in the 'icebox of the nation' talk about how cold it is going to get, that means it is bad. Very bad. There was a lot of apprehension among race participants which included bikers, runners, and skiers, many whom I met during the pre-race meeting. The race director explained that an arctic blast was coming our way: just in time for the race. Many people were re-thinking what they would take with them on the trail. I had brought every item I owned for a worst-case scenario and every bit of it was jammed into my 35 pound sled. My secret weapon ended up being a large down jacket (circa 1972), a loaner from my friend Al Barker. Al bought the jacket to survive the Chicago winters while he attended optometry school. I had never worn anything so large and bulky during a race and almost didn't even bring it. I would soon come to find that without the jacket I wouldn't have had a prayer.

The race began on the first Monday in February 2007 at 9:00 a.m. It took me 45 minutes to get dressed; I found that it's not simple organizing that many layers of clothing. An SUV with a trailer came to my hotel and picked up my sled and I and took us to the start, which was about ten miles out of town. Just prior to leaving the warmth of my hotel room I was watching the Weather Channel. It gave the current local temperature as -42 degrees. I was confidently nervous.

I started running conservatively with my primary goals focused on adapting to the cold, making sure my apparel was working and comfortable, and adjusting my sled belt. My mantra immediately became 'forward steady progress.' The race begins with an unpleasant out and back of approximately 15 miles. My parka was pulled so tight around my face I had no peripheral vision. What I *could* see was painful to watch. The out and back allowed us to see other competitors early on. Their faces were something I will never forget. People were struggling to breathe and get comfortable, and fighting the fear of moving in the coldest weather imaginable. It was not pretty. The first possibility to drop from the race was at the end of the first out and back. Ultimately more than a third of the field opted for this as the next mandatory--and *only* checkpoint was 60 miles away. Once I did the out and back and crossed the highway, I was on the Arrowhead Trail. This felt like the beginning of what was to be an epic adventure. I never saw another competitor during the day. I did see a dog musher out training. It was the first time he had ever run this particular group of dogs. When they saw me, they went haywire: running into each other, getting tangled and some landing upside down. The musher was so patient and calm. He put his brake on while I was apologizing for creating this disturbance; he calmly untangled his dogs and said it wasn't a big deal. He explained his dogs needed to get used to people. We visited for awhile and parted ways, both stretching the conversation longer than it needed to be to prolong the inevitable return to the task at hand. The woods were beautiful and quiet. The sun was shining and the temperature had risen to -25 degrees. It actually felt great! Off went the parka and balaclava. I felt like a detective as I examined animal footprints and scat in the snow.

I started what I called a 'head-to-toe' check very early on. I started by wiggling my toes and rating my comfort level and worked my way up to my head to ensure I was not neglecting anything. I was pulling my 'mobile aid station' behind me. With the temperatures as cold as they were, I had to plan exactly what I was going to do when I stopped to get food or drink out of my sled. Under my Everest expedition gloves were thin liners that offered minimal protection when I unzipped the sled. I had to work fast to avoid frostbite. The hand warmers in my gloves were added 'frostbite insurance.' My primary source of calories during the race was Boost, a milk-like drink high in calories. They were kept in the sled in a collapsible cooler lined with hand warmers. I would try to chug one during each stop; this gave me fluids and calories all at once, effectively taking care of two birds with one stone. I generally had one minute to drink them before they would begin to freeze up. I kept peanut butter crackers and Sharkies in my pocket and ate them as often as I could stand to choke them down. I tried to eat more during the day as I knew the night would be brutally cold and I would not want to stop as often.

The first night was magical! The sky was clear and free of pollution and the stars were absolutely magnificent. The wolves were howling and for some inexplicable reason everything in the world was right. Not many people know this but I found myself actually singing, something I not only have never done in a race, but have never done *period!* I was cruising along and life was great. Daniel's Polar Express was kicking butt! My solitude came to an abrupt end when I spotted the light of another runner. As I caught up with him, I soon realized it was race director and extreme arctic racer Pierre Ostor. We chatted as well as two people can when talking over moving sleds and bundled bodies. Before long I realized he was not thinking clearly. He kept saying 'I need to sleep; I will put my bag down here.' I would say 'Pierre, there is no place to put your bag except the middle of the trail. You have to keep moving right now.' In his French accent he would reply, several times, 'I am too tired, I have to sleep.' We kept moving in silence. We were both jolted when a wolf crossed the trail in front of us! How exciting! A few minutes later, another wolf jetted across the trail! It is gifts from nature like this that revive and renew my spirit. Eventually, Pierre found a place to put his bag and he bivied with a couple of bikers. In the meantime, I became a little bit sleepy. OK, I was *very* sleepy; in fact I actually fell asleep while I was moving. I fell into a snow bank which woke me up rather quickly, something I would repeat three more times before the sun came up.

As the sun rose in the east, my body seemed to accept that it was time to wake up; I would not be sleepy again. I found myself in a boggy, hilly area as the new day started. This would turn out to be the only part of the course I did not enjoy. I had a few sled mishaps including a spectacular roll down a small hill followed by a few choice words. Once I made it through this tough patch, I was ready for a new day of adventure.

In the middle of the day I reached the only checkpoint on the course at the 75 mile marker, Mel George's Elephant Lake Resort. I crossed the frozen lake and was greeted by photographers, locals, and some of the race participants that had opted to drop out. As the photographer was getting ready to take my picture I went to rub the ice off my lashes as I could barely see. All of my lashes came away with my glove! My head gear was frozen and my lashes and hair had icicles in them. At this checkpoint I saw the men's course record holder and defending champion John Storkamp. He was asleep at the table where others were eating. It was a grim picture of runners with black toes and a soon-to-be legendary tale of one runner who became disoriented and was taken to a hospital. The race staff seemed shocked that I was not even considering dropping out after they informed me that temperatures were forecasted to drop into the -40's once the wind chill was factored in. I was reminded that the next checkpoint was 60 miles away--at the finish line, and there was nothing but wilderness between here and there. The only remaining participants in the race were 10 bikers who were all ahead of me. I was now the 'last one standing' of the runners.

After a break that lasted (*was that really*) an hour and some hot food, fellow runner Kerry Owens of Washington, D.C. walked me out to the trail and wished me well. It was late afternoon and I knew I did not have much sunlight left. The trail changes in this part of the Arrowhead region. It has much steeper climbs and descents and is more difficult than the rest of the course...if that's possible. Ten minutes out of the checkpoint I knew that it most certainly *was* possible. I came across a downhill that looked like a super slide...and it most certainly was. I did my best to control my speed on tired legs and ice, but I slid and fell, and the un-chaperoned sled followed right behind me. This happened more than once. When I finally reached the bottom I stood and looked up. Even though I had traction devices on my shoes, I found myself climbing on my hands and knees hoping I wouldn't slide backwards in order to get up some of the steep hills while pulling my mini-Winnebago. There was something very motivating in the thought that I could become the first woman and only finisher on foot in this, the year of the most brutal conditions in which the event was ever contested. I wanted more than anything for Daniel's Polar Express to cross the finish line.

Meanwhile, back in Franklin, North Carolina where I teach at Cartoogechaye Elementary School, my fellow teachers, students, fellow runners, family and much of western North Carolina were following the great online coverage of the race. In time I would discover they knew more about what was going on than I did! There was a tremendous amount of excitement about the ever-developing story of one last human being braving the elements while all others had dropped by the wayside. There was also much trepidation about me heading out into the night, alone, in frigid weather without any checkpoints or aid stations for assistance. Later, once I returned to Franklin afterwards, I discovered that very few of my 'support team at home' got any sleep while I was out in the wilderness. I did know, however, that I had the support and prayers of literally thousands of people. For some strange reason I never really had any doubt I would finish. That was a personal thought and feeling that I would not have shared out loud with anyone. I just *knew*.

I headed into the cold, dark, beautiful starry night with a determination stronger than any I have ever experienced. I was on a mission to complete this epic adventure. Strangely enough, I never got sleepy the second night; in fact it was very much the opposite. My senses were on full alert because I realized there was no margin for error. I maintained my head-to-toe checks, did the best I could to eat and drink (not an easy task) and carefully planned my sled stops to minimize the time my hands were out of my gloves. The only scary moment of the race happened during this second night out on the trail. It was time to change out my hand warmers as I could feel the temperature in my gloves getting colder. I quickly grabbed my hand warmers, had some difficulty opening the package but finally managed to get them into my glove. The hand warmers were supposed to last 10 hours, but in these temperatures the best I hoped for was three. When I got them into my glove, I was not feeling any heat. This particular pair was defective! Between being out of my gloves and not getting the immediate heat, I could actually feel the blood and muscles in my hands begin to 'thicken' and quit working. Instinctively I put both hands into my pants against my skin and rubbed them for warmth. It was scary to try the next set of hand warmers, but I had to do it. After a 40 minute stop (five minutes just to buckle my sled harness as my hands had no dexterity), I had solved the problem and was on my way. This gave my confidence a tremendous boost because I did not panic and I was able to think fast and take care of my problem. In the long run, 40 minutes was nothing because without that stop, I, like several other competitors would have suffered from frostbite and potentially could have lost several fingers.

There are not many signs on the upper part of the Arrowhead trail. At one point during the night, I had that funny feeling in the pit of my stomach that I was on the wrong trail. I actually began hallucinating, seeing signs that weren't there which read 'Arrowhead Trail.' I would get to the sign, reach out to touch it, only to find myself poking at nothing but air. My mind was so desperate to see the signs that it had created them. Again, I did not panic. I stopped and took a look at the map and it appeared I was where I should be, so I kept moving.

Meanwhile, on the online race telecast, it was reported that the snow machines could not locate me. All of my followers thought I was lost in the Minnesota wilderness on one of the coldest nights of the winter. I later found out that the people at home maintained a constant vigil on the school's computers praying for a miracle. My dad wrote a story on the Arrowhead online blog that was active during the race. It relayed the idea that the light would stay on all night, for as long as it took the good people of Minnesota to find me.

As it turned out, I *was* on the trail. As dawn approached on the final morning of the run, I was tired and looking down at the snow. I followed the snow for a while and soon discovered a small mercantile store. I just knew I was in the wrong place. I made the decision to bivy on the porch of a house and hope the owners would eventually show up. It was a painstakingly slow process to get my spikes and shoes off, get my sleeping bag out of my sled and crawl inside with everything on, but I did it. About an hour later, I could hear the sound of car tires 'crunching' in the snow. I was totally enclosed in my sleeping bag so I couldn't see a thing. Car doors opened and I heard a laugh. In a thick Minnesota accent a male voice said 'Is everything OK in there?' I said 'yes, pretty good.' 'Aren't you kind of cold out here? This is not a good night for camping.' I said 'I'm OK: my bag is warm, but I am lost.' The man said 'the back door is unlocked; you could have gone in and gotten warm.' I said 'in the south we call that breaking and entering!' He laughed and invited me in to see if he knew where it was I needed to go. As I had accidentally left my shoes out of my sleeping bag, they were now almost frozen and it took what seemed like forever to get them back on my feet--not the most pleasant experience in the world.

But now I was about to hear the most encouraging, best news I'd heard in days. I had turned off the trail a mere half-mile down the road. I just needed to retrace my steps, get back on the trail, and I would only be 17 miles from the finish line!!! I thanked the kind man and bolted; well, as best I could while pulling 35 pounds behind me. As I moved along, I started doing the math. With a 60 hour cutoff, I should be finished with time to spare. I started feeling very emotional during this time. I knew that I was going to do this. If I could conquer this race, Daniel could conquer his cancer.

It was a beautiful, sunny day; maybe 20 degrees below zero. I shed the infamous parka and kept moving. Soon I was joined by a Brazilian journalist, Rodrigo Cerqueira. Rodrigo had run the first out and back of the race before opting to stop. He had his video camera and asked if I would mind if he ran along with me and asked me to talk about my experience. I welcomed the company. It made the miles pass by rather quickly; at least much quicker than I had envisioned them passing by at this stage of the game. He was very humble and honored that I would talk to him about my adventure. I in turn was flattered that he was so interested. He kept talking about how unbelievable this whole race had been for me. How did I do it? What did I eat? What did I think about? How did I stay warm? I didn't have many good answers at that point. I was so focused on completing my journey and picturing the little boy's photo on the back of my Polar Express. Rodrigo took several photographs, one which would later make the cover of Brazil's version of *Sports Illustrated* along with a great story (albeit in Portuguese).

Rodrigo left me with two miles remaining. I appreciated the gesture, as I wanted to savor every last moment of this incredible experience. I spent a few minutes thinking about the journey I was about to finish, the people I had met, and the stories that would certainly last a lifetime.

I met up with a snow machine that led me towards the finish line. My spirits fell for a moment when I saw a large icy hill that I had to climb. Then, with a sudden burst of energy I charged up the hill! I remember how beautiful the sunlight was in the late afternoon, and how easily and much too quickly the last mile passed by. As I approached the finish line, I began to cry. I was so incredibly overwhelmed with emotion after realizing I had beaten the odds and made history.

My tears quickly froze and actually stung my face, so I forced myself to hold back on this particular physical display of emotion. I had a wonderful welcome at the finish line and was quickly swept inside where it was safe and warm. I was offered a variety of hot drinks, but after 55 hours with virtually no water, all I wanted was a pitcher of ice water! (Yes, *ice* water!)

After three pitchers, I was ready to eat. I did several interviews and laughed a lot with the wonderful people from Brazil that ran the first part of the race. Calls were coming in from friends and my two families, one connected to me by blood and the other through my school. The internet coverage confirmed my historic finish and allowed a lot of people a good night's sleep.

When I arrived back home, the celebration started at the airport. Some of my closest friends and family were there with custom hats that had my face superimposed to make me look like an arctic goddess. They had signs and were cheering wildly; it was awesome! They all hugged me and held on tight as if to say 'I am so thankful you are here and safe.' When I arrived at school the following Monday (the race ended on a Wednesday) there was a beautiful custom banner by the road in front of the school that read:

Congratulations Ms. Lowell
Arrowhead 135 Mile Winter Ultra Marathon
Women's Champion

When I walked in the gym, every teacher on our staff was lined up. Once they saw me, they all started clapping, then crying, and then hugging. The love and support was beyond anything I could ever have imagined. When I unlocked the door to my office I found 135 balloons, assorted bottles of Gatorade, and cards from every class in the school. At 9:00 a.m. the principal played the theme song from *Chariots of Fire* over the loudspeaker while all the students and teachers in the school lined the hallways clapping, cheering and hugging as I walked my victory lap. I was wearing a sash that said 'Polar Princess.' Daniel's parents, grandparents, the Mayor of Franklin and other dignitaries were at the finish line of my 'victory lap.' They ordered pizza and would not let me teach all day. I did several newspaper interviews and answered many phone calls. Again, it was amazing to feel so admired and cared for.

We raised several thousand dollars for Daniel's family, but that was not the most important thing that came out of my adventure in Minnesota.

All of the favorable press that Daniel's Polar Express received brought other families that had children afflicted with neuroblastoma into the public eye. After years of isolation and misunderstanding, we were talking about it, raising money and awareness for it, and bringing people facing its challenge together to support one other and give each other encouragement and hope.

This, the most memorable race of my life wasn't just about running. Nor was it about survival or enduring. It was about *people*.

Of course it involved running, adventure, and challenge, but more importantly it was a race of the heart. It brought our school, community and families closer together in the midst of a crisis. It connected people to this family in need and educated the community as to what they were dealing with. I never dreamed of the far-reaching implications this initially simple idea would have.

Two years to the day of the success of Daniel's Polar Express, Daniel appeared on the local news station as he was preparing to celebrate his 'end of chemo' party. He continues to struggle with the complications due to the cancer, but has a beautiful full head of curly hair and is absolutely adorable. He's a brave soldier winning his battle against cancer. Daniel inspired me to be strong, brave, and selfless. Perhaps he even *taught* this teacher to be strong, brave and selfless.

Racing with your heart will give you strength, confidence and courage you never knew you had. As I said earlier, my involvement with Daniel forever changed the way I will think about running a race. After all, it's not always about setting a personal best or finishing in first place.

It's all about people.

PART TWO:
Extraordinary Gentlemen
✦
(The Back Nine)

Chapter Ten

Lloyd Young

Lloyd Young has run some amazing races.

In fact the race times he is currently running are comparable to mine, yet mine would not be considered 'amazing.'

You see, Lloyd is 31 years my senior.

I'll save you some math: Lloyd Young is 85 years old, and he's still running strong.

I like to kid with Lloyd and tell him his legs are younger than mine (he's been running for 26 years and I've been running for 31 years, so my legs are five years 'older'). But all kidding aside, he is one phenomenal athlete.

What else can you say about someone who is always looking ahead to the next five-year age group to see what the existing world records are?

What else can you say about someone who plans on *beating* them—even if they're five years away—at an age when most people would be having trouble walking to the mailbox once a day?

What else can you say about someone who can still run...*run*, mind you for 12 hours at a time at an age when most people have trouble *staying awake* for that long?

Phenomenal.

That's Lloyd Young.

Lloyd Young

FOREVER YOUNG

In the spring of 2005 I received a handwritten letter from a man by the name of Lloyd Young. Lloyd was inquiring about running in the 4th edition of the Peachtree City 50K in November. He explained he had reservations about air travel, and since he didn't have any credit cards *(he prefers cash, thank you)* whether or not a trip from his home in Pine City, Minnesota to the big city of Atlanta would be wise. After all, Lloyd had just turned 82, and common sense would tell you a lengthy flight at that age to attempt to run 31 miles is a pretty preposterous idea.

But then again, you don't know Lloyd.

I corresponded with Lloyd throughout the summer of 2005 via 'snail mail' *(Lloyd prefers a typewriter and the United States Postal Service, thank you)* about his participation in the race and around Labor Day Lloyd sent in his application. Some good friends of Lloyd's took care of the details—flight reservations and hotel accommodations *(my wife and I offered him a room, but he didn't want to impose; although he said he appreciated the offer, thank you)* and when the big weekend arrived, a trip to the airport in Minnesota. I picked Lloyd up at the Atlanta airport two days before the race and found a quiet, mannerly gentleman dressed in a dark gray sweat suit who didn't appear to be more than 125 pounds—if he was standing outside in the rain... with a 16-pound bowling ball in his hands.

Through our correspondence, Lloyd told me about his background. He was born in 1923 in Reading, Pennsylvania (not more than 15 minutes from the small town my parents were born and raised in—Birdsboro). After his parents separated in 1924, his mother moved back home to Whitebear Lake, Minnesota with Lloyd and his sister Edith.

After graduating from high school in St. Paul in 1941, Lloyd joined the U.S. Navy and served in the southwest Pacific during World War II. After the war, he enlisted in the U.S. Air Force and served one year in Germany on a satellite airlift base in Berlin. Lloyd was married for 25 years and the marriage produced four children, four grandchildren and three great-grandchildren. Lloyd and his wife later divorced when he was 50 years old. For the duration of his career, he worked in the machinist trade, developing naval missile launchers, rocket engines, and lunar landing legs (prior to putting man into space and on the moon).

Lloyd is a man of diversity, as evidenced by his writing credentials as a published author of three collections of poetry. He's won many awards for his writing; but not nearly as many as he's won for his running!

However, before he began his career as a runner, Lloyd battled problems with alcoholism following his divorce. He spent three years at a Christian Bible Camp, and at age 59 he started running. He joined a running club during his five years living in Wisconsin, before finally settling down in Pine City, Minnesota in 1988.

Once he found his stride, so to speak, as a runner Lloyd found immediate success and before long he was setting state and national age group records in a variety of distances.

Among his more notable personal bests:

- A 19:41 5K at the age of 62.
- A 1:00:03 15K and a 3:12:14 marathon at the age of 63. *(It's hard to determine which is more notable: that Lloyd ran a 3:12 marathon at 63 or that he did it after only running for slightly more than three years!)*
- A 39:00 10K and a 5:31:8 mile (on the road, which won Lloyd a National Championship) at the age of 65.
- A 1:35:52 half-marathon at age 71.
- A 6:38 indoor mile—*at age 75*—which is an American and World Best!
- Several time and distance age group records at the 2005 FANS 24-Hour Race, at the tender age of 81.

Once I met Lloyd in person for the first time, I wondered to myself how this quiet, mannerly gentleman could be capable of the many records he had told me about over the summer. But when Lloyd met my friend Al Barker and I the next morning to run the 5.18 mile loop used for the 50K race (in the race, the loop is run six times), all of my questions were answered.

The transformation from the day before when I first met Lloyd wearing his dark gray sweat suit to the next morning was—well, the best analogy I can make is when Clark Kent *(think of Steve Reeves in the Superman television series of the 1950's)* entered a phone booth and exited as the Man of Steel. Lloyd—dressed in running shoes, shorts and singlet—was every bit the Man of Steel. He looked amazing, and was in absolutely phenomenal shape.

Once we started running it was evident that this man was capable of the records he had spoken of. Over the course of our five mile run, Lloyd would occasionally run ahead and each time Al, who would be running next to me, would point at Lloyd and quietly say to me ' *He's 82 years old!* ' Yes, he was indeed 82 years old, and he now had two more members in his fan club.

The morning of the race, Lloyd ran the ½ mile from his motel to the starting line *(I offered to pick him up as I did the day before, but he didn't want to impose on me, seeing as I was the Race Director and would be busy—even though I told him it would be no bother).* Dressed in yet another Man of Steel outfit, Lloyd preceded to run an astonishing 5:53:22. *(Note: Currently the time is being reviewed to determine not only if it is a United States Age Group Record, but a WORLD AGE GROUP RECORD as well!)*

Lloyd turned 85 on July 18, 2008, and now has his sights set on age group records in a variety of events—from 5K to 24 hours. He is a staple at the Twin Cities Marathon every year, and if he's not running in the FANS 12/24 Hour Endurance Run, you will find him there as a volunteer, lending his support and wisdom to the other runners.

Lloyd is optimistic about his chances for more records, because—as he told me excitedly over the phone a few months before his 85th birthday—he's not like the other runners in his age group (who, for the most part, compete at no more than a fast walk) because *he's still running!*

Lloyd is truly an inspiration for runners of every age and every generation. Perhaps Al Barker said it best back in 2005 *(Al was 60 years old at the time)* when he first ran with Lloyd and immediately afterwards said *'When I grow up, I want to be just like Lloyd.'*

That makes two of us, Al.

To Endure is to Live

By Lloyd Young

As a writer of poetry I'm often seeking the best words to define what is being said, thought or written. Another passion I have is running; a favorite word to define the object of competition is endurance. To ENDURE sometimes includes the ability to go beyond pain; or in wisdom, to back off and enjoy socializing with your running friends.

In my first race, I was a 59-year old green-horn. Did I really know how fast I could be...or how far I could go? I enjoyed all that in the meat-grinder of race schedules. Winning isn't everything; I had learned to do what I can with what I have. Second or third place was not a disaster by any means. And now, having had the pleasure of working on the first moon rocket engines and lunar module landing legs, maybe I'm still in the other century. I've tossed my computer along with other electronic devices; all these, cutting into the great passions of my heart. The most valuable tool I still retain use of is my Brother Word Processor.

In 2007 I won a gold medal in poetry at the National level of competition in creative writing. Not bad for a guy who'll likely never be named 'Poet Laureate' of anywhere! In my first year of running competition I wrote my first poem. In it I said, 'I will run with the Elite, I shall be found in their midst!'

This could well be a truth even if I'd never won a race, so I wasn't speaking out of turn. Whatever abilities God has blessed me with, I'm happy where I'm at!

Whatever I do beyond here is a bonus; I'm just as excited as when I first toed the starting line in a 3K race.

Another word I hope to fulfill: LONGEVITY.

To Finish on Inspiration

By Lloyd Young (to commemorate his 85th birthday: July 18, 2008)

'Hey, Lloyd! Are you still running nine-minute miles?' this from a fellow runner.

'Not very likely today,' I replied while preparing for the Lumberjack 10-Miler at age 85.

Another fellow, a stranger to me, noticing a wiping rag in my hand, confided that he left his at home. 'Can't do much without one I sweat so terribly.'

'I'll get you one from my bag; I always carry extras.' I said. Shortly after, I had equipped my new-found 'kindred spirit'—a man in an orange T-shirt, with a clean wash rag.

I didn't see him at the starting line area, what with a sea of 2,000 milling about. Suddenly, off we go! At the two-mile mark I was surprised that I was running an 8:45 pace even though trying to hold back on a largely downhill course.

In the middle stretch I was maintaining nine-minute miles on the gradual upgrade. At the sixth mile I was behind a bit, but not to worry: I'll get it back, as the downhill after the 10K mark loomed with its refreshing promise past Boomsite Park.

Suddenly at my shoulder was my friend in the orange T-shirt. I had earlier briefed him on the course as this was his first Lumberjack 10; now reminding him 'We're entering the enjoyable cool-down part I told you about!'

Then into the final three miles, he was high-fiving many of the volunteers and thanking the spectators. What a guy; a 'spirit of encouragement' to all, and especially to me! His enthusiasm was infectious, having effects on all the other runners and also many curbsiders cheering us on!

With one and a half miles to go I told him 'on this flat part we need to push hard, keeping our stride!' I noticed my friend was struggling somewhat, and sweating profusely. We turned into the finish-line area…I forget, but I think I passed him. And now, 200 meters to go and into my 'grandstand kick,' promising to myself I would be sure to tell my friend just how much he had inspired me.

Beyond my finish that was 90 seconds faster than last year's time, I glanced back at many runners coming to the line, looking for the guy in the outrageous orange T-shirt. Then I looked ahead; where is he? Later, searching for him amongst the thousands, I realized I had lost him. Vaporized?

I believe in angels. In the Bible angels are described as men; I also believe that God appoints just ordinary men to special assignments. I may have met one...and should be aware of my own opportunities.

Chapter Eleven

Tom Adair

If you're a member of the 50 States Marathon Club you probably know the name of Tom Adair. Actually, if you're a member you probably know Tom Adair personally.

In fact, if you're a member I'd be willing to wager that you've posed for a photograph with Tom Adair.

As James Brown once professed to be 'the hardest working man in show business,' Tom Adair is quite possibly 'the most photographed man in running.'

Tom runs all over the country. In fact Tom runs all over the *world*. To decide whether Tom travels so he can run or if Tom runs so he can travel is like deciding which came first: the chicken or the egg. There is substantive data to support either argument, as Tom's total of marathons and ultras is increasing proportionately to his frequent flyer miles.

The next time you sign up for a marathon or ultra, check to see if Tom Adair is on the list of entrants.

If he is, remember to say hello and when the time comes be sure to smile and say 'cheese.'

Tom Adair

A RUNNER AND A GENTLEMAN

My Aunt Freda would have liked Tom Adair. Scratch that: she would have *loved* Tom Adair.

Aunt Freda was my grandmother's sister's only daughter, so technically she was my Great Cousin. However, as Freda had no children of her own, she preferred to call me her nephew, but treated me as if I was her son.

Freda tried her best to impress on me three very important things in life: (1) dress for success, (2) live a Christian life and (3) always—*always* mind your manners.

Those of you who know me understand how miserably Freda failed on item number one. Item number two? Let's just say that the 'end result' is still pending, but I believe I'm on the right track. As for number three, I have to admit that I don't think I've ever failed to say *'please, thank you, yes ma'am, no ma'am, yes sir'* or *'no sir'* when it was appropriate.

But like I said earlier, my Aunt Freda would have loved Tom Adair. Not only does he live up to all three of Freda's expectations, Tom is also one of the finest gentlemen you could ever hope to meet.

I first became aware of Tom Adair in November of 2000. There was an article in an Atlanta newspaper about Tom and his running career, and that the Atlanta Marathon on Thanksgiving Day would be his 100th lifetime marathon (or ultra). A couple days after Thanksgiving Al Barker—who didn't know Tom at the time—called Tom to congratulate him on his milestone. The call lasted almost an hour, as it was filled with Tom's stories of races past, present and future and a lengthy testimonial to the intrigue and allure of the famous Comrades Ultramarathon in South Africa. Tom finished the 54 miles of the 75th anniversary of Comrades on June 16, 2000 with a respectable finishing time of 11 hours and 51 minutes. To this day, Al and I look forward to the day we toe the starting line in Johannesburg—primarily because of Tom's generosity in sharing his stories and his time with a runner he had never met. But that's the type of man Tom is. He is generous to a fault.

In November of 2003, Tom ran in the Peachtree City 50K and was so impressed with the friendliness of the volunteers and members of the host Darkside Running Club he became a member himself in the spring of the following year.

Runners from every corner of the country pay their respects to Tom in his role as the President of the 50 States Marathon Club, an organization he was an essential part of during its original structuring and development. According to Steve Boone, the founder and treasurer of the Club, 'Tom Adair has been an integral part of the 50 States Marathon Club organization since its formation in 2001. His selfless contributions, forward thinking ideas, attention to detail and hard work helped provide the foundation for the club and he continues to be instrumental in the growth and success of the club.' The club, under Tom's steady guidance, has grown to over 2,000 members. Tom certainly leads by example. He completed a marathon in all 50 states for the *second* time on October 1, 2005 (which coincidentally was his 64th birthday). Three short years later, he completed his third cycle of finishing a marathon in all 50 states (November 22, 2008). He has run a marathon on every day of the week (Monday through Sunday)…at one time had a streak of 149 consecutive months with a marathon finish…and in 2004 ran 36 races of marathons distance—or more. From his initial marathon in Atlanta back in November of 1994, he now lists the Big Sur Marathon (which he has run four times), the Marine Corp Marathon (six times), the Umstead Endurance Run (eight times) and the Sunmart Texas Trail (seven times) as his favorites. Boston? You bet; in 1996 and 1998. Tom has also run the Atlanta Marathon 15 consecutive years, and cites Comrades as his most challenging ultra (in 2000, an 'up' year).* In 2004 Tom and a few others ran a 'spontaneous' ultra from Atlanta to Alabama along the Silver Comet Trail (62 miles, or 100 kilometers).

*Note: Comrades reverses its course every year, with even-numbered years being 'up' and odd-numbered years 'down.'

It's hard to believe Tom didn't start running 10K's until 1992, after he was 'burned out' from tennis.

After retiring full time in January of 2007 (he retired 'part time' in October of 2003) Tom began to travel more frequently; not only to run in different marathons but more importantly to honor other runners reaching marathon milestones anywhere in the United States. Tom has served as an inspiration for runners of different abilities and goals, runners from all walks of life, and runners of all ages. Spend ten minutes with Tom and you will find him to be as engaging and charismatic as people who have known him for years can attest.

Tom was born in Memphis, Tennessee on October 1, 1941. After five years of studying English at the University of Alabama, Tom joined the Marine Corp in 1963 and served for six years. Tom still lives by the Marine slogan 'Semper Fi' ('Always Faithful'), both as a person and as a runner. He married Jean, his college sweetheart on the 4th of July in Tuscaloosa, Alabama. In 1972 they moved from Memphis to Atlanta before settling down in Alpharetta (on the northern outskirts of Atlanta). Besides running, Tom fills his 'free time' with his four children, nine grandchildren, staying active in St. Brendan

Catholic Church, supporting his wife's passion of raising and breeding Shetland Sheepdogs for agility and obedience competition, watching college football, and watching television while sipping on a glass of wine or an ice cold beer. Ah, retirement...

Although Tom says he wants to 'slow down' a bit, his list of future running goals offers evidence to the contrary. Tom says he would like to:

- Complete a marathon on all seven continents on March 6, 2010 on King George Island, Antarctica (he's already completed one on the other six continents).
- Complete 300 career marathons (which include 56 ultra marathons) in the summer of 2009.
- Run five miles every day for one year—most likely in 2010.
- Run across the state of Florida with Chuck Savage—again, most likely in 2010.
- Run more local and nearby marathons in Georgia, North Carolina, Alabama and Florida.

Personally, Tom has always had an encouraging word for me (and I like to think that I have had one for him as well). A perfect example was in April 2008 at the Umstead 100 Mile Endurance Run in Raleigh, North Carolina. This was my first time competing at Umstead, and one of the reasons was because Tom had always billed the event as his favorite. I know Tom to be a man of good taste, and I was confident he wouldn't advertise any race as his 'favorite' if it didn't meet his standards of quality and organization. So I entered.

Unfortunately, Tom had slipped on an icy glacier competing at the Antarctica Marathon one month earlier and fractured his right pelvis in three places, so under doctor's orders he wasn't allowed to run for two months. Tom fell at the four-mile mark, but still managed to complete the half marathon. This injury, by the way, is what stopped his streak of 149 consecutive months with a marathon finish. Undaunted, he'll return to Antarctica in 2010 to complete a marathon on his 7th continent, which will entitle him to become a full member of The Seven Continents Club.

But showing both his dedication to the race and his generosity to the sport of running, he made the six-hour drive from his home in Alpharetta, Georgia and spent the weekend at Umstead State Park. Over the 30 hours of the event, Tom supported, encouraged and entertained all 250 participants as they completed the 12 ½ mile lap through the park time after time after time. After one of my laps, Tom had an ice cold beer waiting for me; Tom knows it to be my beverage of choice in runs of 50 miles or more, and I imagine he knew a similar tidbit of information about the other 249 competitors in the event as well. When I completed my 100 miles—at 4:32 a.m. on a rainy Sunday morning—Tom was there to congratulate me, take a few photos, and make sure I had plenty to eat and drink. Again, I'm certain he did that for the other 249 competitors—win, lose or draw—throughout the weekend.

About a week after Umstead, I received a CD in the mail. It was from Tom, and it contained digital photographs of all 250 competitors at Umstead.

Generous to a fault and a perfect gentleman. Freda would have loved Tom Adair.

As for me, I'm just proud to know him.

Run Marathons ... And See the USA

By Tom Adair, Sr.

One of Scott Ludwig's best characteristics is his relentless support and encouragement of other runners like me to do our best. Let me thank Scott from the bottom of my heart for everything, especially for inviting me to take part in this, his second book. Without question, Scott is an outstanding athlete who excels in endurance runs. He sets specific goals and standards for his family life and his running life. With that said most runners who know Scott understand his discipline to train his body uncompromisingly to the point of fatigue. His self-control to train hard is his path to success.

There is one question I have about Scott and his book *Running through My Mind: Confessions of an Every Day Runner* that sometimes keeps me awake at night. I'm not certain I know the answer. How can Scott and I be 'worlds apart' in our sport of long distance running? Yes, we both experience the same love and passion for running. And we both are familiar—*very* familiar, in fact, with the pain and disappointment that comes with the sport.

Okay, we are 'worlds apart' in long distance running and yet we both share a burning passion for running.

Our training is dissimilar, but yet we both benefit from running. How dissimilar? You be the judge:

• Scott trains daily.	I barely train.
• Scott runs 90 miles a week (every week).	I scarcely run during the week.
• Scott always runs marathons under 4 hours.	I usually finish over 5 hours.
• Scott runs fast.	I run slowly.
• Scott is a gazelle.	I'm a turtle.
• Scott wins age-group awards.	I'm happy for a same-day finish.
• Scott is a talented writer.	I can recognize talented writers.
• Scott encourages all runners.	I'm encouraged by other runners.

So, you may be wondering how I ever got involved in long distance running.

For most of my adult life I was a tennis player. I played 'B' level club tennis. I enjoyed the competition, the friendship and the beer drinking after the matches. I thought I'd play tennis as long as I lived. However, I never counted on being 'burned out' on tennis after 18 years of playing almost every week. In high school and college I ran track. I ran 100 and 200 yard races. I was always a sprinter. I never thought of long distance running as a sport I would enjoy. Heck, I used to think an all-out sprint around a 400 yard track was brutal.

So, after I 'burned out' on my tennis career, I looked for something to do athletically. Like many runners, I began to run 5K and 10K races. A few years later I ran a half-marathon. Then in 1994 I ran my first marathon in Atlanta. Although I was not properly trained and my finish was quite honestly nothing to look at, I was hooked.

To gain the training and knowledge I needed to continue with running marathons, I participated in the Jeff Galloway marathon training program for two years. It was an awesome and fun way to learn about running long distances. Admittedly, I learned a lot from the other runners in my group in the Galloway program. One of them, Roger Ackerman, became a good friend of mine. He taught me volumes about ultra running and the training discipline for—good Lord, I can't believe I'm saying this, 100-mile runs. He's an awesome ultra runner, and I learned so much from running with him.

Now fourteen years later, at the age of 68 I've accomplished a few of my goals that were, well, *unfathomable* until I became involved with the incredible athletes of the ultra world.

(1) On November 22, 2008, at the Seashore marathon in Rehoboth Beach, Delaware, I finished a marathon or ultra marathon for the third time in all of the 50 USA States;

(2) On April 9 and August 26, 2006, I finished two 100 mile races after many failures at the distance.
- My first finish was at the Umstead 100 on April 9, 2006 in Raleigh, North Carolina in 28 hours and 58 minutes.
- My second finish was at the Lean Horse Hundred on August 26, 2006 in Hot Springs, South Dakota in 28 hours and 3 minutes.

(3) On February 17, 2008, I finished a marathon streak of 149 consecutive months (12 years, 5 months) starting with the Marine Corp Marathon on October 22, 1995 in Washington, DC and ending with the National Marathon to Fight Breast Cancer in Jacksonville Beach, Florida. Actually, my monthly marathon streak ended on March 5, 2008 at the Antarctica marathon when I fractured my right pelvic bone while falling down on an icy glacier during the race.

(4) Lastly, on September 11, 2007, I finished a marathon or ultra on every day of the week (i.e. a marathon on Monday, Tuesday, etc.).

I'd like to share with you some of the things I've learned and/or experienced over the past 14 years.

Goal Setting vs. Achievement

Early in my marathon running days I met friends who were trying to run a marathon in each of the 50 states, a goal which I thought was extraordinary. It wasn't long before I wanted to try it, too. I eagerly calculated a schedule which allowed me to achieve my 50th state only 18 months later. I followed my schedule religiously and in June 1998 I could proudly say 'I did it.' I had run a marathon in every great state of our glorious country. A few weeks later I told a close running friend of mine that I was thinking about not running anymore. I wanted to quit the sport, give up running altogether. My friend laughed and told me I needed another running goal to replace the one I had achieved. He told me I needed to set more goals which would rejuvenate my passion for the sport. He knew what he was talking about: I set several new running goals and in no time I was happy to be running again. In my opinion, it's more fun to chase goals than to accomplish them.

Running Marathons is similar to my Lifestyle

Life is difficult and fun, and so is running a marathon. Every day of my life is filled with activity, meeting challenges and making decisions. I have moments when I feel good; I have moments when I feel bad. I meet challenges head on: sometimes I succeed…and sometimes I fail. Running is no different, as I experience the same sensations and results when I run a marathon.

I eat, drink and sleep in order to feed my body to accomplish the tasks at hand in my everyday life. I do the same things when I'm preparing for a marathon. I meet new and old friends while running just as I do in everyday life. The list of similar analogies is limitless. The challenges of my everyday life are similar to the challenges of running a marathon.

Spiritual Time to Meditate and Pray

I have been an active member of the Roman Catholic Church my entire life. I learned to believe in God and Jesus Christ. I was taught the importance of helping others. I learned the value of giving more in life to others than I receive. Lastly, I learned the value of daily meditation and prayer. However, it was always difficult for me because I could not find the right time. Training and running marathons and ultra marathons create a large amount of private time that allows me to meditate and pray.   This is a perfect marriage for my interests --- running, meditation and prayer.

Encouraging Others to Run Marathons

As I mentioned earlier, running my first marathon was a bad experience. I was not physically or mentally ready. I was in pain most of the time. It was—in a word, awful. I feared that I would not finish within the allowed time limit. Once I crossed the finish line, however, my pain disappeared and I was happy. How strange: how can 26.2 miles of misery and pain wind up with a happy ending? Of course, I later learned the importance of training properly and learning from other runners. Today, one of my biggest personal rewards is helping and encouraging new runners to run their first marathon. It is a wonderful experience to witness the development of a first time marathon runner. I like to think my suggestions, personal discipline, training advice and daily goal accomplishments have guided a few of my running friends to a successful marathon finish. One recommendation I always suggest to new runners is to have a running partner. There is a wealth of benefits for someone fortunate enough to have a regular running partner.

Lessons in Humility

Most of the problems I faced in my life can be indirectly attributed to my ego. That is, until I started to run marathons. At that time I learned training and running a marathon provides a healthy dose of truth and humility. Marathons forced me to be less pretentious and more modest. Daily runs were reality to my life style. Running has contributed to a more balanced existence.

Lessons in Failure

Failure is a good teacher for future races. I should know: I failed to finish ten different 100-mile races. I never failed to finish due to injury, but rather because I simply did not think I could make it to the finish line. In the words of another runner, a marathon or ultra marathon finish depends on mental stamina; it's your brain that gets you across the finish line. And at the age of 68, my brain has learned how to hang tough. However, the lessons I learned from my failures helped me to finish two 100 miles races in 2006. The lessons I learned (in no particular order) are: (a) avoid mental distractions, (b) utilize a pacer, (c) use my time at the aid stations wisely, and (d) maintain a reasonable body weight (for me it's 155 pounds). While mental preparation is a critical element for a successful 100-mile race, it never hurts to have a wealth of training miles in the bank as well.

In 2008 I failed to finish a road marathon for the first time in my life. It was my first marathon DNF (did not finish). I was running the Antarctica Marathon on King George Island with 175 other runners. At mile four, I fell down on my right hip on top of an icy glacier. My pelvis was fractured in three places although I didn't know it at the time. I continued to walk and jog nine more miles to the half-marathon finish. I was in mortal pain, barely able to drag my right leg as I advanced. I did *not* travel all the way to Antarctica for my first DNF. I was out-of-my-mind with pain in my pelvic area. Mentally I hated the experience of my first DNF. Why did this happen to me? Regrettably, I did not wear Yaktrax (shoe covers to help walk/run on ice). I botched things, the result of poor preparation. Oh, how I wish I had spent $25 for a pair of Yaktrax. Without question, my first marathon failure caused me a great deal of stress, disappointment and force-fed me a load of humility. However, I'm constantly learning what to do as well as what *not* to do in future runs. I always learn from my disappointments...my failures. Anxiously my plan is to return to Antarctica on February 26 through March 12, 2010 for an Antarctica marathon finish on March 6th to give me a marathon finish on all seven continents. My wife Jean will join me for the Antarctica trip and the Antarctica marathon finish.

Membership in the 50 States Marathon Club

In September of 2001 I was an integral part of the 50 States Marathon Club during its formative years. I worked closely with Paula and Steve Boone to get the club up and running. Steve is the founder and treasurer of the club. We all worked together to develop the club rules and regulations, newsletter, website, quarterly reunion meetings, legal incorporation, and board of directors. We spent many hours promoting and growing the club. The club is a non-profit organization dedicated to the promotion of health and fitness, and its members share the common goal of running a marathon in each of the fifty states. The 50 States Marathon Club has grown to over 2,000 members hailing from all 50 states as well as nine foreign countries. I am proud to say that I am currently serving as the club's President.

As you can imagine, the club has provided me countless hours of running enjoyment. Over the past eight years I've met hundreds of new friends in all 50 States. I've enjoyed the camaraderie of runners on all seven continents. Many runners in turn shared their running ideas and knowledge. The mission of the club is to help our members run and finish a marathon in all 50 States. I've enjoyed traveling to all 50 states; finishing a marathon in each of them is merely icing on the cake.

Having finished a marathon in all 50 states three times, I have seen and experienced many different cultures, landscapes and people, all proudly representing the beauty that is the United States of America. It has truly been (and continues to be) an amazing experience.

Here's a fact: There are more people who have climbed Mount Everest and more astronauts who have been in outer space than there are runners (425) who have completed a marathon in all 50 states.

Membership in the Full Hyaku Club of Japan

One of the most interesting and eye-opening events in my life was running in Japan. Eleven years ago (November1998) I was invited to join a Japanese running club known as the Full Hyaku Club after running with the Club president around the Imperial Palace in Tokyo. Roughly translated Full Hyaku means to run 100 or more marathons and enjoy doing so. It was founded in October 1987. There are 278 members with 53 females and 225 males and includes six American members. I traveled to Japan on business annually so this was a good fit. The club supports all marathoners and has a special concern for the middle and back-of-the pack runners. There are 153 who have completed at least 100 marathons. The Club has an annual meeting and marathon. In December of 1999 I attended the annual meeting and ran the marathon in Naha, Japan. Each month they publish a newsletter which includes an article from one of their American members. One member, Giichi Kojima (65 years old) has run 1,170 career marathons. Kojima continues to run 50 marathons a year. Two of the most accomplished women runners of Japan are members: Mariko Sakamoto and Noriko Sakota. My friend Don

McNelly of Rochester, New York is an active member of the club. At 88 years of age McNelly's career marathons are 750, which includes over 100 ultras. McNelly's claim to fame is he has completed the most marathons of any runner after their 70th birthday (471), as well as the most marathons of any runner after their 80th birthday (175 marathons). Don and I were elected vice-president to the Board of Directors of the Full Hyaku Club. It's a token office but an honor we appreciate nonetheless. Hiroyasu Enomoto serves as our key contact for the American members. The other American members include Winston Davis, Chuck Savage, Paul Morgan and Susan Daley.

Falling on My 'Ice'

With 14 years of marathon running, I've made lots of mistakes and bloopers; so many that I lost count. Runners make mistakes and learn from them. A few examples are provided here: I've run too fast early in a marathon and paid the price later by crashing in pain. I've gone to an out-of-town race and forgotten to take my shoes, my running shorts, etc. I've eaten the wrong things the night before a race or during a race and I painfully paid the price. You get the idea.

In 2008, there was an eight-month window (May through December) that I did not run any training miles. I did not train, work out or exercise: nothing. Admittedly I realize putting no training miles on my legs was a serious mistake. However, I managed to finish 30 marathons, 24 of them in the aforementioned eight-month window. Of course, this was not a special athletic feat, just a stupid one! How did this occur? Why did I allow this to happen? Why did I do this to myself? Let's say it is arguably the dumbest thing I've ever done.

Everything started with an accidental fall on an icy glacier in Antarctica. In March 2008 I broke my right pelvis at mile four of the Antarctica marathon. Of course, I didn't know it was broken. It hurt. It was painful. I thought I could 'walk it off' in a few miles. At mile ten, I knew I was done. So, I dragged my bad leg to the half-marathon finish line. It was my first marathon DNF. I was disappointed and emotional. My leg was throbbing. After I returned to Atlanta my doctor said the nature of my pelvic fracture was that 'mother nature' would heal the bone in 60 days. Therefore, doctor's orders called for no training miles for my legs. That made sense, so I was a good patient and followed his advice.

In May I began to run and finished several marathons. I continued to run each month without doing any training miles between races. My pelvic area still hurt. I thought the only logical thing to do was allow more days

of rest and healing…and no training miles for my legs. My hip flexors were a source of agony before, during and after each and every marathon. My doctor recommended I see a physical therapist. The diagnosis of my therapy revealed my hip girdle to be out of alignment. This called for more rest…and no training mileage. In September I had surgery on my right knee to repair a complex tear in my medial meniscus. Following three weeks of recovery, I ran 11 more marathons between October and December. My justification to myself for no training miles during the week was I needed to rest and recover so I could run on the weekends. Maybe I was lazy. Perhaps I was just ......
stupid! Perhaps I should find another sport; but how could I…I love running marathons and ultras.

What happens to a runner (like me) that runs 24 marathons in eight months without any training miles? I paid the price. It was bad. Things got worse. My finish times were slower than my normally slow times. My slower running friends were finishing in front of me. My pain, aches and anguish increased with each race. There was just no time to recover properly. In the words of Olympian Jeff Galloway, *'listen to your body'* and allow enough time to rest, recover and develop a good base of weekly miles.

My 2009 New Year's resolution was to only run marathons or ultras with a good base of weekly miles on my legs. Even a 68-year old can be taught new tricks.

Marathon Idiosyncrasies

- Within a quarter mile of the finish line, I love to ask a person at curb side 'Is it too late to quit the race'?

  Occasionally, I find someone who takes me seriously and says 'No! You cannot quit now.' I love it.

- To my running partner, 'Why race so hard? On Monday, only you and God will know your finish time.'
- As I approach the marathon start line, I often say 'this is the best I'm going to feel for the rest of the day.'
- When I'm bored at a marathon, I listen to Italian opera by Jose Carreras, Placido Domingo and Lucian Pavarotti.
- When my partner says let's sprint to the finish line. I reply *'I'm sprinting now'* (actually I'm walking).
- During a low moment in the race I might say: 'On Monday morning, I'm going to find myself a new sport.'

- To my running partner, at the start of a marathon with no training miles on my legs, I sarcastically whine, 'well, I'm not over-trained for this race.'

Inspirational Running Partners

The Jeff Galloway Marathon program was an enormous asset to my running career. A few of the lessons I learned include the importance of a maintaining a solid mileage base, doing regular long runs, listening to my body, taking walk breaks when necessary, and the value of having good running partners. Admittedly, I've been lucky to have so many awesome and inspirational buddies. What more can a runner ask for? My marathon running partners have been supportive and encouraging. They are always there to pick me up when I got into trouble. I doubt I would be running today without the inspiration of my running friends. Over the 14 years of marathon running I've had wonderful runners to travel with me to each of the 50 States and all seven continents. I'm indebted to all of them for their help and support during the countless miles we ran shoulder-to-shoulder on both roads and trails all over the world. A few of my fantastic running partners include Winston Davis, Paul Morgan, Chuck Savage, Chris Lowery (my son-in-law), Kevin Hatfield, Don McGinty, Roger Ackerman, Norm Frank, Michael Sklar, Rick Worley, Kendel Prescott, Walt Prescott, Bob Parker and Bob Gregg.

Unquestionably I would be remiss if I didn't mention my partner in life, my lovely wife Jean. Without her support, encouragement and inspiration I wouldn't be the runner—or man that I am today.

Love and Marriage on the Marathon Road

Love is everywhere. It's been my experience running marathons and ultras throughout the country to meet couples who met each other while running a marathon or ultra. They fell in love, got married and continued to run marathons together. Fortunately, I got to play cupid one time for two of my close running friends in Atlanta, Kendel and Walt Prescott. Unfortunately, Kendel's father had passed away, so she asked if I would fill-in as the father of the bride. I was honored, and consider it one of the truly special events in my life. It brought me great joy to see two good friends of mine get married to each other. Another couple of friends, Elaine and Jerry Dunn, were married at the eight mile mark of the 1995 Disney Marathon. There are probably hundreds of couples (maybe thousands) who run marathons together and later got married.

Running offers a good lifestyle

Without question, running has changed my entire life. My priorities are different and broader. I am healthier, happier and have more self-esteem. I sleep, eat, and live better. Running is invigorating! Endurance running has encouraged me to meet numerous new friends. Also, I am able to visit and tour places in all 50 states and all seven continents. Aging is inevitable. At the age of 68, I am slowing down. Also, I've lost the passion to run hard every step. It's been bothersome to be at the back of the pack or in some cases, to finish last. I've learned to set my ego and pride aside. Now I am happy to finish the marathon or ultra marathon at whatever the time is on the clock. In my opinion, it's more important to finish than to quit or stay at home.

Perhaps my friend Kevin Hatfield, says it best …'it's better to *burn out* than *rust out.*'

Best wishes to everyone for many years of safe running, health and happiness.

Semper Fidelis Running!!!!

CAMARADERIE RULES AT COMRADES

By Tom Adair, Sr.

The day after, the local newspapers featured photographs of runners carrying other runners like wounded soldiers to the finish line. The spirit of the Comrades Marathon is to help those in need finish.

In 2000 I had the good fortune of participating in the 75th running of the Comrades Marathon, dubbed by many as 'The Ultimate Human Race.' In its infancy, the event was viewed by the athletic establishment as a form of freakish pedestrianism. Today, it is widely acknowledged in running circles as the 'Mount Everest' of road running.

'*Mount* Everest' is appropriate to describe the course, a hilly 87.3 kilometer (54 mile) route from Durban to Pietermaritzburg, South Africa. The course includes five challenging mountains (please note—the South Africans refer to them as 'hills'):

- Cowies Hill, which rises 137 meters over 1.5 kilometers
- Fields Hill, which rises 231 meters over 3 kilometers
- Botha's Hill, which rises 150 meters in 2.4 kilometers

(At this point the halfway mark in Drummond is reached)

- Inchanga Hill, which rises 150 meters in 2.5 kilometers
- Polly Shorts *(the bad-ass of all hills)*, which rises 737 meters in 1.8 kilometers

Comrades began in 1921. It is always conducted on June 16th, a National Holiday in South Africa commemorating the soldiers who died in World War I. In South Africa, English is the prevailing language (although the natives speak with a strong British accent). However, there are still 12 Black languages spoken. The racial mix in the country is about four to one black to white. In the race, the racial mix was 2/3 white and 1/3 black. Every other year the course is run in the opposite direction. In 2000, for example, it was run from Durban to Pietermaritzburg, this 'uphill' version measuring 54 miles. (In 2001, the race would be the 'downhill' version, which inexplicably measures in at 56 miles).

June is in the midst of the winter season in South Africa. Durban is the same latitude as Orlando, Florida. The temperatures race day featured a low of 64 degrees and a high of 73. Humidity was at 48%, and the wind was slightly blowing at eight miles per hour. Along the course there were 56 aid stations. Runners were required to wear two race numbers: one in front and one in back. The numbers were color-coded, indicative of the country you were from (which led to continual and unexpected cheers throughout the day).

The aid stations offered a choice of three beverages (PowerAde, Coca Cola and water) but only two food items (bananas and oranges). It's best to run Comrades with a chronograph as there are only three official time clocks on the course: at the start, the half-way point in Drummond, and the finish. The course had 87 markers for each kilometer…but they were placed along the course in *descending* order (i.e. 86km to go, 85km to go, etc.). It is a Comrades tradition.

At the time, Comrades was the first race in which I had prepared a complete racing strategy and had myself mentally prepared with periodic goals throughout the race. I carried a pace chart with my target times for every 5 kilometers, which worked out great. My goal was to run each kilometer in 8 minutes (the equivalent of 13-minute miles).

With my 8-minute-per-kilometer target, I projected a finish in 11:36, which allowed me a 24 minute cushion with respect to the 12 hour cutoff. It was reassuring to monitor my progress every kilometer. I found myself playing a game to determine if I could shave off a few seconds from my 8 minute target. In the first half of the race I got a little carried away, and ran several kilometers in 6 or 7 minutes. When I reached Drummond, I was 20 minutes ahead of my goal.

However, somewhere after Drummond (between those last two 'hills') my body turned on me, and I started giving back much of my time cushion. I heard over a loudspeaker that the winner, Vladimir Kotov crossed the finish line in a record uphill time of 5:25:33. This certainly didn't make my job any easier.

I learned a new phrase as I climbed (notice I didn't say 'ran') up Polly Shorts: false summit. As I approached an uphill, I was intimidated by the vertical climb in front of me. I pushed on, and when I reached (what I thought was) the summit, I would travel around a curve in the road only to find the *next* summit. I repeated this traumatic experience about a dozen times during the second half of the race.

Once I reached the top of Polly Shorts—still 7 kilometers from the finish, I was cramping in agonizing pain. I considered quitting. The pain was brutal. Somehow I managed to get to the finish line in (officially) 11:51:36. I would like to mention that, although we were wearing timing chips, it *did* take me a full six minutes to get to the starting line (the 2000 Comrades had 24,505 registered runners for the event, and approximately 20,000 officially made it to the finish line).

After crossing the finish line, I was both exhausted and dehydrated. Although I visited the medical tent, the volunteers said they had 'thousands' who were in worse shape than me. So they 'released' me without giving me any assistance. On the one-hour bus ride back to Durban…well, let's just say I'm glad I had my airline motion sickness bag with me.

The next day the newspaper reported that thousands went to the medical tent (the volunteer told me the truth!), and ultimately 55 runners were admitted to the hospital (of which three went to ICU and one actually died). All of a sudden, vomiting didn't sound like a bad option.

After the race—and suffering no injuries, I enjoyed the rest of my time in South Africa. Naturally, I went for my first swim in the Indian Ocean. The people of South Africa were incredibly friendly and truly made me feel welcome.

It was truly an honor and a privilege to run this prestigious international race. I am eternally grateful and proud I was able to finish within the allotted 12 hour time limit.

Creigh Kelley of US Sports once said of Comrades:

The Comrades is the greatest race of them all. Running Comrades is like having a baby; you forget the agony very quickly.

However, I will not...I repeat, *will not* run this race again.

Maybe if I ever had a baby I might think differently.

Footnote: The 2000 Comrades Marathon became the largest ultra marathon in the world, with over 20,000 finishers.

Chapter Twelve

Jack McDermott

I've watched Jack McDermott run for many years, and if I were forced to select one word to describe his running it would be 'tireless.'

By definition the word means 'incapable of tiring,' which might make me think twice about using it to describe *anyone*.

So I did. I thought about it again. I was right the first time: 'tireless' it is. Jack McDermott is tireless.

I've watched Jack McDermott run for many years, and the way his legs pump up and down remind me of two pistons fueling a tiny, powerful engine.

Two pistons that allow Jack to cover amazing distances in an even more amazing amount of time.

Tirelessly.

Jack McDermott

BACK OF THE PACK

If you didn't know Jack McDermott, at first glance you can instantly tell by his build that he's athletic--but you may have a hard time figuring out in which sport he excels.

Football, perhaps. His physique resembles that of a cornerback — or perhaps split end for a Division 2 college football team.

Maybe rugby. His stout, broad-shouldered upper torso may remind you of someone who likes to push groups of large men around for fun in his spare time.

Quite possibly swimming. It's obvious Jack is sporting a huge pair of lungs inside a massive rib cage that is disproportionately larger than the lower half of his body.

Running? Not with his top-heavy body supported by nothing more than stumpy but muscular legs. The thought of Jack as a long distance runner is ridiculous.

Not so fast. It may surprise you to know that Jack McDermott has run 1500 meters in 4:35...5K in 17 minutes flat...and a marathon in 2:50:15.

Inside that massive rib cage is not only a huge pair of lungs but an incredibly strong—and large *heart* as well. Working in unison with the aforementioned pair of ever-churning legs, they have provided Jack the tools to develop into a top-flight distance runner.

For many years, Jack wrote a regular column for the monthly newsletter of Tallahassee, Florida's Gulf Winds Track Club (GWTC) called 'Back of the Pack.' The truth of the matter is Jack ordinarily runs at the *front* of the pack, whether the distance is 3.1 miles or 50 miles. Don't let his appearance fool you: this man can flat out *run!*

Jack was born in Portland, Oregon to a family of non-runners. He fell in love with running as a child and later became a four-year letterman at Stayton Union High School (Oregon) in cross-country.

His pursuit of higher education led him to the northeastern United States, where he earned a B.A. in Political Science at Colgate University and later graduated from the John F. Kennedy School of Government at Harvard University.

Jack moved to Tallahassee in 1996 where he initially worked as a political consultant before starting to work at the Florida Office of Insurance Regulation one year later.

Once he began 'working for a living,' Jack's running tapered off significantly; he even began smoking a pipe. His weight, as he says, 'ballooned' to 198 pounds and at the encouragement of a friend and co-worker, Jack got into shape and ran his first 5K in 22:17 in February of 1999. He also gave up the pipe.

Jack joined a running group, the Sunday Streakers as well as the GWTC in 1999, and trained with a few members of the Streakers for the 1999 Jacksonville Marathon. The training was a success: Jack completed his first marathon—at age 30—in 3:32. His initial thoughts of never running another marathon had no lasting effect, as he ran a 3:06 marathon (Mardi Gras) a mere 14 months later, a time that qualified him for the prestigious Boston Marathon.

Jack's travels took him abroad, and he ran his first international marathon in Rotterdam in April of 2001. He paced a friend, Laurel Slyck, and began a personal tradition of pacing friends in races.

His first sub-three hour marathon coincided with the three-year anniversary of his marathoning career, as he ran a fine 2:57 at the First Light Marathon in Mobile, Alabama in December 2002, finishing in sixth place. Five months later he ran his PR 2:50 at the Newport Marathon in Oregon, finishing in third pace.

The man can flat out *run!*

Jack moved to the ultra in June 2003, as he finished second in the difficult Pennar 40 Mile Run with an excellent 5:26. Soon he would realize his first overall win since his high school days, at the Tallahassee Marathon in February 2004; his time was 2:55. Jack was unable to defend his title the following year, as he assumed the position of co-director for the race in 2005 and ultimately director in 2006.

Jack is ambitiously working towards his goal of completing a marathon or longer in all 50 states (he's a member of two 50 states clubs as well as the Marathon Maniacs); so far he's finished 33 states as well as the District of Columbia. He completed his 100th marathon or longer at the Mardi Gras Marathon in February 2008, while carrying on his tradition of pacing others in races. This time the 'pacee' was his future wife, Laura Reardon (McDermott).

Jack has continued his winning tradition established at the 2004 Tallahassee Marathon. His impressive list of wins:

- 2004 Tallahassee Marathon (2:55)
- 2005 Draggin' Tail 18-Mile Run (1:55)
- 2006 Hot 2 Trot 8-Hour Run (50.2 miles)
- 2006 Draggin' Tail 18-Mile Run (1:55)
- 2007 Hot 2 Trot 8-Hour Run (51.3 miles)
- 2007 Run with the Horses Marathon in Wyoming (3:20)
- 2007 Peachtree City 50K (3:34)

- 2007 Tallahassee Ultradistance 50-Mile Run (6:41)
- 2007 Christmas Marathon in Olympia, WA (3:02)
- 2008 Delano Park 12-Hour Run (78 miles)
- 2008 Draggin' Tail 18-Mile Run (1:55)
- 2008 Tallahassee Ultradistance 50K (3:36)

A quick note about the Delano Park win: it was a course event record. The man can flat out *run!* With 12 career wins, 25 marathons under three hours, and 25 top-10 marathon finishes, Jack is in his prime.

When you meet Jack for the first time, just remember: you can't judge a book by its cover.

Looks can be deceiving.

And don't expect to find Jack at the back of the pack.

After all, the man can flat out *run!*

TRANSCENDENTAL RUNNING

By Jack McDermott

In the era of fast-food, Nintendo, and general lethargy --- a counterculture has emerged to battle the obesity epidemic. This counterculture is not characterized by superhero Olympians; instead, it features weekend warriors who participate in endurance events in a futile attempt to stall the aging process, and shore-up their dismal dating prospects. This is not the most glamorous group of individuals; some do not have jobs, while others are not considered 'sane' by the medical community. I am one of these people.

Getting Started

> *'It is hard to fail, but worse never to have tried.'*
>
> -- Theodore Roosevelt

The year was 1998 – at Happy Hour after work, two female running friends challenged me to run a local 5K in November. I agreed. I had not run actively in years, and figured it would be easy. The next day, I went to the local track and jogged three laps and had to stop before the onset of cardiac arrest. It was only then that I realized how 'out-of-shape' I had truly become.

In high school and even college, it was easy to exercise. There was never a shortage of physical events, pick-up basketball games, and the desire to look your best. Only a decade later, convenience, job pressures, and a slowing metabolism had conspired to turn me into what the fictional Ahab called 'the white whale.' I was a fat, overweight, out-of-shape, and very unhealthy 29 year-old --- basically, a typical American. It would take four months to adequately train for a 5K.

Initially I did not run for the health benefits, or to reconnect with my childhood exuberance of running. I needed a new challenge, and was having difficulty coming to grips with my adulthood.

Really Getting Started

'The foundation of humility is truth. The humble man sees himself as he is.'

– Henry Fairlie

Before graduation, high school seniors stood up in my college prep class and announced their life goals which included everything from being president to landing on Mars to founding a computer company. Very few individuals even vaguely came close to achieving their goals. *(My goal, of course, was to go to Europe and become a mime.)* The moral of the story is that there is a big difference in saying you will do something, and actually doing it.

Now, 12 years later, I did not enter the 5K race in November that I promised. I faked an illness, an injury, and a deceased grandmother for good measure as I knew I would be humiliated. It would take three months of hard training to muster the courage to appear at an event. My first event in 12 years was the Cookie Run in February 1999 – near my 30th birthday.

While I finished my first 5K in a respectable 22:17 – I was passed by men, women, and children – even a guy who was hung-over beat me. It was a humbling experience for someone who considered himself a good high school runner. It was then that I learned an important lesson --- you need to compete against yourself.

Joining the Running Community

'Pain is real when you get other people to believe in it. If no one believes in it but you, your pain is madness or hysteria.'

– Naomi Wolf

On June 7, 2003, I awoke at 2:30 am in the morning to arrive at Pensacola for my first ultra race. After checking into my hotel the night before, the attendant looked at me strangely – probably figuring I had a drug deal to attend, as who else requests a 2:30 am wake-up call?

When I gathered with a group on Pensacola Beach at 4 a.m., I was tired from a night of driving and overall lack of sleep, but excited to be running my first ultra *(a distance longer than the 26.2 mile marathon distance, in this case, a 40-miler that went to Navarro Beach and back).* I realized that I was attending more than a race – it felt like a family reunion. I was the 'new' guy, or the 'ultra virgin' despite the fact I had completed 27 marathons, qualified for Boston and was a relatively well known local runner.

People will tell you a multitude of diverse reasons why they began running, but what keeps people running is always the same: the friendships and camaraderie they develop along the way. Running is kind of like body odor. If you are the only one with body odor – you are soon the pariah of the group. If everyone has body odor – you fit right in. Runners know each other, are friends with each other, and commonly *(as in my case)* end up dating and marrying other runners. The reason is that to some running becomes more than just an event, it becomes a lifestyle and a set of values that binds people together. But that was in the future …

Finally – A Goal

'Because it is there.'

– Sir George Mallory

When asked my favorite quote, I always turn to Sir George Mallory. A reporter from the *New York World* once asked him why he wanted to climb Mount Everest. There was no money, little fame, risk of death, and no scientific knowledge that would be gained – in essence – why challenge yourself? Sir George Mallory's simple response, of course, soon became legend: *'Because it is there.'*

If I were asked one enduring questions by non-runners it is this: Why do you run and challenge yourself with endurance events? Part of the reason is that simple – you should challenge yourself simply for the sake of challenging yourself. Because it is there. To gain confidence, to focus your goals and energies, to find out how tough you really are. Only then can we truly transcend our daily lives and understand ourselves.

I have accomplished a few things in my life: a graduate degree from Harvard, work accomplishments and personal achievements but in many ways these pale in comparison to the accomplishment I feel every time I finish an endurance event *(hopefully my wife will not read this)*.

When I began running in 1999, I enjoyed the atmosphere, the competitiveness, the novelty and the (positive) changes in my body and psyche that developed due to running. However, I did not have any real focus – I was running for fun. One day, someone in my running group mentioned running a marathon. I lamented the fact that I had never run a marathon; now at age 30, I was practically middle-aged and 'too old' to run this type of endurance event.

I was wrong. It was other 'older' runners in my running group that inspired me, and gave me confidence that I could accomplish the distance. My first inclination was to run the Boston Marathon – it was internationally known and a dream of mine since I was a child. Unfortunately, I was soon informed that this was the one race that I could *not* run – I would first have to achieve a qualifying time -- a time that seemed prohibitively out of reach.

My First Marathon – Jacksonville Marathon, December 1999

'Sweat is the cologne of accomplishment.'

– Heyward Hale Broun

I was nervous when my training group arrived in Jacksonville, Florida. After dinner, I bid everyone adieu and announced 'Now I'll go to bed and stare at the ceiling for six hours,' which proved prophetic. My roommate was Jack Brennan who, to spite me, slept soundly. Nobody should be allowed to sleep that soundly before a marathon. I was so stricken with jealousy that I overcame a temptation to poke him with a sharp object to awaken him.

I had barely shut my eyes when my alarm went off. There had been rain in the forecast, and for the first time in modern meteorology, the forecast was accurate. By the time we arrived at the start of the race, there was a drizzle that would become progressively worse. One of the people I knew from Tallahassee was Kate McFall. She asked if I had slept the night before. My answer: 'Yeah --- about 20 minutes. But it could be worse. It could be raining.'

I made it to the halfway mark on pace, and picked mile 15 to make my surge. My surge, if you can call it that, lasted about 100 yards. By mile

16, I hit the wall. It is difficult to describe 'the wall' to a non-runner; it is the moment when you lose your energy, your will to live and want to cry '*Mommy.*' Unlike walls in real-life – this wall moves. I carried the wall for the last eight miles.

The irony is, I was dehydrated. What was I thinking? I'm a lizard? A runner has to *drink* water, and unlike a lizard, cannot absorb it through his skin. I recovered a little, but the wall came back and slapped me at mile 18. I remember seeing a women drop out at mile 21 as she stopped a car...with tears rolling down her cheeks. She begged a guy to drive her to the start line. Of course, she had nicer legs than I did; I had no choice but to trudge onward.

I tried to cling to an 8-minute per mile pace, and saw it slip away in the late miles. I finished in 3:32 and felt like I had been through a war. Ann Guillen was one of the first to see me at the finish line, and asked how I liked running my first marathon. My verbatim response: 'That was terrible! I'm never doing THAT again! I need a new hobby -- like ping-pong.' After finishing, I thought of the quote by Tim Robbins in *Bull Durham*, 'Sometimes you win, sometimes you lose, and sometimes it rains.' In Jacksonville that year, it rained.

From First to Worst --- My Second Marathon

'*Genius is 1 percent inspiration, 99 percent perspiration.*'

– Thomas Alva Edison
[By that standard, I should be a genius – Jack McDermott.]

In 490 B.C., Pheidippedes ran from the Plains of Marathon to Athens to report that the brave Athenians had defeated the Persian hordes of Darius the Great. Upon arrival he announced, 'Rejoice! We Conquer!' and abruptly died. It has become apparent to me that in 2,500 years of recorded history we have learned absolutely nothing from his experience.

After my first marathon experience, my marathon-voyeur friends in the office betting pool were disappointed that I was not dead (paid off at 5-1), permanently maimed (odds 2 to 1), or in the hospital (even odds). They would not have to wait long. With reckless enthusiasm I embarked upon my second marathon, the Blue Angel Marathon in Pensacola – a mere two months later. I was over-confident and under-trained. I was still recovering physically and psychologically from my first traumatic marathon attempt and assumed I could rely on my 'experience.' After finishing, I felt like I had just given birth – to Frank Shorter. Here is what I learned:

- If you are late, do not speed 50 miles an hour in a 35-mph zone. According to the law enforcement officer, medical emergencies and giving birth may be legitimate excuses to break the speed limit, but speeding to make the marathon packet pick-up is not. If you offer to give a friend a ride to the race, make sure they understand the purpose of time zones; otherwise they may call your room at 4:45 am with: 'Where are you? I'm in the lobby! We have to leave! We're late!'

- If you are shaving your legs the night before the race in your motel room to reduce 'wind resistance,' be sure to bring Band-Aids. *(If you are a guy shaving your legs for the first time, be sure to ask your female friends for some leg shaving tips. I attempted this in the bathtub, and before I finished, there was more blood in the water than in a Jaws movie.)*

- If you are going to ditch your shirt at the 11-mile mark, be sure to bring a shirt you never want to see again, not a $30 Mickey Mouse T-shirt you just bought in Orlando. I also learned that if you pass military volunteers at the four-mile mark do not sing 'In the Navy.' *(Apparently active military personnel are not big Village People fans.)* Another problem, if you need to stop and pee at the 14-mile mark, do not urinate on a fence next to an 'angry neighbor dog' that may startle you and force you to pee on your shoe.

- If you have only been running 20-30 miles a week, never expect a personal best. As a matter of fact, do not expect to walk the next day. Another important piece of advice – do not expect this will qualify you for a handicapped parking space. Apparently it is like gaining a purple heart in the military – they do not give credit for self-inflicted wounds.

I labored to a 3:40 – the slowest race I ever ran. Even to this day, I am still bitter about my sub-par performance at the Blue Angel Marathon. Therefore, I would like to sue the organizers of the race *(the U.S. Navy)* for $7 million dollars. I am seeking $2 million for 'emotional trauma' *(having to look at my unsolicited race photos)*; $2 million for 'defamation of character' *(yeah ... like any woman would date me after looking at those race photos)*; $3 million for 'pain and suffering' *(did I mention the race photos?)*; and $46 for uncovered medical expenses *(mostly Advil)*.

You may ask why I am pursuing my bogus lawsuit. I guess it is because the theme of the 19th century was 'If at first you don't succeed … try, try again.' The theme of the 20th century was 'If at first you don't succeed … try something easier.' The theme for the 21st century is 'If at first you don't succeed … try to find a lawyer and sue the **** out of somebody.'

Why We Keep Running

'Death is the final finish line.'

– Jack McDermott

Any veteran runner must confront a few uncomfortable realizations: 1) Your performance is declining due to age; 2) you need to find new goals; and 3) at least two of your toe-nails will never grow back. When you begin running the prospect of 'faster' or 'longer' is a self-evident goal. Soon you may be contemplating races in Antarctica, the Mojave Desert, or the Chunnel – all of which were created to quench this thirst.

I have two distinct goals. One is to finish a marathon (or longer) in all 50 states. There are several national clubs dedicated to this goal, which at my ability level is more a matter of finances and travel logistics than physical ability. Another goal is to finish a 100-miler. My first attempt at the distance was a fiasco owing partially due to my poor health *(I had to withdraw after 62.5 miles due to the flu).**

By the time this book is published, I will have reached the magic age of 40 – middle-age by some standards. I hope this is merely mile 12 of the marathon of my life, and that there is more life in front of me than behind me. As we age, it seems natural that we simultaneously contemplate our own mortality and its role in our running adventures.

The goal of running is not the quantity of life *(although a multitude of studies confirm that exercise helps people live longer)* – it is about the *quality* of life. My goal is to live to be 91 – and see my native state of Oregon's bicentennial – February 14, 2059. However, I do not want to be hooked to tubes, lost in dementia and bedridden; I want to be out running around the capitol building. It would be a bittersweet moment. Many of my friends featured in this book or in the Darkside Running Club will not be around. But the greatness of the running community is that it is evolving, expanding, and multi-generational. I am sure I will have new and younger running friends to carry on the tradition after I can no longer run on this planet.

Running in Our Society

'The goal of every culture is to decay through over-civilization.'

– Cyril Connolly

We in the United States of America are over-civilized. We are one of the wealthiest nations in the world *(please ignore the federal debt for a moment, I am using this as a literary device)* and one of the most advanced societies in the history of mankind. We no longer need to plant our own vegetables, hunt and forage for food, sew our clothes, build our house or walk to work. We live sedentary lifestyles, and most of our material needs can be purchased at Wal-Mart with a credit card.

This decadence comes at a cost. We are becoming one of the laziest and most obese nations on the face of the earth and must confront a multitude of new health problems. The running community really is a counter-weight to this societal trend, an emerging counterculture that others would be wise to notice. Given all of our modern conveniences, it seems almost primordial that a few odd and eccentric individuals would feel the need to run. The reason is not complex. We run for joy – the physical, psychological and spiritual joy derived from this simple and noble endeavor.

*Jack's DNF at 100 miles was at the 2008 Umstead Endurance Run.

Jack was credited with his 8:15:50 finish at the 50-mile distance, placing him 6ᵗʰ overall.

MARATHON RACE DIRECTING:
WHO PUT THIS IDIOT IN CHARGE?
By Jack McDermott

A few people in my local running club had the misguided notion that I would make a good race director. They were wrong. It is akin to seeing an inebriate languishing at the end of the bar and suggesting, 'Hey, you would make a good bartender. Or better, yet --- you should own your own bar!'

Making me a race director was like throwing gasoline on a fire. Only after the tavern is engulfed in flames as the vagabond owner belatedly realizes grain alcohol is flammable do we realize this travesty could have been easily avoided. (*Besides – I cannot spend too much time with the race director details – I have to focus on my own marathon training!*)

Marketing a Tough Marathon

Prior to 2004 the Tallahassee Marathon was held on a very hilly course, due in part to the title sponsor (the Tallahassee Nurseries) wanting the race to start and finish at their establishment – on top of a hill, which meant a grueling final mile climb. Rule number one: never bow to the whims of a race sponsor.

A one mile uphill finish would have been great for an ultra, but not for a marathon. One of the main differences between an ultra and a marathon is not the mileage, but the marketing. Ultra runners enjoy races with names like 'Masochist,' 'Endurance,' 'Challenge' or 'Mountain' in the title. You even hear Ultra race directors bragging that '*only four people have ever finished the real course*,' or '*we had a good year last year --- we only lost 12 people.*' For an ultra, if your pre-race packet contains a compass and a flare gun, you will get your money's worth.

Marathons, on the other hand appeal to a different breed of (*how can I say it delicately?*) pampered people who either want a Boston qualifying time and/or lots of music and cheerleaders to ease their pain. If the words 'scenic' or 'rolling' appear in the literature – the race most likely will not financially break-even.

The challenge for my home-town marathon was how to market a 'less than easy' course. Our first thought was to obtain a big-name corporate sponsor. Most of the premier marathons have them: Seattle (*Harrisdirect*), New York City (*ING*) and Mardi Gras (*Nokia*) – just to name a few. In 2000 we did a mass mailing to all Fortune 500 companies touting our event. The good news is we found a highly-visible multi-national corporation to sponsor our race. The bad news? It was the Enron Corporation.

Unfortunately the Enron Tallahassee Marathon never came to fruition as their offices were raided by a joint task force of the FBI and Securities and Exchange Commission agents. There were three reasons that I knew we were in trouble even before the pre-registration ended: (1) According to our website, the charity runners were asked to raise money *for Enron*; (2) someone hocked our finishing medals at a pawn shop in Houston; and (3) instead of mailing finishing certificates, the sponsors were planning on mailing 100 shares of Enron Stock.

Despite this corporate debacle, the race went on as planned with 100 participants --- large by ultra standards, but not in the top echelon of marathon participation. Therefore, we did what any marathon would do --- we gave up and found a faster venue. This did not stop me from developing my own 'Top 10 Advertising Slogans' to save our hilly course, which I will now pass along for the benefit of other race directors should they find themselves in a similar predicament.

10 It will Scare the 'Hill' Out of You
Also in this genre are 'To Hill and Back' and 'Just for the Hill of it.' The point being the race has hills, and instead of camouflaging this feature with words like 'scenic' or 'rolling,' the race director should embrace the fact the course is brutal and unforgiving. Truth be known, the only thing that is 'rolling' will be your stomach and the only thing 'scenic' will be the one port-o-john at the half-way point.

9 More Roadkill than any other Marathon
In Tallahassee the smell of victory is the smell of a dead armadillo on the side of the road. As long as the race directors see more dead carcasses of animals than runners, you know we had a better year than most.

8 And you Thought the Bataan Death March was Fun...
Running a tough marathon is like the Bataan Death March except it is not in the Philippines, there are a few more water stops and if General MacArthur were there, he would never vow 'I shall return.' If you do use the Bataan Death March in your race literature, just be sure to stress the fact that you enjoy plodders and do not 'shoot the stragglers.'

7 Smallest Finishing Medals in the South
Small marathons do not qualify for the bulk-rate discounts for finishing medals, so you have to be creative. One idea is to use city bus-tokens and yarn. Another option is to use play

pieces from Chuck E Cheese. If the finishers do not elect to keep the token --- at least they could get a free game of skee-ball.

 # 6 *It's Capital Punishment* If you are short on race-volunteers I suggest you contact the local jail. Many of them have 'prison-release work programs' and can provide numerous smiling 'volunteers.' If I were elected governor one of my 'get tough on crime' initiatives would be to make all convicts run a marathon. Although the Supreme Court may think it violates the Eighth Amendment prohibiting cruel and unusual punishment, I am sure it would reduce recidivism rates.

 # 5 *For Those of You Who Like Signing Waiver Forms* Tallahassee has more lawyers per capita than any other city in Florida. *(In an amazing twist, the local tourism bureau fails to include this in most brochures.)* If your marathon is short on race volunteers, tell the runners if they experience hardship to just fall down and start twitching --- usually a lawyer will arrive in a matter of minutes – with water in hand.

 # 4 *Traffic Control at Over Half the Intersections* You know you are in trouble when you arrive at a race being the only one without a bright orange vest or blinking lights. This reminds me of the best advice I ever received an old ultra veteran: 'Never run a trail ultra during Elk season.'

 # 3 *Because Mickey Mouse is Just a Rat* All small marathons have a difficult time competing with larger ones with bigger sponsors. The 900-pound gorilla in our neck of the woods is the Disney World Marathon, also run in Florida at the beginning of the year. All races need a mascot, and if the Disney Corporation's mascot is linked to bubonic plague -- you should be able to choose almost anything with four legs and do better. I prefer rabbits. If a rabbit's foot is good luck --- then a rabbit should be really lucky because he has four of them.

 # 2 *The Race that Never Fills Up* Most people think the reason I waited so long to get married is because I am eccentric, bizarre, and have only eight toenails. Another possibility is that I force girlfriends to wear 'I'm with Stupid' T-Shirts and stand next to me at social functions during the dating ritual. The truth is I fear commitment. This carries over to the fact that I never pre-register for races which is problematic for marathons. Some of the premier marathons in the country like Grandma's, Marine Corps, or St. George require you to sign up months in advance. Small marathons can accept race-day registrations, which is great for people like me.

 # 1 It's Like Taking a Hammer and Hitting Yourself in the Head One of my college roommates asked me why I ran. I told him that it feels so good when I stopped. He told me that was equivalent to saying 'I like taking a hammer and hitting myself in the head because it feels so good when I stop.' I am not sure where I am going with this other than to say that marathon runners are not normal people. Running a tough, hilly marathon is abnormal even by running standards. Good luck with your race…whatever slogan you choose!

Conclusion

After co-directing the Tallahassee Marathon with friend Toma Wilkerson in 2005, and then on my own in 2006 I surrendered the reigns to superior race administrators. While I helped add some interesting additions to help modernize our marathon (for example – our website at http://www.tallahasseemarathon.com), I never achieved the breakthrough to make the Tallahassee Marathon a premier event.

I also learned some important things. At the top of my list is to never complain to a race director again! It amazes me that people who are professionals in every day life morph into nervous children with bladder-control problems the day of the race. Honestly, how many port-o-lets do you people need? It also exposed me to the most bizarre demands that I could imagine – from providing VISA help with the State Department for a runner from Morocco to babysitting some woman's kid while she ran the race to a woman asking how far apart the medical tents were. *(My concern here was not that she needed medical tents – but that she planned on needing multiple medical tents. Perhaps she should try an easier sport – like backgammon.)*

The current race directors, Jay Silvanima and Nancy Stedman-Laux have transformed the event to the point that it now touts over 200 marathon finishers and 400 half-marathon finishers. The race even has a real race sponsor (at the time of this writing Capital Regional Medical Center) and offers prize money. Another advantage is that it switched weekends and is now the first week in February *(in races, as in life, timing is everything)*. Although I am making progress, I have not quite convinced them to change the name. One day it may be the Groundhog's Day Marathon/Ultra. If the Groundhog does not see his shadow spring is here, and the race is over after a marathon. If he sees his shadow, well then we'll run six more miles and the race turns into an ultra.

Some people are born race directors.

I however, am not one of them.

Chapter Thirteen

Bob Dalton

Bob Dalton is not only one of the finest runners I know, he is also one of the finest *people* I know.

I've known Bob for many years; in fact I've known him longer than anyone else you've met or will meet in the pages of this book.

Many other people have known Bob for many years as well, or at least have known *of* Bob. He's been winning races in the Atlanta area for a long time and his name has been announced at race awards ceremonies and printed in running magazines arguably more often than anyone else in the state of Georgia. While it may be a stretch to refer to Bob as a legend, it's not a stretch to say that his running accomplishments are legendary.

When my family experienced a tragedy several years ago, Bob was the first person to call me and offer his support and encouragement. I'll never forget his words and how much they meant to me and my family.

On that day, as far as my family was concerned Bob became a legend.

Bob Dalton

STILL GOLDEN

I knew his name for many years before I actually met him. On most weekends I would follow him in local 5 or 10 kilometer races—at first a few yards behind and by the time I reached the finish line as much as a mile behind— and became quite familiar with his long, graceful stride and shaggy, almost surfer-blond hair flying parallel to the ground as he cranked out mile after mile at under than a six-minute pace. I knew his face only because it would inevitably appear next to the Race Director as the award was presented to the overall winner of the race. On most weekends that winner was Bob Dalton, sporting a perennial tan that is best described as a brilliant shade of gold which he maintains with his daily noontime training runs used to break up his day from a demanding job as a Senior Intelligence Analyst at Third Army Headquarters at Fort McPherson, Georgia.

Bob, a self-described 'Air Force brat' was born at Bolling Air Force Base in Washington D.C. A mere six weeks after he was born Bob's father, a career Air Force pilot, was transferred to Wright-Patterson Air Force Base in Ohio. His father's career then took the family to New Mexico, back to Ohio, to San Bernadino, California, and finally to Eglin Air Force Base in Florida where he ultimately retired from active duty. Bob graduated from high school in Georgia, where his father began a second career with Lockheed in Marietta.

Bob attended Georgia Tech for a year before continuing his education at the United States Military Academy at West Point. He met his future wife Teresa while being assigned to the U.S. Modern Pentathlon Olympic Training Center at Fort Sam Houston in San Antonio, Texas. Teresa had recently graduated from the University of Alabama with an ROTC commission and a nursing degree, and wound up in Texas to complete her nursing degree. Before long Bob had a wife and companion as his Army career took him from one place to another.

Teresa, an 'Army brat' (her father was an Infantry First Sergeant and Viet Nam veteran) is from Hamilton, Alabama. After graduation she completed four years of active duty as a nurse at Fort Sam Houston and two years in the reserves. Bob and Teresa's son David became the third member of the Dalton family in 1986. David, a Georgia Tech graduate is a full time musician while Teresa works as a Registered Nurse at Southern Regional Medical Center (just south of Atlanta) in the maternity ward.

Bob's roots in running can be traced to his high school days. After unsuccessful attempts at basketball and soccer Bob explored sports which 'didn't require as much coordination,' so he ran both track and cross country for his high school. A few years later he found himself competing for three different teams in college: marathon, cross country and triathlon. However, to realize the extent of Bob's talent and versatility you've got to examine his college and military athletic credentials a little bit closer. Bob was a member of the:

- West Point Marathon Team (1973 – 1976)
- All Army Track Team (1978)
- U.S. Modern Pentathlon National Team (1978 – 1983)

His talent and versatility is best exemplified by his invitations to compete in the 1980 and 1984 Olympic Trials in the Modern Pentathlon (run, swim, shoot, fence and ride). In 1980 President Carter boycotted the Moscow Olympics in retaliation for Russia's invasion of Afghanistan, and in 1984 Bob's assignment in Germany—which required 12-hour days and an absence of convenient training facilities—precluded him from participating in the trials. After steadily progressing through the rankings every year...and after four years of daily training and competing at the national and international level, Bob was ranked 7th in the nation in 1983 when the Army transferred him to Germany. However, Bob will never know how he would have fared against the world's best, but it's fair to say that with his talent and *heart* (the man *loves* to compete!) he would have given everything he had towards earning a gold medal...or two. But yet Bob has no regrets, and he eventually retired from the Army after devoting 20 years of his life to it.

Before long, Bob began an amazing run of success in sports which 'didn't require much coordination.' In 1980 and 1981 he was the National Triathlon Champion, when the event consisted of running, swimming and shooting (in lieu of biking). Then he ventured into the world of road racing where his talent and heart took him to another level.

Bob modestly admits he has no idea how many lifetime road race wins he has, but admits 'it's in the hundreds.' Among the running credentials Bob lists as his personal bests are:

- 20 marathons, including six Boston Marathons and a personal best (2:32) at the 1986 Berlin Marathon and the Masters Course record (2:38) at the 1998 Jacksonville Marathon
- Georgia State Age Group Record (ages 45 – 49) in the 12K (42:07) and 15K (51:13)
- Georgia State Age Group Record (ages 45 – 49) in the Half Marathon (1:13:24) until, as Bob says 'John Tuttle demolished it'
- 5K PR of 15:59, 10K PR of 32:30, 10 mile PR of 54:27 and Half Marathon PR of 1:12:00

- Georgia State Age Group Record (ages 50 – 54) in the 15K (54:46)

Certainly a gold medal resume if there ever was one.

Bob's love for the sport extends beyond his personal competitions. For the past 12 years Bob has been the coach of the Third Army/Army Central Road Racing Team (of which he is an active member as well). In nine of those years Bob's team has won its division in the Army Ten Miler (the largest 10-mile road race in America) while finishing in second the other three years. Since 1999 Bob's team has won its division in the Atlanta Corporate Challenge seven times (and taking second the other three years). Bob served as President of the Peachtree City (Georgia) Running Club from 2006 through 2008. He was asked to serve an unprecedented third year (the normal reign of a President is two years) due to his tremendous popularity among the members who love and respect him as a leader, a runner and a man with a heart of gold.

Bob's heart—and soul, for that matter are immersed in his position as the Race Director of the New Hope Harvest Classic 5K, a position he has held since the event's inception in 2001. Rich Terry, the Director of Missions at New Hope Baptist Church in Fayetteville, Georgia was looking for a way to raise funds for future youth mission trips when he came up with the idea of hosting a church-sponsored run. He enhanced his idea by asking Bob to be his Race Director, and as one might expect Bob took the idea and ran with it. The race has been tremendously successful and become an enduring legacy and a firmly established race that is well known throughout running circles in the metropolitan Atlanta area.

Bob, a new member in the 55 – 59 age group continues to compete in road races and recently in sprint triathlons. Not content to keep his feet firmly planted on the asphalt, Bob earned his private pilot's license in 2000. He enjoys flying a couple of times a month and taking friends and relatives sightseeing. Bob particularly enjoys taking his flying companions for a ride over their own house so they can see it from the air for the first time.

Shortly after turning 55 Bob ran a quick 38:14 at the prestigious Peachtree Road Race 10K in Atlanta against a very competitive field. Had there been age group awards at Peachtree (oddly, only overall and masters are recognized in a field of 55,000 runners), Bob would have finished first in the 55 – 59 division.

Bob Dalton. Fifty-five years old. Complexion, talent, heart…all still golden.

LESSONS LEARNED ON THE ROAD – A TRILOGY

By Bob Dalton

Although I ran track and cross country throughout high school and college, my running career almost ended only a few short years after it began. As a brand new Army Lieutenant stationed in South Korea on my first assignment in the late 1970's, I would often train in the surrounding mountains and rice paddies. One weekend there was a five mile race hosted by the 2nd Infantry Division headquarters at their sprawling compound just south of the Demilitarized Zone (DMZ). The race started at the gym on the base, went out the back gate into and through the local 'ville' (GI slang for the surrounding village), around the perimeter of the base, and back in the front gate finishing back at the gym.

In those days, for various security reasons you had to show a valid military identification card not only to get on base, but also when departing. During the pre-race briefing we received instructions on the course and assumed the gate guards had been briefed about the race since it would be ludicrous to stop everyone going out the back gate and re-entering again through the main gate. Or so I thought.

After the race started, we ran on the compound for a couple of miles and then headed out the back gate. I had a pretty nice lead by this time and as I whizzed by the Military Policeman standing guard, he hollered at me to HALT!! I ignored him and continued to run like hell as I didn't want to lose my lead. But I heard footsteps behind me and turned just in time to see him with his big black baton drawn and raised high in the air ready to bash me over the head with it. I promptly pulled up as he yelled at me to produce an ID. I explained I was leading a race and pointed to the crowd quickly closing in on us. As he turned to look, his jaw hit the ground at the oncoming horde and I took advantage of his distraction to take off running again. Apparently the guards on the main gate had been briefed and didn't challenge me as I raced through although I slowed as I was wary of a repeat of the rear gate incident. Needless to say the race director got an earful after the race about his failure to brief the rear gate guards. Fortunately I avoided a head bashing and lived to race another day.

Lesson Learned: Always make sure the race director properly briefs <u>*everyone*</u> *involved with or affected by the race course.*

Fast forward a couple of decades later. I was taking part in a running club Grand Prix event called an Adventure Run that entailed finding the correct point among four or five different stations located around town manned by volunteers who you had to check in with. Once you reached a point, the volunteer would tell you whether you had reached the correct point by stating either 'this is it' or 'this is not the correct point.' The first runner back to the start with the correct point was the winner. At the starting location at a local shopping center, the event director described the location of each point. One was located at a boat dock on a popular nearby lake. The director stated that he didn't know the name of the volunteer at that particular point, but he knew she was a new member of the running club and had blonde hair.

If you strategized well enough, you could go the closest points first and if they weren't the correct one, you could race on to the other points and still hope to be the first one back. The closest one happened to be the boat dock, so when the starters' gun sounded a lot of us took off for the boat dock. Being the first to reach it I began scouring the area for the club volunteer manning that point. There were quite a few people around. Some were feeding the ducks, some were in the adjacent picnic area, and some were just enjoying the quiet early morning hours on the lake front. Finally, I spied a blonde-haired lady standing on the boat dock who fit the description so I ran up to her and breathlessly yelled loud enough for everyone around to hear: 'Please tell me those three little words you know I want to hear!' (i.e. '*This is it.*')

Her reaction was priceless. She eyed me curiously and then cocked her head to one side and said 'I beg your pardon?' Just then I heard a woman's voice behind me say, 'This is not the correct point.' I turned to see another blonde lady sitting at a picnic table about 20 paces away. I then turned red-faced to the first blonde and stammered, 'Oh, I beg YOUR pardon.' I then took off running as fast as I could to the next point leaving the surrounding onlookers wondering what was going on and who the crazy running guy accosting women was.

Lesson Learned: Always make sure the race director properly briefs <u>everyone</u> involved in all the details of the race.

A few years ago I was co-leading a 15K race with a couple of other runners. About two miles into the race we started hearing a flapping sound. After awhile I asked 'What's that noise?' One of the other runners pointed at me and replied 'Dude, your shoe's coming apart.' I glanced down and sure enough the sole of my left shoe was peeling away from the forefoot. Every time my left leg came forward, the sole would slap against the upper.

I had bought these racing flats at a running expo several weeks before. I had followed the runner's adage that you never try anything out for the first time in a race. Accordingly, I had worn them around the house for a few days to break them in and then wore them on a few training runs. They were a brand name shoe and named after a very well-known and accomplished runner. The fact that they were on clearance for a mere $20 struck me as a great deal, not that there might be something wrong with the quality.

You can imagine my dismay as the slapping got louder and more pronounced as the sole continued to peel away from the shoe with practically every step. Torn between wanting to stop and fixing the problem but not wanting to lose the lead, I struggled for another mile until finally it became apparent that I was not going to be able to continue. Something had to be done. So at mile three, I stopped and pulled the offending sole from the bottom of my shoe, tossed it aside and continued running. I was now forced to continue with no sole on my left forefoot. I was able to finish apparently none the worse for wear, but could only hold on to second place overall.

I retrieved the offending sole the next day and took it and the shoes back to the dealer from whence they came. He offered to replace them with the same model and I agreed. Surely it was a manufacturing defect and couldn't happen again.

A couple of months later, I was warming up for a race with the replacement shoes when sure enough I began to hear the dreaded slapping sound. Fortunately, I had brought another pair of racing flats for just this contingency and was able to change into them before the race. Needless to say I gave up on that brand and model and have never again trusted another 'special edition' shoe that happens to named after a famous runner.

Lesson Learned: A 'good deal' on a 'special edition' shoe is not necessarily always the case.

MILITARY INTERVENTION

By Bob Dalton

I feel fortunate to have competed in all 15 editions of the U.S. 10K Classics (held on Labor Day in Marietta, Georgia) since the inaugural running in 1994. Deep down, I dream of being the Bill Thorn of the U.S. 10K Classic (Bill is the only person who has run each and every Peachtree Road Race in Atlanta). 1998 holds the fondest memory for me as I finished 2nd to Bill Rogers in the Masters Division. Less than two months later I won the Peachtree City (Georgia) Classic 15K in front of my hometown crowd, which was an incredible feeling. I've had success through the years competing at a variety of distances, but it's always nice to run well in my backyard.

However, personal success takes a back seat to the satisfaction I derive from coaching the Fort McPherson (Georgia) Road Racing Teams I have had the privilege to be associated with for the past 13 years. During that time we have competed in the Army Ten Miler, the largest race of that distance in the country every year and won first place in our division nine times and captured second three times. We have also competed in the annual Corporate Challenge in Atlanta for the past ten years, winning our division seven times and taking second the other three. Our team also won the annual Army Hooah 10K (Atlanta) race the past three years and fielded winning teams at the annual Atlanta Track Club Ekiden (marathon) relay the last two years. It's great to see people work hard together and then see them reap the fruits of their labor as part of a larger team effort. I feel blessed to work, train, compete, and win with some of the greatest American patriots you could ever find anywhere: the Soldiers of the United States Army!

Hooah!

Chapter Fourteen

Andy Velazco

I first met Andy Velazco when he introduced himself to me at the starting line of the 2002 24-Hour Endurance Run in Olander Park, Ohio. Andy spoke to me like we had been lifelong friends. After our five-minute conversation before the start of the race I felt like we were.

That's how it is with Andy: if you're a runner then you're his lifelong friend. He wouldn't have it any other way.

Andy has the most intricate network of running support of anyone I know. His family and friends are all participants of long distance running. His family and friends are all *supporters* of long distance running. His family and friends have all run races while being supported by Andy. As I said, a most intricate network that extends throughout the country.

They say that you can judge a man by the company he keeps. That being the case, Andy Velazco is one very successful man.

Andy Velazco

MARATHONS RUN IN THIS FAMILY

Allow me to introduce you to the family of Andy Velazco.

There's wife Kathy, an anesthesiologist by profession and the mother of their five children: three sons and two daughters.

Son Geoffrey, who lives in Los Angeles, is a car designer for BMW.

Daughter Kristin is a producer for ABC television in Los Angeles.

Daughter Kari is a Manager for LA Fitness in Atlanta, Georgia.

Daughter Kati recently completed her Master's degree in Archeology after studying abroad in Southhampton, England. She now lives in Washington, D.C.

Son Alec, the youngest of the children, is currently attending the University of Colorado in Boulder where he is majoring in Aerospace Engineering.

Then there's father Andy, a physician and orthopedic surgeon originally from Peru who used to drive race cars in his spare time.

The Velazco family's interests and career paths have been as successful as they are diverse. But one thing they all share is a love for marathons.

Kathy has 102 marathons to her credit, including one in each of the 50 states.

Kristin and Katie both have completed one marathon. Kari has run seven marathons. Alec, the youngest of the children at 19, already has 98 marathons and one ultra on his resume. Geoffrey, alas, has not yet been bitten by the marathon bug. Operative word: *yet.*

Andy, who has been running just over 20 years, has run 150 marathons and 76 ultras. He finished a marathon in all 50 states in 2002 (beating Kathy to the punch by five years) and 'accidentally' is only a mere four marathons away from a marathon finish in all 50 states a second time.

Quick tally for the Velazco family: 359 marathons and 77 ultras. Ask Kathy or any of the children (except Geoffrey for the time being!) who or what inspired them to venture into the land of 26.2 miles and they will all look in one direction: towards dear old dad.

Andy, now a spry 60 years old says he 'became a runner by default.' After moving to Atlanta in 1976 he spent all his energy on his family and his medical practice. But then, Andy says 'that all changed in 1986 when a friend dared me to run a 10K. I was successful at it and actually liked it. My interest in running started then and there.'

At first Andy found running difficult, but over time it got easier and easier. He started to read and learn as much as possible about running, not only about the sport itself but the science related to it as well. For several years he read as much as he could about it (now Andy writes for several prominent running periodicals). In time he found himself wanting to run not only better, but farther as well. Andy participated in many races around Atlanta put on by the Atlanta Track Club. He joined a weekend running group led by Hugh Toro, an experienced runner in Jonesboro, Georgia who currently works as an Assistant Track and Cross Country coach at Clayton State University. Andy learned a lot from Hugh, and soon he was running or racing every weekend. Soon Kathy got the running bug as well, laying the groundwork for a most perfect husband-and-wife activity in the very near future.

Kathy and Andy participated in a training program culminating in both of them competing in the Atlanta Half Marathon, traditionally held on Thanksgiving Day. A successful completion of the hilly and challenging 13.1 mile course led to a mutual decision to train for the New York City Marathon, which would soon become the first marathon finish for both of them.

Andy says he made 'as many mistakes as possible' during the New York City Marathon. 'Instead of enjoying my first marathon, I tried unsuccessfully to qualify for Boston, break the world record, and win the event.' He didn't do any of those, but he *did* finish, running a personal best in the process. After all, it was his first marathon, remember?

One marathon a year evolved into two, which soon became three. Andy tried to convince Kathy that a good way to have a 'guiltless vacation' was to run a marathon in their destination of choice. Then, after Andy complained about the theft of his 'stashed' water bottles during a long run, Kathy suggested he should 'just run a marathon somewhere and let the organizers worry about supplies.' Talk about killing two birds with one stone.

Andy utilized marathons for training purposes as well. If his training called for a 15-mile run, he would run hard for the first 15 miles of a marathon and then jog the rest. Two weeks later he might run hard for 18 miles and cruise in to the finish line. Kathy, however, is not fond of speed work. In fact, she settles into a single speed and holds it throughout—regardless of the terrain, the temperature or the conditions.

After meeting many of its members during their travels, before long Andy and Kathy joined the 50 States Marathon Club. Soon they were focused on traveling to and finishing a marathon in every state. Their running vacations increased. Andy enticed Kathy with the suggestion of a charm from each state for her bracelet to celebrate her success. Andy admits that while it was a fun idea, it became quite expensive.

Andy's 'Other' Family

Andy also travels with his 'running buddies' all over the *world* to compete in international events. He enjoys sitting in his office and looking over the photographs on the wall that show 'a snippet in time of an event, (although) they don't show the struggles and difficulties of the race, the satisfaction of finishing, the hotels, the rental cars, and the shared meals.' He cites Mike Smith (aka 'younger,' or 'bad Mike'), Mike Brooks (aka 'older,' or 'good Mike'), Walter Prescott and Carl Hunt as his closest friends in the ultra world. Although they all live and work in different parts of the country, they all share a common passion for long distance running.

In 2002 Andy served on Mike Smith's crew at the Badwater Ultramarathon. It was this experience, helping a friend complete the toughest footrace on the planet (as it is known) which cemented their friendship. They discovered that even though they were from different backgrounds they were very similar in their love for running and testing their personal limits. This band of five agreed to return to Badwater and crew for each other in the future. Since that year, they have returned to Death Valley three more times and thus far they are a perfect four-for-four in successful Badwater ventures. *(Walter—they're still waiting for you to bite the bullet and enter!)*

Their 'Badwater bond' extended to other endurance races. Soon Andy was running 24-hour endurance events, 50 mile runs and then a 100-mile race. Attempting to run these long distances made Andy realize that everyone has strengths and weaknesses, and that everyone has good days and bad days while running.

Andy likes to joke that for most runners, if you ask them what they're running and they answer 'four or five,' they would be referring to miles. For Andy's group, they would be referring to hours.

As mentioned earlier, Andy is known for his writing skills *almost* as well as for his running skills. There is a lot to be learned from this spry, active 60-year old physician from Jonesboro, Georgia by way of Peru.

One thing I personally learned from knowing Andy Velazco is the absolute confidence and optimism he has in his athletic abilities and his passion for competition. One day during the fall I asked Andy if he had any resolutions for the following year. Andy said: 'Next year I would like to complete an Ironman. But first, I need to learn how to swim.'

About 11 months later I saw Andy and asked how he did with his New Year's Resolution.

Andy said he had been successful and completed an Ironman.

Three of them, in fact.

WHY I RUN

By Andy Velazco

I feel alive when I run, and enjoy the feeling of finishing a quest.

Why do I run endurance runs of 50 miles…100 miles…or even longer? Why do I set out to finish a race that will require me to run through the day and night and sometimes the next day as well? It's a legitimate question that's not easy to answer.

I could simply say that I run because I am insane, as my daughter Katie would have you believe. Or that I 'fried my brain' in Death Valley running the 135-mile Badwater Ultramarathon, as my wife Kathy insists to be the case.

For the record, I would like to state that I run because I want to know my limits. Besides, the absolute truth of the matter is I run because it allows me to be free. I don't worry about paying the bills, working around the house, or spending the day in surgery. I appreciate the fact that I become entwined with my body at a cellular level. Specifically, each of my body cells report to me: 'I am OK; I am running low on fuel; my tank is at 80%;' etc. My toes and quads complain about the downhills, while my neck and back muscles struggle with the uphills. My abs ask me how I could have been so lackadaisical with my training and subsequently subject them to this living hell.

As I run along the trails, all I can hear is the scraping sound of my shoes on the leaves and the hood of my jacket slapping me on the back. Occasionally I hear movement in the bushes next to the trail and I sense an animal running, although despite glancing towards it I fail to see the hidden creatures, perhaps because I have frightened them. I look up in the sky and see a glorious hawk circling, searching for prey. Perhaps that is why I was unable to spot the creature in the bushes. I hear the sound of running water way before I actually reach the stream. As I approach it my brain computes the best path to take; where to place my foot to avoid slipping or getting it too wet. Occasionally my brain computes the best spot to put my foot in the inevitable mud to avoid having my shoes sucked off of my feet.

During my runs I have been lucky to run into deer, moose, and once I saw a bear that (fortunately) was content to watch me pass by. There is something special about seeing dawn and dusk on the same day during a run, or seeing the trail change during the course of the day. At dawn, the frogs sing as the morning cold and fog are replaced with warmth and sunlight. Occasionally the hoot of an owl, the whine of a horse or the bark of a dog can be heard. As the sun moves up in the sky warming me up, I shed my jacket and don my sunglasses. Soon midday passes and the shadows of the trees on the trail change sides. As the shadows grow longer the trail becomes more difficult to see. Passing between brightly lit areas and shadows make the surface of the trail difficult to see. My brain reminds me to lift the tips of my shoes to avoid catching it on an unseen root or rock.

As the sun sets I enter a twilight zone. There is too much ambient light to use a flashlight, but not enough light for me to see well on my own. My legs continue to move, although now operating more on memory than by conscious effort. I decide the general path to follow but it is muscle memory, reflexes, and training that allow my feet, ankles, and knees to do the tweaking needed to advance without mishaps.

As the night settles and the temperature stabilizes, my eyes adjust either to the moonlight or to a headlight, and running—albeit significantly slower than before is possible again. During the daytime I can run for hours without seeing another runner; at night I can see the flashes of light from the headlights and flashlights of the runners ahead of me as well as behind me.

Every so often I can hear voices or music. Suddenly bright lights or a roaring campfire can be seen in the distance. An aid station appears out of nowhere staffed by a group of enthusiastic volunteers that praise you, wait on you hand and foot, or perhaps offer you a chair while they fix you hot soup. After a minute or two they encourage you to get back out on the trail. They know that you cannot get too comfortable for fear you may lose your desire to continue. So you bid them farewell and head back out into the darkness of the trail ahead.

Both time and distance always seem to pass by quicker at night. As morning approaches the temperature usually drops yet again before the rising sun warms up the day. Soon the trail becomes visible again, lights and people appear in the distance and you realize the end is near. There is not a more satisfying or rewarding feeling than knowing you have battled the course, the weather and yourself and have won. You realize you overcame moments of exhaustion, depression, and perhaps injury and ultimately succeeded. As you receive congratulations from the other runners, volunteers and running enthusiasts you encounter at the finish line, for one shining moment time stands still as you reflect on what you have just accomplished.

That, my friends, is why I run.

WHAT I HAVE LEARNED

I have been running for over 20 years and have participated in about 250 marathons and ultra runs. I have completed a marathon in all 50 states, finished almost 80 ultras, and run at least one 100-miler in each of the last ten years. Just recently my friends and I took up triathlons, and now we are all proud to say we are Ironmen.

As for endurance running, any distance can be accomplished if you follow these suggestions:

- Start slowly.
- The longer the distance, the slower you should run (or walk).
- Take rest breaks, beginning with the first mile.
- Eat and drink as much as possible.
- Nutrition starts with the first mile.
- Run your own race. (Even your best pal or training partner can be faster on you on a given day; do not go faster than what you have trained to do…or are *able* to do.)
- Train with the same equipment you will be using during the race. (I run every training run with the fuel belt, handheld water bottle and food I intend to use in a future race.)
- Keep moving forward. (Everyone has a bad patch; if you eat, take salt and slow down; soon you will feel better and resume running.)
- Break the run into smaller portions. (Few people can look at a 100-mile run, 24-hour run or mountain course like Leadville or Hardrock and not be intimidated. If the course is broken into smaller pieces it can be swallowed and digested better. For example, I set my sights on first making it to noon, then midafternoon, then dusk, and then ultimately dawn. Before long the run is almost over.)
- Talk to other runners; they are looking for company also.
- Enjoy the day. This may be the most important tip of all. We all run for personal satisfaction. Most of us don't win prize money or awards; therefore, there is no reason not to stop to look at mountain flowers, a stream, a waterfall or the animals in the forest. Enjoy the trail, enjoy the scenery, and enjoy being outdoors.

UPHILL BATTLE

By Andy Velazco

The Badwater Ultramarathon is a 135 mile invitational running race starting in Badwater in Death Valley (elevation 280 feet below sea level) and finishing at the Whitney Portals on Mount Whitney (elevation 8,360 feet).

Badwater is recognized as 'the toughest footrace on the planet.'

In March of 2003, I eagerly awaited a letter from the Race Director of the Badwater Ultramarathon advising me whether or not my application for the event had been accepted. A friend of mine had already been accepted, and I feared that my application had been denied. How did I feel? Both relieved and dejected at the same time. *Relieved,* because I knew the amount of training needed to complete the run and how difficult the run would be. *Dejected,* because even though I knew how difficult the run would be, I wanted the chance to test myself against my running heroes.

Then a few days later my fears were gone. I had been invited to compete in the Badwater Ultramarathon in July. Within 24 hours I had my support crew lined up: Mike Smith, Mike Brooks, Jeff Titus and Walt Prescott were all willing to give up a week of their lives to support me in my attempt to cover 135 miles in the most difficult conditions known to man (more on that later). My son Alec would be joining us to represent my family. I am grateful to them for giving up time from their jobs and families in a hot and inhospitable place where they will be faced with limited rest (let alone sleep), limited nourishment and a few days in the most undesirable conditions imaginable.

Acceptance into the race signaled the beginning of some serious training. Athletes who make their living running have the time and ability to train at high mileage. Athletes like me—who have a full time job, family responsibilities, and community obligations don't ever seem to have enough time to train adequately for an event of this magnitude. So the important question was not *how* to train, but *when* to train. A year ago I trained to be Mike Smith's pacer at Badwater, but that was different: I didn't have to run the entire way nor did I have the responsibility of supporting an entire team. Now as I begin to plan my run, I am overwhelmed by the planning and logistics: hotel reservations, car rentals, equipment and supplies. Besides all of that, I need to find time to run.

By the time May drew to a close my mind was sold on the idea of finishing Badwater. I had run several marathons, completed several long runs, lifted weights, rode many miles on a bicycle and walked on the elliptical trainer for hours while catching up on movies rented from the local Blockbuster. Many nights I would start walking at 7 or 8 p.m., and would continue until I was finished with my rentals.

Before I knew it June arrived. It was time to increase my heat training in the sauna at the gym. I also need to work on my abs more, not to mention my upper back. On the logistics front, I have to review my supplies and double check my hotel, car and flight reservations. Things are starting to come together. I was notified that I am in the 8:00 a.m. starting wave at Badwater (the other two waves begin at 6 and 10 a.m.). I am happy with my 8:00 start as it will give me a few miles in the shade of the valley's walls before the sun pushes the temperature in the desert up towards 130 degrees. Or more.

Then feelings of uncertainty rush over me. I realize the most difficult thing is to get *to* Badwater and actually toe the starting line. I know that I have been eating well, and I have even trained to endure the lack of sleep and desire to quit when I am exhausted I know I have trained well and thoroughly planned my journey, but still the feeling of uncertainty is difficult to avoid. I know that other runners have trained more than me. Do I have what it takes? Have I trained enough? Although I feel stronger every day, I continue to ask myself these questions.

I feel fortunate that my son Alec is coming along with me. Hopefully he will learn that tremendous things are possible if you really want them. More than anything, I want to finish. With a 60 hour time limit, I believe it to be possible. Earning the coveted belt buckle—signifying a sub-48 hour finish, would be icing on the cake. At this point it's easy to allow doubts and fears to creep into my mind with the unknown challenges I am about to face. Mentally I am able to counter them as I have the utmost confidence in my training, preparation and experience. I have been training for this moment for years, and am ready to face the ultimate challenge of mind and body. I just have to be smart and remember what I have learned. I have a great group of close friends supporting me, giving me an added incentive to do well.

It's now early July. I have been doing some weight workouts with my wife Kathy and the kids. My muscles are sore, but I am maintaining my weight. I have increased my protein intake. I am running longer. I ran 20 miles one day without any problems whatsoever; in fact, it felt virtually effortless. I am ready.

Badwater is one week away and I'm getting my equipment together for the trip. My plans are made and I trust they're adequate. If not, it's too late now. I have the courage to start, but do I have what I need to finish? I'll find out soon enough.

It's two days before my 8:00 a.m. start, and my crew and I are at the Furnace Creek Ranch in Death Valley where we'll be spending the next two nights. It's 2:00 p.m. and the temperature in the desert is a blazing 119 degrees. In the shade.

The next morning Mike Brooks and Walt want to run the first 17 miles of the course, from Badwater to Furnace Creek. We decide it would also be a good trial run for our rental vehicle. Mike and Walt take off running at 6:30 a.m. Alec will join them for a few miles in a little while. While the three of them were running, Mike Smith and I discussed plans for tomorrow. The early morning shadows began to recede and the temperatures quickly soared into triple digits. Mike Brooks and Walt had a good run—four hours and 56 minutes for 17 miles in 110 degree heat. I was proud of Alec, who fared quite well for as little training as he did; it's obvious he has his mother's genes. The three runners hit the pool before we had lunch and we all attended the mandatory meeting for both runners and support crew members.

The meeting was both hot and long. I met several of the runners, and saw some I knew from last year. The Race Director showed a video of last year's event (*very good!*) and went through the rules of the run again and again (*very boring!*). After photographs of all the runners were taken, we left to finish our preparations, recheck our ice and just simply rest. Before I fell asleep, I taped my feet and toes and put on my socks. I was asleep the minute my head hit the pillow.

Race Day was finally here. I woke up at 5:00 a.m. and got ready quickly. I had my normal breakfast—a protein shake—and took my gear to the vehicles. My crew was already there. They had restocked the ice and had all the equipment loaded neatly into the vehicles. We drove slowly to the starting line, 17 miles away. As we drove I felt calm, comfortable and ready. I felt like I do when I am about to perform difficult surgeries; my mind is settled since I know that I am going to be successful. Also, I had the best crew available who were more than willing to work and suffer for me.

Before we knew it, we arrived at the starting line in Badwater, 285 feet below sea level. We took some photographs along the salty crusted pond of minerals and collected water. I was interviewed by two television crews. We took our official group picture and at the crack of a pistol we were off. I tried to run slowly and settle on a pace while my crew kept telling me to 'slow down, slow down.' Soon enough I was locked in on a good pace. The sun moved overhead, and the temperature began to rise from the 100 degrees at the start. I was drinking a bottle of water and/or carbohydrate drink and taking a salt capsule each mile.

Soon my starting weight of 145 pounds had climbed ten pounds, to 155. I was urinating very little. I spoke with another runner—Mike Karsh, a fellow orthopedic surgeon about my situation. He agreed with me that since I was running well, I was probably drinking more than I needed. *(Now we could both write the trip off as a business expense!)*

We reached the first checkpoint at Furnace Creek Ranch at noon. My crew provided a chair and a fresh pair of socks. I was relieved to discover I didn't have any blisters. Mike Brooks assumed his duties as a pacer at this time, and we passed the Borax mines and headed into the bowels of Death Valley. The heat continued to rise and the sun kept baking the asphalt road on which we were running. There was a distinct possibility that our running shoes could melt, as the temperature on the road was much higher than the temperature in the air, perhaps as much as 70 degrees. During the afternoon, the heated air began to rise, hitting the valley walls and creating convection currents that turned and blew towards the valley floor. The heated currents of air created whirlwinds that would hit and burn us. My crew placed a wet towel over my head and sprayed my shirt with water every mile. The shirt would be dry in less than three minutes, and the towel shortly after that. I had never felt so much heat. During the afternoon the air temperature reached 133 degrees. The highest recorded temperature on earth is 134 degrees. My skin was burning. I wanted to quit several times. The miles passed by. Slowly.

We passed the Sand Dunes and reached the outskirts of Stovepipe Wells and the Mountain Range. My crew immediately directed me to the hotel swimming pool, which I jumped in without removing the first piece of clothing. Water never felt so good! There were other runners cooling down in the pool and lying on the lounge chairs. I was asked to take care of a fellow runner's heel blister; after draining and taping it, I ate a plate of spaghetti. I changed my shirt, socks and replaced my running shoes with running *sandals* and began the long 19-mile climb to Towne Pass. I was urinating every 30 minutes, so I felt good about my hydration (ah, the little things). However, for some reason I had the strongest desire to quit…badly, in fact. However, the thought of not wanting to disappoint my crew was even stronger, and this thought kept me going as we approached the mountain. It was now dusk as we began the climb. We experienced large blasts of heated air blowing from the desert up the mountain and hitting us in our backs. I took my glasses off to keep my eyes from drying up; since we were running without headlamps, we couldn't see much anyway. The wind finally died down after we reached 2,000 feet in elevation. We passed other runners—and were passed by other runners—as darkness came, and the miles continued to pass by. Slowly.

We finally reached Towne Pass. It was after midnight. After a couple of photographs I took a quick 20-minute nap. Feeling much better, Walt and I ran down the mountain towards Owens Lake. The road across the dry bed of Owens Lake is a boring and virtually straight line close to seven miles long. We crept towards the outskirts of the Panamint Mountain range and to our next rest stop, the Panamint Hotel. My crew had arrived ahead of me and had an egg burrito ready for me to devour. Before long I was back on the road, starting yet another climb towards Father Crowley's Pass. This climb is shorter yet steeper than the first. As we climbed, the sun began to rise. We had a crew change, and Mike Brooks was now serving as my pacer. During this second climb we were entertained by several military fighter jets doing climbs and attacks on the dry lake floor. I felt my lower back tightening as we reached the top of the mountains. As we passed Father Crowley's there was a lady with a massage table and an umbrella offering her services. I lay down on her table for a five-minute back massage, which felt quite good.

We ran along the mountain range at an elevation of 4,500 feet. The mountains suddenly were filled with a greenish-color attributed to its abundant plant life—one huge difference from the earlier mountains at the lower altitude. We passed the west boundary of Death Valley National Park and entered the Argus Range. We were now 80 miles into our adventure. There were some long gradual flat stretches and some long (but not long enough) downhill stretches. We passed Joshua trees, jackrabbits and curious small rodents that resembled chipmunks—except they moved much, much quicker.

A couple miles later brought about another crew change: Walt was now my pacer as we headed to Lone Pine. We met up with the Canadian runner whose blisters I had tended to in Stovepipe Wells. She was running well, which pleased me, and she was very grateful for my assistance earlier. Together we passed the 100-mile mark; we could see Mount Whitney in the distance.

Dusk settled in and we all put on our reflective vests and lights for a second time. I decided to use my headlamp. My regimen now consisted of running two minutes and then walking two minutes. My back was tight once again, but I was making progress. I couldn't eat trail mix or dry pineapple chunks anymore, and started eating peanut butter and jelly crackers. Normally I don't eat peanut butter, but with the heat the peanut butter had liquefied to the point that I could swallow it easily. We could see the lights of Lone Pine in the distance, yet it was demoralizing to run forward while the lights remained the same size in the distance. Were we really making progress?

A car approached us, and I noticed that Walt was leaning sideways to the right at a 45-degree angle. I told him that he was leaning and that he could actually touch the ground if he stretched his right arm. Wait, no one can do that. I closed one eye at a time to see if the picture changed. It didn't; I saw the same image through each eye. I shook my head to see if my equilibrium was off; it wasn't. Walt was still leaning, however, and I was not hallucinating. I looked at my legs and saw that they were leaning as well and then it hit me: Walt wasn't leaning, *I* was. The road was not sloping; it was my head tilting that gave me the visual impression of Walt leaning. I was amazed that I had been running and walking for 50 miles bent sideways and never realized it. My crew had known for some time, but had kept it from me since I continued to move forward. I also now understood why I had been stepping off the road and onto the road shoulder so much, and why my crew tried to keep me moving closer and closer to the middle of the road.

Finally we reached Keeler. We were now only 19 miles from Lone Pine. I was really tired, and my back was sore and trying to spasm. We continued to move forward, although I had been having hallucinations for a while. I knew that I was having them and they were distracting, but they did help to pass the time. I wasn't sleepy at all, nothing at all like the first night. I was able to make the hallucination appear and disappear at will. I was seeing a red hologram about a foot in front of me, then a table, two peoples' heads and something jumping. I also felt like I was running in a chute with side walls, like a gutter in a bowling alley; it was my perception of the white highway lines and the road. I also had 'feeling' hallucinations; one I felt as if something was hitting me on the back of the left shoulder over and over again. Looking upwards to the sky, I was able to see all the stars connected by a road of light—like a 'space city.'

Slowly the miles passed, and we finally arrived in Lone Pine. I was extremely tired. The two miles on the road to the Dow Villa Hotel, the last checkpoint, seemed to take forever. I was cranky and refused to eat or drink. All I wanted was to get this thing over with. As we entered the 13-mile stretch of road leading to the Whitney Portal it began to rain. My crew was encouraging me to finish under 48 hours. I just wanted to finish, regardless of the time. I told them I would go as fast as I could. I pushed as hard as I could while it was still dark.

Dawn arrived with five miles remaining. The long, ascending switchbacks of the mountain road were demoralizing to see. I was passed by two runners, Mike Karsh and Marshall Ulrich at this point. No matter how hard I tried, I could barely move forward. My back was tired. *I* was tired. Finally the cone signifying the beginning of the final mile miraculously appeared. The last mile was long; *very* long.

At long last we reached the portals. My crew gathered around me as we crossed the finish line as one. I was happy, but more than anything I wanted to sit in the chair and give my back—hell, my entire *body* a rest. I received my medal from the race director and had photographs of my crew and me taken. They were all happy for me, and I was happy that I had not let them down. It was the culmination of a dream of mine, one that I've held on to for many years.

Amazingly, as tired as I was, I had already started to think about what to do better the next time I take on 'the toughest footrace on the planet.'

• •

Andy Velazco finished the 2003 Badwater Ultramarathon in 48:54:12, missing the coveted belt buckle by less than an hour.

Crew member Mike Smith finished the 2002 Badwater Ultramarathon in 45:12:10, and crew member Mike Brooks the 2004 event in 46:17:10, both earning belt buckles. In 2005 Andy's good friend Carl Hunt completed Badwater.

Andy crewed for all three of them.

Chapter Fifteen

Craig Snapp

I was only a couple hundred yards into my quest for mileage at the 2004 24-Hour Endurance Run in San Diego, California when I heard someone on the side of the road calling to me and asking me if I was Scott Ludwig.

When I answered affirmatively he said his name was Craig Snapp and that he had been asked by the United States Running Streak Association to write a story about me. I was flattered not only that someone would want to write a story about me but that I was recognized while being almost 3,000 miles away from home by a total stranger.

That, of course is where I was wrong. In the world of Craig Snapp there *are* no total strangers.

Craig has a personality that instantly makes you feel at ease and as if you've known him all your life.

Craig's running…and his *writing* about running have made him a favorite of many across the nation.

His fan base includes my late parents. The story Craig would write about me was proudly framed and prominently displayed in my parents' home until they both passed away in the fall of 2007.

In my parents' home Craig was no stranger; after all he had written a flattering story about their only son.

In my parents' home Craig Snapp was family.

Craig Snapp

SNAPP OUT OF IT

To say that Craig Snapp's life revolves around numbers is an understatement.

The man lives for numbers. He knows how to put the 'anal' in 'analytical.'

Give him a number—or better yet, a series or list of numbers and he'll stay busy for hours. Imagine giving a kitten a ball of yarn or an avid reader a copy of *War and Peace*. You get the idea: endless hours of entertainment.

The man is so fond of numbers that when he retired at the tender age of 50 after owning a convenience store for 20 years, you just knew the store had to be a *(what else?)* 7-11. Craig always remembered the advice of his father, who had suffered a heart attack when he was 50: 'I don't know what you inherited from me in regards to heart-health, but if you're able to retire early, do it!' He did just that and has never looked back.

Early retirement meant more time for his two (well, three if you count 'number-crunching') favorite activities, running and writing. As for the writing, Craig says that his '666 articles about running have probably covered just about every step he ever took.'

The statement may be an exaggeration, but if Craig were to tell you *how many* steps he has taken while running, don't doubt him for a second. The same applies if he were to tell you the price he paid to see the Rolling Stones for the first time when he was 19 years old ('$7.50, and it was the most expensive seat available') and that the opening acts were B.B. King and the Ike and Tina Turner Revue. Or if he were to say that when he was 14 he saw Jim Ryun defeat the defending Olympic 800 and 1,500 meter champion, Peter Snell, in the mile by running a 3:55:3, a record which stood for 36 years.

Craig was born in San Diego in 1950, the son of a fifties' housewife mother from Kansas and a workaholic, over-achieving father from San Diego. They were married in Kansas, and their Best Man was Milton Eisenhower, whose brother Dwight became President of the United States six years later. His father, a 1949 University of Southern Cal graduate, started his own insurance agency with a workforce totaling one employee ('eventually he moved up,' Craig says). At one point his father was simultaneously the National Vice President of the Air Force Association as well as the President or Chairman of the San Diego Aerospace Museum, the City Planning Commission, the Elks Club, the Kiwanis Club and the Little League. Soon afterwards he was elected the mayor for the city Craig still lives in today (El Cajon), which has doubled in population from 50,000 in the 1950's to a bit over 100,000 today.

While Craig's dad served as mayor, at the age of 18 Craig had the honor of chauffeuring his father in a convertible Camaro at the front of a Presidential motorcade for Richard Nixon. Craig says his hair was noticeably longer than the other chauffeurs, and after the event he 'borrowed' a traffic cone from the V.I.P. parking area, stuck it in the trunk of the Camaro and kept it as a 'Nixon souvenir.'

During Craig's second year of college he received a new draft card which changed his draft status from 1-A to School-Deferment. As the end of the Viet Nam War was still six years away, Craig counts his blessings to this day. In fact, he mailed his old draft card to his aunt who was working in Saigon, who ceremoniously burned it for him.

Craig graduated from San Diego State University ('when they had a football team that could actually win') with a BS in Business Administration. However, for the past three decades he has adopted his father's alma mater as his own.

When Craig was 26, he began his running career.

Craig admits he was fascinated by 'the magic that is running' at a very early age. His grandfather told Craig that when the two of them were sitting on a park bench when Craig was five years old they saw two runners fly by. Craig asked 'what are those guys doing?' Grandfather answered 'Well... maybe they're running from the law!' At the time, the humor flew way over Craig's tiny, crew-cutted head but he found the two runners mesmerizing. Craig and his grandfather continued feeding the pigeons and singing songs from the Mickey Mouse Club and then, about an hour or so later the two runners flew by again. 'WOO,' Craig says, 'the template was struck!'

Even though fascinated by running at an early age, he didn't attempt running personally until many years later. In elementary school, Craig admits he was unathletic in any sport he tried. In fact, during his last two years of Little League his batting average was .000. (Craig, an admitted numbers-nerd, says he still has the end of season batting average lists). Before starting 7th grade, Craig's parents enrolled him in a physical education class. During summer school.

At the end of the class—a class in which he wasn't doing very well, his teacher ('Coach Rose') said that if anybody could run two miles without stopping they'd receive extra credit. So Craig tried...and made it. Although his time is forgotten (perhaps the only statistic the number-nerd can't recite), he'll never forget the accomplishment.

Soon after that Craig's body stopped growing. Well, it stopped growing *up*, but not necessarily *out*. After high school, Craig stood 5'3' tall and weighed 159 pounds. These dimensions were not particularly conducive to a career as a runner, and had a negative effect on any running fantasies Craig harbored from the successful 'Coach Rose Run' in summer school. So Craig maintained his interest in running as a spectator and found himself going to many track meets.

After witnessing the aforementioned performance by Jim Ryun, one of Craig's best friends bet him he couldn't run five miles without stopping. Craig did it and (of course) he still remembers the time: 53:11 which, Craig adds 'is not too bad for a short, fat kid.'

The summer before college Craig says that 'Mother Nature woke up Father Puberty' and by the end of his freshman year he stood 6'2'…and still weighed 159 pounds. Running then became a lot easier. For the next several years Craig had fun with running but never got too serious about it. In his early 20's, another of his best friends bet Craig that he couldn't run more miles than him in a period of 24 hours. Craig ran six different times during those 24 hours, accumulating 19 ½ miles, but lost the bet by 4 ½ miles. This, as were the two runners in the park many years ago, was another eye-opener. His first glimpse of 'the loveliness of the long-distance runner,' as he calls it.

At the age of 26 Craig was living with another of his best friends who challenged him to 'start a running career.' Craig officially christened his running career with a run of three miles. The friend encouraged him to record his accomplishment in a notebook. Later that evening the two of them had a long discussion which ended with yet another bet: that Craig couldn't run 26.2 miles without stopping within the next twelve months. Twenty-eight days later Craig won the bet. Craig now felt comfortable calling himself a runner.

Craig has had quite a career as a runner. His impressive list of personal bests includes:

- 5K – 17:21
- 10K – 35:28
- 10 Miles – 59:28
- Half Marathon – 1:18:25
- Marathon – 2:42:24
- 50K – 3:49:01 (Craig has only run the distance one time, and actually it was more of a fun run than a race)
- 50 Miles – 11:25:02 (Craig has only run the distance one time, and actually it was more of an 'initiation' into a club of accomplished ultrarunners)

Perhaps the most impressive number of all for the admitted numbers-nerd is the number of prizes he's won in races, which includes overall, masters or age-group awards:

- 0

Explaining Absolutely Nothing

You may be wondering how someone with such quick personal bests could never have won an award for a performance in a race. The blame might be attributed to Bill Rodgers and Frank Shorter, whose performances in marathons during the 1970's captured the imagination of a country and inspired the famous 'running boom' in the United States. These two men were responsible for inspiring runners as well as wanna-be runners all over the country, resulting in performances we may never see again.

To see what Craig was up against, look no further than a quick analysis of performances at the Boston Marathon presented by our favorite numbers cruncher. Specifically, the number and percentage of finishers who completed the Boston Marathon in less than three hours since 1979:

Year	# of Finishers	% of sub-three hour finishers
1979	3,031	50.8%
1981	2,899	51.8%
1983	2,647	49.1%
1987	1,625	30.2%
1991	1,423	18.6%
1995	1,031	12.4%
1999	756	6.7%
2003	582	3.4%
2004	319	1.5%

What can we derive from these statistics?

Well, you can draw you own conclusions. But it certainly helps explain why Craig's 'running awards batting average' was only .000.

JUMPING OFF THE PAGE

By Craig Snapp

Guttenberg and his gang invented the printing press so that umpteen eons later we could have textbooks about running. At some other point in time, another person invented Windows so that in 2009, the aforementioned textbooks could be flung out the later-mentioned window.

As my Grandpa Dementia says, 'the first rule of running is that there ain't no stinkin' rules!' Since you're reading this, I'm guessing that you might have also read advice about running before, with the 'same ole same ole' information. Well, this ain't that!

That being said, for me the most important part of running is to have fun. There is a cornucopia of side-effects, like improving health, improving self-esteem, losing weight, getting faster, getting stronger, and 94 others. They are all wonderful and are to be thoroughly enjoyed. Yet, for yours truly it starts with having fun.

The sometimes-flip-side-of-the-shoe to having fun is to 'listen to your body.' If it would indeed be 'fun' to run 20 miles, yet were experiencing a sharp shooting pain in your leg for every step of your first two miles, then 'listen' trumps 'fun' and you should stop. However, I have seen too many folks that *don't* 'listen to their body' when it's 'having fun' and say 'well, the textbook says that I should stop at X miles today, and even though I'm feeling great at X I'll stop.'

CAUTION: You are about to enter the 'no logic zone!' Do not try to replicate any of the following at home. As Grandpa Dementia says, *'be what you want to be…but if you're gonna be a bear, you might as well be a grizzly!'*

A buddy—Pete, had done several marathons and did a twenty-miler every Sunday. On one particular Sunday, he hooked up with a guy to do the 15-mile loop around the bay. As they were approaching the end of the loop the guy asked my buddy if he would like to start another loop, and Pete said 'well, OK.' As they were approaching the end of the second loop (Pete had never gone a step beyond 26.2 miles) the guy asked the same question and got the same answer.

They finished the third loop and Pete thought 'damn…I just did 45 miles! I guess that 26.2 is *not* my limit!' He went on to do 50-milers, 100-milers, 24-hour races (setting an American single-age record of 133 miles at age 42) and even a six-day race (where he circled a quarter-mile track during an April heat wave for 1,656 laps, or 414 miles!).

Another buddy—Mike went to a half-marathon where the course consisted of one-mile loops. He was not interested in what he might be able to do for the full distance, but rather wanted to see how many loops he could do at a certain pace (6:30 per mile). When he could no longer hold that pace he would step off the course and be happy with whatever he did.

His first mile was right on pace and he thought 'OK, now how much longer can I go before my body says *no mas!*' He'd never gone beyond six miles at this pace so as the miles rolled by, his goal became getting past six miles. Well, he never got any faster—but never slowed down either, and ended up doing the entire race at 6:29 pace. He said 'damn, I could *not* have done what I just *did!*'

My running partner—Debbie started her running career with a quarter mile effort that left her breathless and swearing (both in profanities and in oaths) that she'd never do it again! A few weeks later her longest run was already up to three miles. We went to a half-marathon finish area, ran in circles until the winner came in, then went out and back several times trying to help friends make it to the finish. When we finally stopped she'd tripled her longest run, completing a total of nine miles.

A couple months later, her longest run had been extended to 18 miles and a few months after that she did her first marathon. Her career is now at eleven years and she's finished 39 marathons and one 50-miler. She also has a streak of running every day (a minimum of three miles) that hit ten years in March 2008, averaging slightly less than ten miles per day. Recently she said 'damn, that first quarter-mile *still* hurts!'

Another idiotic buddy—OK, actually this would be me started his running career with a three-mile run. Although I hadn't been running I was only 26, rode my bicycle to and from work—since I didn't own a car—and played some racquetball, so I wasn't exactly a la-zee boy. I then took two days off and, to win a big bet, ran 13 miles.

In the next 24 days I ran seven times, never exceeding 10 miles. On the 29th day of my running career—to win a *really* big bet, I ran 26.2 miles. 'Damn,' I said. However, I wasn't sure if that comment was in appreciation of what I'd just done or a curse on the person that had 'forced' me to make the bet! (I'm choosing not to share the fact that I didn't run a single step for the next 10 days, or that I didn't go beyond 10 miles for the next 79 days) What I *am* choosing to share is that on day 80 following the 26.2 miles (to win one last really, *really* big bet) I ran another 26.2 miles.

I'm not advising that any (sane) person ever attempt to do anything like this. What I am advising is to be aware of the amazing potential of the human body! So when some day you've gone out to do what the textbook says is your limit and you ultimately approach that point and you still find that you're feeling, well…pretty good, simply find that window of opportunity, throw out that textbook, and exclaim:

Look out world, here I come!

As Grandpa Dementia says, 'folks used to do whatever *Runner's World* said because it was the Bible. Well, Pluto's not a planet anymore, either.'

BREATHLESS IN BOSTON

By Craig Snapp

Of the many races I have run, the 1979 Boston Marathon earns the honor of being my absolute favorite. Although I would later do a few marathons faster--and would even run seven more Boston's in the years ahead--this was, after all my very first and for that reason it's still my NUMBER ONE!

I didn't start my running career until February of 1977; however, I'd been a fan of the sport for as long as I could remember. In 1970, I actually wrote a letter to the BAA asking what one needed to do to run Boston. (Of course, I still have their reply.)

I did my first 26.2 miles in March of 1977 in a modest 5:12. The Boston Qualifying Time at the time was 3:00 so I didn't honestly believe that I could shave *two hours and twelve minutes* from my time. Somehow, with a lot of luck and a little bit of work I sneaked in with a 2:57 marathon in August of 1978. Then in December of 1978 I dropped another two minutes off my time and one month later I dropped another four minutes, running a 2:53. My Boston Marathon application was mailed in the next morning!

When I arrived in Boston it was MECCA to me, both as a runner and as a fan. The entrants included Bill Rodgers, Frank Shorter, Toshihiko Seko, Jerome Drayton, Tony Sandoval, Ron Tabb, Brian Maxwell, Garry Bjorklund, and Tom Fleming. Most of my buddies had no idea who these guys were (and today, even fewer would have any clue!), but I worshipped them then, and I still do now.

In the corral right before the start I was (literally) jumping up and down. Part of my excuse was that I wanted to see those gathered in front of us. But more importantly, I was simply too excited to stand still. My mentor/running partner Will (as in 'Where there's a ... ') said 'Snapper! Calm Down!' My reply was a loud and vociferous 'THIS IS THE BOSTON MARATHON!' *(Truth be told, I used 'The F-Word' in the middle of that declaration.)*

When the gun went off, so did I. Will had instructed me before the start: 'Trust me! There are no mileage markers, so simply follow me and you'll run the right pace.' This was good advice--partially because he knew me and partially because it was raining and my glasses were all fogged-up, so I couldn't see much beyond him anyway.

It took us slightly over a minute to reach the starting line, so this small delay would not be a major detriment to our finishing time. Following Will as closely as I could, I knew I was running 'over my head.' However, with the unbelievably large and loud crowd screaming us on, I decided to go with the flow.

At one point Will said 'I think we're approaching 10 miles.' Right after that we noticed a man on the back of a pick-up truck with a small clock which displayed the current time of day. It appeared to say 1:02, and since the race allegedly started at 12:00 I was a bit concerned. *If* it was indeed 10 miles, and *if* it was 1:02, and *if* we'd started at 12:00, this would indicate we were running a pace of 6:12 per mile. My personal best was only three months old, was run on a flat course on a dry day, and I managed a pace of 6:40. When I mentioned this to him he said 'follow me!'

Shortly after the guesstimated 15-mile mark I was still feeling great, yet realized that my leader was feeling even greater. After informing him of both he said 'Well, if you slip behind, keep me in sight and catch me later.' That 'slippage' did occur, but I was still 'flying' by my definition, so our separation didn't bother me at all.

At several points along the course there were leader boards listing the top ten runners as they had passed that particular spot in the race. The running fan in me read as much as my 'foggle-goggles' would allow. For the first few, Fleming was at the top, and then it was Bjorklund. Yet, Seko and Rodgers were always somewhere near the top of the board.

Approximately a mile or so after I'd slipped behind Coach Will's slip-stream, I'd lost visual contact with him. That didn't mean I'd slowed much; rather that my vision challenges combined with the density of runners made it virtually impossible to differentiate one runner from another. I kept looking forward to see him because for the donkey in me, he was my 26.2-carrot-gold.

My brain-on-rain was slightly confused about the uphills on the course. I'd read about the number of them and their various descriptions. So when I'd crested one I asked the stranger next to me 'Does 'Heartbreak Hill' start soon?' 'That *was*,' he answered, 'Heartbreak Hill'!' WOO! I was not trying to be a wise-heinie. Honestly, I did not know. What I *did* know was that after Heartbreak, the course was all downhill. And my running style made me feel upbeat about running downhill.

My father had come with me to the race, and our motel was on the course, somewhere near the 23-mile mark. When I got there, I looked for him but couldn't find him anywhere. Somehow, someway he not only saw me but also took a picture and hollered 'You're Doing Great, My Son!' My eyes got blurred. And not from the rain.

(My folks had separated the month after my high-school graduation, when I was still the 5' 3" 159-pound 'SFK' (short fat kid). They divorced the following year. Therefore I was never living with my father when Mother Nature finally made me the 6'2" 159-pound 'TSK' (tallish slow kid).

Running with the emotion stirred in me by my father I flew over those next few miles, made the turn onto Hereford Street, looked at my watch and said to myself 'Oh, my God!' I knew the distance from there to the finish, and realized I was going to shatter the personal best I had run only three months earlier. Taking the turn off Hereford Street, I could see the finish line and realized I could get into the 2:47's. I was right, finishing in 2:47:25. Immediately I got that blurry-eyed-vision again. And, I must admit, it was wonderful.

When I exited the finish chute I went straight to the wall where Honeywell had thumb tacked partial results. It was then and there I discovered that Bill Rodgers had won his 3rd Boston, in 2:09:27 with Seko only 45 seconds back. I knew that Mister Rodgers' time was a course record, an American Record, and the 4th fastest time in history! (I had this thing about numbers even back then.)

After absorbing as many numbers as I could I went into the underground garage of the Prudential Building looking for the famous hot beef stew. And that's when I saw Billy! He was being escorted out and I yelled over to him 'Congratulations on 2:09:27!' He yelled back 'Thanks! How'd *you* do!?' 'I did a PR by six minutes!' He yelled, 'Congratulations to you!' WOO!

I found my mentor/pacer Will right after that and heard that he'd finished 109 seconds ahead of me. We'd later learn that evening that in those 109 seconds, 175 runners finished between us! And remember, I'd run a 6:23 pace! So I knew why I'd lost visual contact with him. I also knew that this had been a race for the ages.

(I could very easily overdo my statistical analysis of the race, yet I'll try to restrict myself to the following):

- 3,031 of the 5,958 runners ran sub-three hour marathons, which translates into 50.8% of the field. This established a new percentage record (for sub-three hour marathons in a field), and it has been exceeded only once anywhere—at Boston in 1981, with 51.8%.
- With fields almost four times as large, the last five Boston Marathons (2004 – 2008) have averaged 842 sub-threes, or only 3.9% of the field. With fields over six times as large (London, Berlin, New York, Chicago), the average is around 1,200, or 4.2%).

When I finally arrived back at our motel room, I set a personal best for longest hot shower ever taken. Remember, having lived in San Diego all my life my body had never been through anything like Boston before: the temperature at the start was 41, it rained the entire way, and the temperature when I finished was 38.

That night there was a 90-minute highlights show on television. I sponged up every moment of it, while drinking up every Michelob we had and eventually eating up every awesome ounce of a 'Boston delicatessen sandwich supreme.' Believe me, I earned (and burned) every bit of it!

That day brought about a major change in the way I viewed myself as a runner, as well as how I looked at life. Though the weather had chilled me to my Southern California bones, it was the perfect storm and the Boston Marathon remains my favorite race.

Chapter Sixteen

Gary Griffin

Gary Griffin has been an incredible source of running knowledge and inspiration.

I met Gary at the two-mile mark of the 2002 Callaway Gardens (Georgia) Marathon. We ran the rest of the way together, trading historical tales of our past and sharing aspirations of our future. It was an instant connection. We found that we were alike in many ways, particularly when it came to long-distance running. I mentioned that I wanted to run the Badwater Ultramarathon—hopefully in 2003, and Gary immediately volunteered to serve on my support crew.

Seventeen months later Gary was running beside me, handing me water bottle after water bottle in 133-degree heat through Death Valley for well over 50 miles as I was living out my fondest running dream. His running knowledge and inspiration was invaluable to my success at Badwater, and for that I'll always be grateful.

Gary is not only an accomplished distance runner but a veteran Race Director as well. Gary and his wife Peg were co-race directors of the Tallahassee Marathon for several years and are presently the co-race directors of the Tallahassee Ultra Distance Classic (TUDC).

In 2007 Gary dedicated the TUDC to my parents, who had both passed away in the six weeks prior to the event.

I'll never forget it.

Gary Griffin

RELENTLESS FORWARD MOTION

Don't stop 'til you get enough.

-Michael Jackson

There are all types of runners. Some are like the hare in the old parable: they run quickly for as long as they can, only to fizzle out at the end and crawl to the finish. Some are like the tortoise, just plodding along at the same consistent pace until they comfortably arrive at the finish. Then there are those who have the uncanny ability to combine the better qualities of both the hare and the tortoise (quickness and consistency, respectively) and truly excel in the sport of ultra distance running. One of them goes by the name of Gary Griffin.

Gary, a runner for the past 25 years runs—and *lives* by his credo of 'relentless forward motion.' Born in Homestead, Florida in 1949, he retired in Tallahassee in 2007 after a career with the Internal Revenue Service as a Property Appraisal and Liquidation Specialist (which Gary claims is a fancy term for 'auctioneer') spanning 32 years.

In 2008 he celebrated 31 years of marriage to his remarkable wife Peg as well as his 59th birthday (*this last fact is important for a point to be made a little bit later*). On the running front, Gary completed his 100th lifetime marathon and/or ultra when he crossed the finish line of the Stump Jump 50K in Chattanooga, Tennessee.

Spreading the Wealth (Non-running version)

There's more to Gary than his running. Gary serves his community and fellow man through his involvement in a variety of charitable and religious organizations. He is an Executive Committee Member of the American Cancer Society (Leon, Florida Unit) and in 2003 served as the Leon County Chairman of the Relay for Life, an event he continues to support as both an active volunteer and participant. He is an Elder for the Faith Presbyterian Church and a Lay Preacher for the Seafarer's Chapel in Shell Point, Florida.

Gary is also very active with the Tallahassee-based Gulf Winds Track Club, both as a member and competitor. For many years he and Peg served as co-race directors for the Tallahassee Marathon, and in 2006 they were 'promoted' to the position of co-race directors for the annual Tallahassee Ultra

Distance Classic, traditionally held on the second Saturday in December. Gary calls it a 'reunion' for ultrarunners everywhere, but primarily for those in the southeast. Every year many ultrarunners show up to complete either 50 kilometers or 50 miles on the famous 2.07 mile loop at Wakulla Springs. In all honesty, it's worth the price of admission just to hear Gary's pre-race announcements and thank you to the volunteers (including who he refers to as the *real* race director, Peg), capped off by his always-eloquent dedication of the race to someone near and dear to the hearts of the tight-knit family of ultrarunners assembled for the event. Minutes later, Gary toes the starting line (usually for the 50-mile event) after handing the reigns over to Peg and the rest of the staff of dedicated volunteers, comfortable and confident that they are all up to the task at hand.

Spreading the Wealth (Running version)

Gary has excelled at a variety of distances and on a variety of surfaces in his running career. His impressive list of personal bests includes:

- 5K – 18:23
- 10K – 38:23
- 15K – 58:30
- Half Marathon – 1:28:10
- Marathon – 3:01:48
- 50K – 4:01
- 50 Miles – 7:15
- 100 Miles – 19:02:30

Of particular significance are the personal bests at 50 and 100 miles, as they were both run when Gary was *58 years old!* The latter distance is the most noteworthy as (a) it was the 4th fastest 100 mile time by a 58 year old male in the United States and (b) if Gary had run the time six weeks later when he turned 59 his time would have bettered the existing all-time best 100 mile time by a 59 year old...*by over 40 minutes!*

Gary's outstanding 100 mile time was run at the *2008 Lean Horse Endurance Run in Hot Springs, South Dakota.* He made the trip west hoping that 'somehow, some way, perhaps in some sort of a dream' he could break 20 hours. The rest, as they say, is history.

Gary cites two other events at the head of his 'best ever performances' list:

Fall 50 Mile Run in Door County, Wisconsin, October 2007 Three months after Gary retired he was able to 'ramp us his mileage' and eclipse his former 50 mile best by over 20 minutes, running the year's second-fastest 50 mile time (7:15) in the United States for the 55-59 age group.

Croom Trail 50K in Brooksville, Florida, September 2002 The race served as the Southeastern RRCA Championship, and Gary not only finished second overall but first in the Masters division with an outstanding 4:08 at the age of 52. About the race Gary says 'My feet had wings; I never felt better in my life, in spite of 90-degree temperatures, high humidity and a soft, sandy hilly trail.'

Gary's running career has literally taken him all over the world. Among his favorite ultras is the prestigious Comrades Marathon in South Africa, an event he summarizes as 'wonderful.' Obviously he has a soft spot in his heart for the Lean Horse Endurance Run as well, but his absolute favorite is the Mountain Mist 50K, 'a nasty little rocky 31 miles on Monte Sano Mountain in Huntsville, Alabama.' Gary considers it to be the perfect course for an ultra, as it is totally challenging yet fair in the sense that you can run it. He believes that too many ultras have become nothing more than 'hikes' in ridiculous terrain that level the playing field far too much; Mountain Mist, on the other hand still rewards the runner.

As for marathons, Boston is at the top of Gary's list, if only for that half mile stretch past Wellesley College in the middle of the course.

Boston is also near the top of Gary's less-than marathon list; Boston, Georgia that is. The Boston Mini-Marathon is 'an incredibly sweet out-and-back half-marathon through the rolling countryside of south Georgia' in late October. Gary says he's run the event at least ten times and loved every single step.

The Spiritual Advisor

On a personal level, I've known Gary since January of 2002. We met while running together for 24 miles of the Callaway Gardens (Georgia) Marathon. During the three hours we ran and talked literally non-stop, and during the lengthy conversation I mentioned I'd like to run the Badwater Ultramarathon one day. Instantly Gary said he wanted to be a part of my support crew. Seventeen months later Gary and I and the other four members of my crew had the most eventful week imaginable as we blazed a 135-mile trail across Death Valley and up to the portal of Mount Whitney. Gary was assigned the role of 'spiritual advisor' for our adventure, and I'll be the first to tell you he took the assignment seriously. During the event we had our share of highs and lows, but if you ever have the opportunity to talk to Gary about his trials and tribulations after pacing me for 60 miles across a blazing 133-degree desert—without drinking an adequate amount of fluids, believe me—you want to take advantage of it.

While the assignment was a temporary one, I now know that it wasn't even necessary to make in the first place. Gary's whole life could be described by the title 'spiritual advisor' as he lives each and every day the same, which is to say he is the most optimistic, positive and encouraging person I've ever known.

If there is ever a need for an ambassador for the sport of running, I know just the right person.

He lives in Tallahassee, and if he isn't busy running, helping others, bird-watching or cheering on his beloved Miami Hurricanes....well, just consider yourself lucky you found him. After all, it's difficult to find him standing still; the man is undeniably relentless forward motion at its finest.

JUST LISTEN

By Gary Griffin

It is interesting to reflect upon the giving and taking of advice I've been a part of over the 25 or so years of my running career. I do recall that during the formative years, I did a lot of <u>listening</u>, for I came into the sport knowing only that it required a pair of shoes that one wore while going from point A to point B. As evidence of the fact that I knew little about even the basic shoe requirements, I ran in a pair of $19.99 J.C. Penney tennis shoes for the first several years before graduating to my beloved Nike Pegasus (the originals, not the pretenders that are marketed today!) that could be found at the same J.C. Penney for $49.99.

I still try and do a lot of listening, even these days, as I have had the extreme good fortune of finding myself in the presence of gifted and experienced runners who know far more than I do or ever will. Having said that, I have two very strong opinions about advice I think are critical to all of us in this age where one need only pick up the latest running magazine or newsletter, read the plethora of running blogs and opinion columns out there, or if worse comes to worse, do a Google search on the running question of the day. Simply put, it is this:

1. Listen to the opinion of only those who you trust and respect.

2. Listen first and foremost to yourself.

Seeking and getting advice from a trusted source is wonderful, and something to consider and experiment with if you think it might work for you, but remember this is your body that you're trying to propel from Point A to Point B and it is not the body of the one who dispenses the advice.

We are all different, the 'experiment of one' we read about. The thing I love about distance running is that it is really pretty basic – just as it was 25 years ago. Lace 'em up and go out the door and do the relentless forward motion thing until you're half-tired, then hope that you've not gone out any further than you have to go to get back to your home/vehicle. Pretty darned simple, huh? Not for many folks.

Nowadays (a word my grandfather used a good bit) it seems to be that so many think the formula for running success can be found in the latest development in shoes, or in some high-tech gel or replacement fluid. It ain't so, gang. The secret is still in doing the work – the training – and furthermore it is what beats in <u>your</u> chest and resides in <u>your</u> mind that far outweighs anything that anyone will ever dispense in the advice arena. Nope. All the wisdom and advice in the world cannot and will not replace that. The Psalmist put it so eloquently in saying that we are 'wonderfully made.' Know it to be so and trust in it.

Graduation Day –
The Lean Horse 100 Mile Run

By Gary Griffin

It all started back in the early 1990s. I had just begun to get my feet wet in the ultrarunning world when the idea of running 100 miles first struck. In many ways it seemed far beyond comprehension; one of those things accomplished only by the best of the best. So when I found myself in the presence of an ultra veteran months later I felt compelled to ask what I thought was a fairly simple question: How do you run 100 miles?

Maybe I was expecting to hear some sort of textbook training routine or perhaps a recommended regimen of 50 mile races, followed by a 100K or two before attempting the distance. I figured there surely must be a formula – some sort of secret routine that would guarantee success should I ever bring myself to such a level that I could even consider a 100-mile start. What he said, though, remains indelibly etched in my mind, for his response was simply this: 'You need to *learn* how to run 100 miles.' I believe that in the annals of wisdom imparted to me over the years, those words are near the top of the list.

'You need to *learn* how to run 100 miles .....'

Some things we set out to accomplish have a steeper learning curve than others. My daddy taught me how to change the oil in the car without spilling it all over the driveway in two lessons, and I learned how to be a pretty decent auctioneer in a week of auction school. On the other hand, I've still not mastered the TV remote or come anywhere near to being competent with any number of simple computer operations.

Learning how to run 100 miles fell into the latter category.

My first attempt came in 2003, a few months following a high mileage summer coupled with the elation of running 60 miles or so over two days with my friend Scott Ludwig as he powered to a 6th place finish at the Badwater Ultramarathon – a 135 mile journey through Death Valley. Brimming with confidence from that experience, I accompanied Scott to the US 100 Mile Championships at Olander Park (Ohio) and proceeded to have a disastrous experience. Oh – I finished, and even finished with a somewhat respectable 21:52 -- but it wasn't pretty. I walked much of the last 50 miles after going out far too hard, and had blisters so bad I could hardly walk for a week. Two years later I was back at Olander Park, duplicating the 2003 mistakes, and even adding some major nutrition/hydration failures to the mix. Somehow I made it to the finish, shaving a whopping seven minutes off my 2003 time. My desire waned. I was frustrated. I had gone to the starting line twice with lots of miles under my belt; something I thought constituted the basic requirement for 100-mile success. As I continued to reflect on those two attempts, I recalled the words from years gone by:

'You need to *learn* how to run 100 miles …..'

I am the first to admit that I am hydration and nutritionally challenged. My running partners call me 'the camel' – a moniker hung on me for my seeming ability to run miles and miles in the summer heat without water. Furthermore I have traditionally taken very few calories in any form in races of any duration. I ran my PR marathon in 1991, taking no water and zero calories for 26.2 miles. I also remember the day I ran the 30K at St. Marks (Florida) followed by several hours of yard work without taking anything to drink. This proves absolutely nothing except that the human body is capable of great adaptation when exposed to a certain routine over an extended period. It was not only ridiculous behavior for one striving to be the best he could be, but it was also not healthy.

Improper hydration and nutrition were not the only barriers to 100-mile success. There were pace issues and blister issues as well, along with who knows how many other things that could surface out there beyond the 50 mile mark. As fate would have it, I found myself in the presence of two gifted individuals who had mastered two of these elements. In October 2007 I got a lasting lesson on pace during a 50-miler on a glorious fall day in Door County, Wisconsin from David Yon. David's plan called for patient 8:35-8:45 miles for the first 40 – a pace that I would normally eschew -- and dearly pay for late in the race. By following David's lead, though, I had the race of my life to that point, eclipsing my 50 mile personal best by nearly 30 minutes. Two 30-hour adventure race experiences with Ed Baggett in 2007 and early 2008 forced me to deal with my nutrition and hydration issues. Ed was counting on me, and he continually and patiently urged me to feed my body to enable it to keep going. Finally, a breakthrough of sorts, I learned that by pounding down the calories I was able to perform at a higher level. I still wasn't where I needed to be, but I had certainly turned the corner, so to speak.

One other thing just 'happened' that really seemed to equip me for the 100 mile stage. I learned how to run. I'm not talking about pace or hydration or nutrition. I'm talking about running form, and it came about totally by chance.

I had been troubled by chronic hip and hamstring issues for years – conditions I just learned to deal with. Every step hurt, but being a runner I assumed that that was how it was supposed to be. Besides, as an ultra runner I wasn't taxing my legs in the same way the 5K/10K crowd was, and could do the 'ultra shuffle' for hours and hours and just deal with the pain. Yet while casually running alone on the single tracks at Maclay two years ago I suddenly realized that I was running without pain. As I continued along I observed I was running upright and it wasn't my legs that were carrying me forward as much as it was my center. Now, I am not a student of running form or much of anything else when it comes to running, but I believe that what I found myself doing (and which has become the norm for me now) is that after 25 years I finally discovered how it is that we are supposed to move ourselves forward. My hamstring and hip issues had vanished, and it seemed as though my legs were no longer doing the work. The 'cooked shrimp look' that my friend Dana Stetson uses to describe one's posture during the latter stages of a long run was gone.

In early 2008, while dealing with a two-month layoff following a stress fracture, I felt that maybe I had learned some of the things I needed to learn to run well at 100 miles. It was time to go back to the starting line, and the Lean Horse 100 in Hot Springs, South Dakota in August seemed to have my name written all over it. . .

In the mind of an ultrarunner, a sub-20 hour 100-miler is akin to a sub-three hour marathon. In my 1991 personal best marathon I missed that goal by less than two minutes. The idea of running 100 miles sub-20 was not even in my thought process. And yet, as my summer training progressed I felt I was becoming more capable of it. Friends had told me about the course – 16 miles of rolling country gravel road, followed by 34 miles of the mostly flat Mickelson Trail (a converted rails-to-trails on cushioned, finely crushed stone), repeated in reverse for the final 50. I was 'cautiously confident,' fully aware that much can go wrong in 20 hours or so of running and that one mistake can turn 20 hours into 25.

In the days and weeks leading up to the race I was blessed with encouragement and wisdom from family and friends who had been along this road with me. *Their* confidence in me helped to raise *my* confidence in me – an essential ingredient in any success. At the pre-race meeting, featured speaker Scott Ludwig reminded the 170 or so entrants in the 100 and accompanying 50-miler that getting to the finish can be far more mental than physical. Confidence and the ability to fight through occasional darkness are mandatory components of endurance running.

After days of pretty intense heat (the hottest day of the year was two days before the start!), race day dawned cool and dry. My wife Peg was to crew for me and put up with my whining and puking and whatever else I was going to endure, and urge me to hold fast to my pre-race plan calling for the approach that David Yon had held me to in Wisconsin. She was also going to insist that I 'drink, drink, drink and eat, eat, eat.' The best laid plans . . .

The 16 mile section at the beginning was hillier and a bit rougher than expected; nonetheless, it was cool and dry, and I kept myself hydrated (!) and by mile 20 was 20 minutes ahead of a sub-20 hour pace. I had projected to hit mile 50 in nine hours, but found myself there at 8:20. Nonetheless I was feeling very well in relation to how I had felt at the same stage during my 2003 and 2005 experiences. It was far too early to get caught up in heady thoughts of having a happy ending – after all, I still had 50 miles to go. At mile 70 I was still comfortably ahead of my projected pace but was having trouble drinking and had totally stopped eating. I held on through mile 75 but hit a bad patch from miles 75 to 83 where I was faced again with that hilly gravel road. Somewhere around mile 80 I felt my time goal slipping away and made peace with the fact that it was OK – I had done all I could do and I should just enjoy the night. Rural South Dakota is dark, and the sky was filled with more stars than I had seen when I worked in New Hampshire nearly 40 years ago. As coyotes howled around me and bats swooped in and out of my headlamp, I thought of all those folks who had urged me on from a distance, of how lucky I was to be out there with Peg, and of how good it was going to be to lie down and sleep. These are the things that I really live for and there was no place that I would rather be. Going into that 16-mile stretch, I was dreading the uphills, and didn't have any great expectations for the downhills.

But – something magical happened out there. I found that I could run the downs with authority and concentrated on relentless forward motion on the uphills. I refused to look at my watch to avoid the disappointment I thought it would reveal, and pressed on until the final aid station at mile 96. Looking at my watch I thought I must have been hallucinating -- 18:04. 'No way,' I said. 'You don't have your glasses on and you can't see.' I looked again. 18:04 it was. I had gone from 20-hour pace at mile 83 to having an hour in the bank at mile 96. The effort had left me pretty tapped out, and the last four miles weren't anything to write home about, but I was fine with that. It was over. When I crossed the line Peg said 'You did it.' I said, 'No honey, *we* did it' and it was so, so true. I did it, along with Peg and all of those who encouraged me and urged me to change things in my program that had served as obstacles in attaining my goals at this distance. There was one other person who played a role in that 19:02 as well. I'll never know his name but I'll always remember what he said:

'You have to **learn** how to run 100 miles …..'

Chapter Seventeen

Jerry Dunn

Amy Yanni suggested to the Race Director of the Lean Horse Ultra that he consider me as a guest speaker at the annual pre-race meeting in 2008. Amy explained to him that my autobiography had just been published, I was registered to run the race and my fee for speaking would be reasonable (*free!*).

When I found a voice mail message from Jerry Dunn asking me to be his featured guest speaker, I was honored. After all:

It was *Jerry Dunn, America's Marathon Man*
inviting *me* to speak at *his race!*

I quickly returned his call and accepted.

I've spoken at running stores, running club meetings, Team in Training dinners, race expos, clinics and running club cookouts, but this was the first time I was invited to speak to runners the night before an event of this caliber.

Before the start of the race Jerry dedicated the race to his mother, who had recently passed away. As it was only nine months after I lost *my* mother (and only ten months after I lost my father), his words meant a lot to me.

I met a lot of interesting and amazing people after my speaking engagement throughout the course of the 100-mile race during that August weekend in Hot Springs, South Dakota. Many of them went on to become good friends of mine.

I consider Jerry Dunn one of them.

Jerry Dunn

IT'S A DUNN DEAL

Jerry Dunn is a man on a mission.

His insatiable thirst for adventure led him to running the original New York City Marathon course in Central Park for 28 consecutive days in 1998, culminating in the completion of the actual event on the 29th day. Questioned by a reporter after crossing the finish line what the future held for him, Jerry instinctively replied that perhaps he would run 200 marathons in the year 2000.

Just when he completes one mission lasting a month (29 consecutive runs in New York City of 26.2 miles) he's already committing to another that will consume an entire year.

Expect nothing less from Jerry Dunn, who was given the moniker 'America's Marathon Man' by the late Jim Murray, one of the most popular sportswriters of the twentieth century.

Jerry was born in 1946 in Indianapolis, Indiana, the only child of Raymond and June Dunn. He attended 'PS 72' for the first seven years and remembers walking ¾ of a mile to and from school each day. When he entered Manual High School the commute extended to a full mile each day which he walked until his junior year when he was old enough to get his first car: a 1949 bullet nose Studebaker.

At the age of 10 Jerry landed his first job delivering the evening newspaper. Two years later he began delivering the *morning* newspaper which required him to wake up at 4:00 a.m.—seven days a week, 365 days a year. He held the job until he turned 18 and graduated from high school.

Jerry believes this is where he developed his lifelong habit of being an early riser, and why getting up at 'dark-thirty' to start an ultra event doesn't seem out of the ordinary. As the Race Director of the Leanhorse Ultra in Hot Springs, South Dakota (a race he founded in 2005), the traditional 6:00 a.m. start allows Jerry—by his definition of 'early,' to sleep in.

His diminutive stature and his 'career' in the newspaper industry kept Jerry from being a jock in high school. He did, however play intramural basketball (what would you expect from a boy growing up in Indiana?) and reserve tennis (he had two matches: one he lost and the other was rained out) during his freshman year. Thinking back to 4th grade at PS 72 Jerry recalls a Field Day event where the boys were classified by their size. 'A' were the bigger boys, 'B' the medium-size boys and 'C' were…well 'C' was Jerry and Kenneth Wilde, who both won ribbons in whatever events they chose to enter.

Jerry admittedly wasn't a jock in high school, but he *was* musically inclined. Concert choir, the men's glee club, concert band, marching band, all musical productions...his plethora of interests were the epitome of 'musical cross-training.' His instrument of choice was the tuba or as he calls it 'the get-inside-and-carry-it-on-your-shoulder-kind-of-tuba.' His stature, all 'five-foot-nothing' of it made it hard for him to compete with the other five (larger) tuba players in the marching band at the football games on Friday nights, but he somehow managed to 'rock with the best of 'em.'

Being an honor student throughout high school, Jerry was 'accepted with distinction' at Ball State University. However, they forgot to invite him back for his sophomore year. Something about his GPA being below the accepted standard. Seeing as Jerry thought GPA stood for 'good party atmosphere...' Fortunately, Uncle Sam was not as selective in his call to service.

Jerry spent 31 months in the United States Army from February of 1966 until November of 1968 when he was granted an 'early out' to return to Ball State. He put his newfound freedom to use and completed a degree in, well... alcohol consumption with a minor in pharmaceutical experimentation. For the next two decades Jerry put his 'college degrees' to work. But all that changed the morning after he turned 37.

On that day Jerry met a man named Bill W, and to this day over 26 years later they remain friends. Bill taught Jerry quite a lot. Like figuring out the 'marriage thing.'

Jerry's current wife, Doctor Elaine Doll-Dunn allows him (occasionally, as long as it doesn't become a habit) to refer to her as 'W4.' Jerry no longer has any contact with wives W's 1, 2 and 3 but is fairly certain they wouldn't like being referred to as W's 1, 2 and 3.

Jerry and Elaine have celebrated 14 years of (literally as well as figuratively) running around together. They both agree that the strongest bond they share is this 'running thing.' Naturally there are a few other things that they are both passionate about that keeps their love alive. But running? Besides their love for each other, that's the strongest bond they share.

Jerry was only 18 when his father passed away, which left him with a huge hole in his heart. As his 'college degree' might indicate, he filled the huge hole with all sorts of addictive behaviors: alcohol, drugs and women. That is, until 1993 at the age of 47 Jerry found himself in the middle of a desert in Nevada. It was then and there he made peace with his dad as well as his running addiction.

Ah, his running addiction. Where did it begin?

Jerry was tending bar at nights in Sarasota, Florida...the 'perfect job,' as he recalls for an alcoholic with a degree in drinking. During the day he hung out on the beach when one day his girlfriend's brother (who happened to be the head lifeguard) told Jerry he should run with him. Jerry told him in no uncertain terms 'no' as he had all the running he needed at Fort Knox, wearing fatigues and boots while carrying a pack and a rifle.

But his girlfriend's brother wouldn't quit until finally Jerry gave in and said 'OK, a half mile and that's all.'

That was 1975.

The rest, as they say, is history.

Since that time Jerry has had an extensive career in running, both as a participant and a promoter. In 2002 Jerry and Elaine founded the Mickelson Trail Marathon, a race which *Runner's World* magazine refers to as 'the best-kept secret in marathon competition.' It was Jerry's vision and imagination which brought together the best nature has to offer with the best life has to offer (running!) to form the perfect event in the beautiful Black Hills of South Dakota.

As a runner Jerry boasts an amazing litany of credentials, including a 1,900 mile run and 807 mile bicycle ride across the United States to raise awareness for Habitat for Humanity in 1991, completing 104 marathons in 1993 and an amazing 200 runs of marathon distance in the year 2000. When he turned 60? A celebratory run covering 480 laps of an indoor 1/8 mile track (60 miles for the mathematically-challenged!).

Olympian Jeff Galloway says of Jerry:

Jerry Dunn has the energy to make things happen.

What would you expect from a man who says he 'still gets chills watching anyone complete his or her first marathon.'

Jerry Dunn is a man on a mission.

On second thought, Jerry Dunn is a man on *many* missions, and he knows how to get them done.

I find it extremely difficult to express what running has meant, and continues to mean to me, and when I'm asked to make some intelligent or motivating statement that sums up how running has impacted my life, I usually fall back on this little piece I wrote about 10 years ago.......

WE RUN AS ONE
By Jerry Dunn

We're not elite, and seldom fleet.
Not much like racers, more like pacers.
The thing for us is long, slow distance,
Which plays quite well with our persistence.
We live to run, but not too fast,
But even then, we're seldom last.
We move along at our own speed
Rarely do we find ourselves in the lead.
The joy for us is just to run
And better yet just to be done.
The finish line is just the same
For runners fast and runners lame.
The prize is ours just past that line
Evoking tears most every time.
We've conquered more than others do
You're part of me, I'm part of you.

As long distance endurance runners we are family. We share a common experience. We have a mutual respect for one another. Some members of our family run like the wind, and we applaud them. Some of our brothers and sisters walk more than they run, and we are equally proud of them. The elders of our clan are held in high regard for their commitment to continue on. The young in our midst are encouraged to grow and to learn. Everyone in our family is a winner. Even the last one home is crowned *The Slowest of the Winners......* a victor just the same.

Our family has no ethnic, political or religious restrictions. We are one.

We come together in the early morning with a single purpose and a common goal, and we do whatever we can to help each other finish the day with a personal victory.

We look at the one running next to us and we see a sister or a brother, another human being: nothing more and certainly nothing less. And as we look at them, we smile. We offer a word of encouragement. We want them to succeed. We want them to be proud of what they have accomplished that day. We run with a single purpose....to finish what we came to do.

So remember: Run your own race and share the joy.

DON'T LIMIT YOUR CHALLENGES: CHALLENGE YOUR LIMITS

By Jerry Dunn

- Mark Covert - 40 + years as a Streaker
- Dean Karnazes - 50 Marathons – 50 Days – 50 States
- Marshall Ulrich - Quadruple Badwater
- Jerry Dunn – 200 Marathons in 2000

Most humans place self-imposed limits on what they think they can do.... they **limit their challenges.** Other humans, like the ones listed above, take the opposite approach and **challenge their limits.** The latter call the former 'lazy' and the former call the later 'crazy.'

If I were forced to choose one of these two options as a way of living the remainder of my days, I would most assuredly choose to be in the 'crazy' crowd......we're a much more interesting group.

I officially adopted **DON'T LIMIT YOUR CHALLENGES ~ CHALLENGE YOUR LIMITS** as my mantra back in the early 1990's. I had unknowingly been adhering to this philosophy since that beautiful fall day in 1988 when I ran my first 50K at the *Midwest Running Festival* in Muncie, Indiana. Getting out beyond 26.2 opened a new and exciting world of mega distances, multi day events and journey runs. My imagination and yearning for modern day adventures was set free, and I was off and running.

December 1988 - Frankfort to Louisville, Kentucky 50 mile road race – This is the race in which I learned how to walk. It's a known fact human infants need to learn how to walk before they can run......and so do ultra runners. What a miserable last 20 miles, not to mention that my inexperienced crew allowed me to get off course by about a mile....which forced me to run an extra two miles......which felt like 10.

June 1989 - Solo run from Athens to Marathon, Greece – After a couple of loops around the same downtown area of Athens, and after asking numerous non-English speaking locals 'which way to Maratona?' I finally headed in the right direction. (Quick aside: when running in new/strange cities I like to look at it as an adventure run, a sightseeing run, and in the good ole U S of A, getting lost was never really an issue.....but deciding to run from Athens to Marathon, unaided, without a cell phone ...*a what?*...was a really dumb idea). It didn't help matters that unbeknownst to me this was a national election day in Greece and almost all businesses were closed and there were hardly any motorists or pedestrians on the roads. Die hard that I am, I made it to Maratona. As I came into town there was a political banner of some sort stretched between two light posts on the cobblestone street and I imagined myself finishing the race to the sound of the roaring crowds...... the imagination is a wonderful thing. I found a bakery and bought a loaf of the world's best bread; found a grocery store and bought a few grams of salami and a liter of Coke. Then through a combination of pointing and scribbling and mostly looking desperate, I found that there was a bus back to Athens leaving in a little while. (Not having made any plans whatsoever for my return trip was part of the 'adventure.') I found the bus stop...sat on the bench...inhaled my food.....boarded the bus, and made it safely back to Athens. God is good.

October 1989 - Glacial Trail Run 100K I completed the race in 11 hours and 39 minutes and earned by best-ever finish in an ultra: *4th!*

une 1900 - 43 miles as a pacer at the Mohican Trail Run for Jim Dill who was running his first 100 miler. This was my first night time running experience.

July 1990 - Vermont Trail 100 mile run. My finishing time of 22:42:31 earned me the title of 'fastest Hoosier at a 100 mile distance.' Not bad for a rookie 100-miler. Lesson learned: never trust your crew when they tell you at the last aid station 'oh yeah, we just put fresh batteries in your MagLite.' Have you ever been in the heart of a strange forest at 1:00 a.m. dead tired, all alone, within a few short miles of finishing your first 100 miler, on a moonless night without any source of light? Well, I hadn't either, and for a brief second or two, I panicked. After realizing I wasn't in last place, I simply waited for the next runner to come by (*surely* they would come by!). Eventually Dick Collins and Robert Woodworth found me babbling to myself in the middle of the trail. Talk about male bonding.....it was instantaneous. The only bad part is they were working together off of one light. They said 'if you want to be the third man on the light (another first for me to experience) then come on.' A short time and a few tumbles later we crossed the line holding hands, high in the air yelling some indiscernible victory cry. (*We* placed 62nd out of 126 finishers.)

November 1990 - 150 mile stage run across Indiana as a fundraiser for Habitat for Humanity (50 miles a day for three days). Over Thanksgiving weekend, in a borrowed luxury motor home, I attempted my first journey run/multi-day ultra......alone. (There were no other runners doing the whole thing. I *did* have a crew and some running company for a few miles each day, however.) This was the first of my 'titled' events/ stunts....**ACROSS THE STATE IN 28**. My goal was 28 hours total running time from the Indiana/ Illinois border to the Indiana/Ohio border using State Road 36 and US 40 as my route. Result: 29:54:54.

June through September 1991 - San Francisco to Washington D.C. I began running in San Francisco in early June with the goal of running to the nation's capital. The total distance was 2,707 miles, of which I ran 1900 and cycled the rest. This was an awareness raiser for Habitat for Humanity called **'Shore to Shore in 104.'** I arrived in Washington, D.C. on September 27, 1991. There are too many tales tied to this journey to relate to you here, but it was during this solo, transcontinental journey that I came face to face with a lot of things. As I made my way across the desert in western Nevada on The Loneliest Highway in America, US 50, I had my moment of Zen. It didn't come in a clear cut vision with color and sound, but more like a massive flooding of feelings washing over me. I was 47 years old. 29 years earlier my father had died at the age of 47. I was dedicating this entire journey to his memory. I had been running for close to 20 years and really wasn't sure why. But it was a result of this 'moment' that I came to the gut-wrenching realization that I didn't really need to know **WHY** I was running....just that I needed to keep on doing it. This *running thing* was my gift from God. It was my salvation, and as long as I continued to run--and run with a purpose I was fulfilling the Master's plan. It became as simple as 'Let go and let God.'

September 1992 - Invited runner in the Trans Colorado 500K (50 mile per day stage race to raise money for the homeless shelters of Colorado). Another journey run with a compassionate purpose and an even more compassionate organizer.....Marshall Ulrich. His was a name that was already becoming legend in the ultra family and I was honored to be invited. This one was 50 miles a day for six days; crossing the state from south to north. I made it 3½ days and then switched over to crewing for the remaining four runners. My excuse for bailing out was that come January 1, 1993 I would begin my quest for 93 in '93 and I didn't want to take the chance of injuring myself just three months before my next adventure.

1993 - Successfully completed **104 marathons in a single calendar year**, which at that time was an 'unofficial' record. (Actually, it's STILL 'unofficial' as noted in the U.S. Congressional Record of 2/6/94.) Okay, this is the year the ultra purists came out of the woodwork. *'If you're going to count a marathon as completed and chalked up in your total column it has to be...'* Well, y'all know the rest of the sentence. 'It has to be publicized; it has to have at least three entrants; results have to be posted; it has to be........' HEY, did I say I was trying to lay claim to anyone else's record? Am I the first person ever to run a marathon race course alone, the day before the event and then come back the next day and run the event and call it two? Maybe yes, maybe no. It matters not. All I'm about here is seeing if this human being, Jerry Dunn can complete 26.2 miles on 93 of the 365 days in 1993. I did. In fact the 93rd was the New York City Marathon on November 14th which left me with six more weeks in the year with nothing to do. I was already in the groove of running 26.2 miles on Saturday and 26.2 miles on Sunday, so why stop in November? The result? 93 in '93 turned into 104 in '93. (Another reason to take it out to 104....Ed Barreto was claiming 101 marathons, so why not?).

August 1994 - Invited runner in the **Siberian International Marathon in Omsk, Siberia** - with Elaine.

January 1995 - Married during The Disney World Marathon. Seen live on the *Today Show*. Quick rewind to September 1993...Numbers 86 and 87 of 104 in '93 were run on the Black Hills Marathon course in Rapid City, South Dakota. STORYLINE....Marathon Man meets Wonder Woman. Fast forward to Disney Marathon II. Marathon man marries Wonder Woman (Elaine Doll-Dunn) in front of the Castle at Disneyworld in Orlando. Elaine's two favorite lines about her 'Fairy Tale Wedding:' 'Jerry carried me across the finish line, so I beat him by a hip' and 'we had 4,000 guests at our wedding and not one gift.'

January 1996 - Ran 49 miles to celebrate my 49th birthday. All the hard core runners do this, don't they? I moved to Spearfish, South Dakota in early January 1995. All the runners in a four state area are psyched up to do this weird four-miler called FREEZE YOUR FANNY over in Sundance, Wyoming just 39 miles away from my new hometown. So what is The Marathon Man going to do to perpetuate his reputation as this 'weird guy who runs more than anyone has ever heard of before?' What else....run a 10K around Spearfish, run 39 miles over to Sundance and be waiting at the starting line of Freeze Your Fanny at 9:00 a.m. to finish off the day with 49 miles.

March 1996 - 'A Marathon of Marathons' As part of 93 in '93 I ran the Boston Marathon course on three consecutive days....a piece of cake. So I figure why not up the ante a bit and do the infamous Boston course on *twenty-six* consecutive days? I asked for a little help with this one and God sent me a guardian angel in the form of a fellow 'friend of Bill' named Gere Munro. Gere and I became very close over the 25 days leading up to the 100ᵗʰ running of the Boston Marathon. He picked me up every morning at 5:15, drove me to Hopkinton, prayed with me, threw me out in the street and said 'see ya down the road a ways.' And by golly he did just that. About every five miles there he was making me eat; making me laugh; making me cry; and making my day. Gere, Elaine and I ran the 100ᵗʰ Boston Marathon together with another of those photo finishes involving three people holding their heads and hands high as a symbol of accomplishment......an accomplishment of *way* more than just running.

September 1997 - Megan's 24 Hour Track Run. I ran 74 miles in 16 hours, took a five hour nap and then ran the Portland Marathon in 5:31:23, thus accomplishing my goal of 100 miles in less than 30 hours elapsed time. I also managed to raise $600 for SIDS (Sudden Infant Death Syndrome) in the process. I hadn't successfully run 100 miles since 1989 at Vermont, and here it was eight years later and the *isn't-it-about-time-you-pushed-yourself-a-little-for-a-change* bug bit me in the butt and said: 'betcha can't do a 100, betcha can't do a 100, nah na nah na.' So I said; 'OH YEAH....just watch me.' I couldn't find one that I could do right away so I improvised. It went something like this: go to Portland with my wife and a few of our runnin' buds who were signed up for the Portland Marathon and as a prelude to the marathon I ran 74 miles at Megan's 24 Hour Run during the day and part of the night before the Portland Marathon. How long it took me to log 74 miles on the track would then determine how much sleep I would get before heading to the start line of the Portland Marathon. It wound up being about five hours, on hard ground, in a make shift tent.....woe is me. I had some breakfast and made it to the starting line with time to spare. Given that my goal for completing 100 miles was 30 hours I had to run the marathon in six hours or less. Thanks to the sacrifice of my wife Elaine (and it really was a sacrifice for her because she was at the top of her game training wise, and had just moved into a new age category and probably could have placed that day, but she chose to help me achieve my goal that day) we finished in 5:31:23. *(I owe you BIG TIME for that one dear).*

March 1998 - 13 consecutive days running the **Los Angeles Marathon** course - just for something to do in the springtime.

October and November 1998 - 28 consecutive circuits of the original New York City Marathon course in Central Park and then on the 29ᵗʰ day I participated in the 29ᵗʰ running of the modern day New York City Marathon.

The next night I had an interview with Keith Olbermann on whatever show he had going at the time and one of his questions was 'what's next for America's Marathon Man?' And without thinking, I said; 'Oh, I'll probably do something major for the turn of the century......eh, maybe 200 in 2000. You know, challenge my limits.' Me and my big mouth...

March 1999 - 14 consecutive days on the Los Angeles Marathon course. A tune up for 2000.

2000 - 200 in 2000. My challenge was to complete 200 marathon distances, each one on a certified marathon course. Boy did this one irritate the purists, but by now they had all realized I'm only dangerous to myself, not to anyone's record. I mean come on; this is totally nuts, and no one is going to believe me anyway. However, it's true: I did it. It went something like this: January 1, 2000, Elaine and I ran the San Diego Marathon course in Carlsbad, California all alone while everyone else in town was recovering from New Year's Eve. Then later that afternoon I put my bride on an airplane bound for home and spent the next 14 mornings running that same course by myself. The night of the 15th day Elaine flew back in and on January 16th we ran the San Diego Marathon together. In February I ran 16 circuits of Las Vegas Marathon course. In March, 16 circuits of the very familiar Los Angeles Marathon course. In April, a return trip to Boston for 17 repeats of the most hallowed 26.2 miles in marathon history. It went on like this for the remainder of the year (you can find them all listed on my website: www.marathonman.org). On December 10 in Tampa at the inaugural HOPS Marathon I finished my 200th marathon. Somehow I managed to run my fastest marathon of the year: 4:05:30.

January 2006 - (*Is it really six years later and I haven't done anything worthwhile?*) **60 Miles on my 60th Birthday.** I covered 480 laps on an indoor track to celebrate my 60th birthday and to celebrate 19 years of alcohol-free living. As an added bonus I raised over $1000 towards the new climbing wall at our local middle school. This one wasn't pretty, but I got 'er Dunn.

My time for the 60 miles was 14:45:30. That included the time out I took to eat birthday cake with the kids.

Chapter Eighteen

Al Barker

I've known Al Barker since Thanksgiving Day 1993.

We met after the Atlanta Marathon. We've been to every one since.

In my first book *Running through My Mind*, Al suggests he and I have 'run a zillion miles together.' No doubt an exaggeration, it's not far from the truth. Al and I have run a LOT of miles together.

Al and I formed the Darkside Running Club. Today the club boasts a roster of members from all over the country and includes some of the finest people and most amazing runners you'd ever want to meet.

Al Barker is certainly one of them.

Al was with me when I finished the Badwater Ultramarathon. Al was on my support crew. His oil painting *'Badwater 2003'* is on the cover of my first book.

I was with Al when he ran 100 miles at the age of 60 in less than 24 hours. I was his biggest cheerleader.

Al and I attempted the Western States Endurance Run. Twice. We entered via the 'buddy system' in 2004 and 2006 and were selected to both times via a lottery system. Al missed a checkpoint cut-off time both years, so he turned to another event to realize his dream of completing a 100-mile trail run. In 2007 at the Umstead Endurance Run his dream became reality.

In the near future Al would like to run the Comrades Marathon. He'd like to run 100 miles…just one more time. He'd like to return to the Boston Marathon once more to make it an 'even dozen.'

As he is on the doorstep of his fifth decade in the sport of running, Al Barker continues to dream.

Al Barker

Making the Team

As a child, Al Barker never played any organized sports. Throughout his years in school he never tried out for a team: not baseball, not basketball, and at *his* size *certainly* not football. The only true athletic memory he has of school is running the quarter-mile and the mile in P.E. (barefooted and on a dirt track, no less!) and although Al posted the fastest times in his class (64 seconds and 6:38, respectively), the coach didn't have the wherewithal to notice that the heart of this wisp of a young man bore the spirit of a true competitor. Al's career as a runner would have to wait for another day; first he had to get his education out of the way.

Trying Out

Al fell in love with running at an early age. It was just the sport for him, as it allowed him to test his mettle against the toughest opponent he could ever hope to find: himself.

June 1, 1975. With college and a degree in optometry behind him, Al started running.

Al began by mastering the shorter distances, eventually realizing the ultimate goal of the amateur short-distance runner, a sub-five minute mile. This spurred Al to success in other distances as well as he progressed from impressive personal bests at 400 meters (58.5 seconds) to 800 meters (2:16) to the mile (4:55) to two miles (10:21) to 5K's (17:13) to 10K's (35:49) to 15K's (57:41) and the half-marathon (1:21).

Al not only tried out; he made the cut. He was unequivocally a runner.

Surviving the Cut

It wasn't long before Al became enamored with the marathon. Spurred on by the nation's love affair in the decade of the '70's with the likes of Boston Billy (Rodgers) and Olympian Frank (Shorter), Al was ready to see if he had what it takes to be competitive for 26.2 miles.

Boy, did he ever! Before the decade drew to a close, Al proved he had the talent…the *mettle*, to qualify for the prestigious Boston Marathon, setting a personal best of 2:53:30 in the process. If only his P.E. coach could see him now. Al was now competitive against the finest runners—not in his high school, but in the *world!*

After two decades of running as an individual, Al was ready to play for a team.

Playing for the Varsity

In 1994, Al tried out for the famous Atlanta Track Club Men's Masters Competitive Team. This was new for him as up until this point in his life—nearly 50 years—he had been flying solo. Not any more.

He posted qualifying times for the team at several distances and before long he was flying to Boston and St. George (Utah) and Chicago to compete as a member of an official team for the first time in his life. His distance of choice? The marathon, of course.

Al, always known for his strong finishing kick, dusted off his old 'miler' skills in the late '90's to be a member of two different relay teams, which resulted in his ownership of 1/100th of two different world records:

- The men's masters 100 (runners age 40 and older) X 1 mile relay world record team
- The men's grand masters (age 50 and older) 100 X 1 mile relay world record team

Wanting to share his experience and knowledge with others, Al signed up to be a volunteer coach for the Atlanta Track Club. He's had a variety of students over the years, the most successful arguably being Susan Lance, the successful ultramarathoner you read about in Chapter Four.

Earning a Letter

Al's running career took a decidedly different path towards the turn of the century, and before long he was discovering success at distances virtually inconceivable to him when he was posted his 5K and 10K PR's while in his thirties. If his new-found success earns him a letter for his varsity sweater, it will be the letter 'U.'

'U,' as in 'Ultramarathon.'

After crewing at the Badwater Ultramarathon in 2003, Al's fascination with distances longer than the marathon was ignited. He immediately set his sights on the granddaddy of all ultras, the Western States Endurance Run.

After posting a qualifying 50-mile race with a time of 9:30, Al focused his training on a 100-mile jaunt through the Sierra Nevada Mountain Range.

Although putting himself through an arduous training regimen to get ready for the event, including a three-day training camp along the very course he would be trying to conquer in June 2004, he failed to make the time requirement at the 43-mile checkpoint and was removed from the race. Undeterred, he tried again in 2006, only to miss a time cutoff even earlier in the race. However, he looks at his experiences out west in a glass-half-full sort of way, as he says 'if you don't test your limits you'll never find them.' As it is with many runners, successful road running didn't necessarily translate to successful trail running for Al.

However, Al's successful *road* running did translate to a successful 100-mile run at the San Diego 1 Day in 2005. Al completed 100.07 miles (to be exact) in 23 hours and 30 minutes at the age of 60, an amazing accomplishment for a talented runner 30 years his junior. Al truly pushed himself to the limit in San Diego, as after completing the 100th lap of the exactly one-mile loop, he jogged several yards, walked several yards, and then performed a perfect pirouette before falling face-first on the infield grass. He rolled over on his back and remained there for another 30 minutes, silently reveling in his accomplishment.

An All-Star

While Al hopes to run until the day he dies, he is the only runner I personally know who touts the following four accomplishments on his running resume:

- A sub-five minute mile
- A sub-three hour marathon
- A sub-24 hour 100 miles (at age 60, no less)
- Over 100 marathons

An all-around runner, one might say. Except, perhaps, his P.E. coach.

Extracurriculars

An optometrist by profession, Al is not only an accomplished runner but an accomplished artist as well. One friend suggests that Al doesn't travel the world running races, but that he travels the world so he can find fascinating scenery to paint. He spends much of his free time painting in his mountain cabin in Nantahala, North Carolina. His paintings adorn the homes of many of his friends. In fact, Al's painting depicting our adventure at Badwater (that was me he was supporting in 2003) not only hangs in the home of Cindy (my wife) and I, it also serves as the cover for my autobiography, *Running through My Mind.*

On the home front, Al and his wife Hope live in Fayetteville, Georgia. Hope had a short but successful career as a runner early in their relationship, winning a 5K and competing in distances up to 30K. Al admits that Hope is the top race-winner in the Barker household. They have a newlywed (and now college graduate) daughter Ashley who has been known to show up at races proudly holding up signs and banners encouraging her father as he runs by; smiling, of course. As for Ashley's personal interest in being a runner like mom and dad, let's just say that the running-gene skips a generation in the Barker family.

Al also loves to read, study astronomy and bird-watch. As there will never be a time for Al to sit back and reflect on his career (remember, he plans on running until the day he dies), he does have a few favorite running events:

- *Big Sur Marathon,* on a course Al describes as the most scenic of those he has run
- *St. George Marathon,* which Al says is the best for a fast time (he ran it in 3 hours at the age of 50!)
- *Boston Marathon,* which Al has run 11 times and is the best for 'hoopla'
- *Atlanta Marathon,* which is his favorite for fun with friends

In 2008, Al and I ran the entire 26.2 miles of the Atlanta Marathon in our slowest time ever—four hours and 15 minutes—and we loved every second of it. It happened to mark the 15 year anniversary of our friendship, and we'll both continue to run it—together, most likely—until the day one of us dies.

That's OK with me, because it ensures I'll continue to hear one of my favorite stories (and he's got many) Al likes to tell now and again. Daughter Ashley married several years ago and Al—with an incredible fear of speaking in public was dreading the thought of giving a toast to the bride and groom at the reception following the wedding. Although he had rehearsed it over and over again, he wasn't sure he would be able to actually go through with it (presenting the toast)…until he abruptly stood up at the reception, attracted everyone's attention…and proceeded to give the most eloquent, heart-felt toast you could ever hope to hear.

The part of the story I like best is when he says it's a moment he will 'remember for the rest of his life.'

This then opens the door for me to say 'more importantly, it's a moment she will remember for the rest of *her* life.'

A HAPPY CHILDHOOD

By Al Barker

June 1st, 1975 was a very special day in my life - graduation! It was the turning point that opened a door to a freedom I had never known, but always hoped for. I knew that my life was about to make a change for the better. I also knew that the end of all my studies would leave a huge void in my life, and I had often thought about how I would fill it.

Always, in the back of my mind I saw myself becoming some sort of an athlete, but I didn't know what kind. Maybe tennis? No. I was too uncoordinated to hit the ball. Swimming? No. Too impractical. I needed something I could do in a moment's notice without much preparation. Simplicity was the key here.

Aside from being fun, my new found sport would have to be one that would help me maintain maximum fitness and health. My family history of heart disease (my father died at age 61) had always weighed heavily on my mind, but in the mid 1970's not much was known about the health benefits of exercise. It was just generally expected, but there was not nearly as much compelling research evidence as there is today.

I did a lot of searching and the one book that finally caught my eye was Kenneth Cooper's *Aerobics*. Cooper was a respected cardiologist and the head of the Aerobics Institute in Dallas, Texas. It was probably the most popular and convincing book on the subject at the time. I decided to give it a try.

It wasn't long before I found myself on our local high school track, trying to run a mile without ending up lying on my back afterward! I somehow remained persistent and gradually saw some improvement. Someone told me to stick it out for six weeks and I'd be hooked. They were right! I had found my elusive sport! A few months later I ran my first race and that was the day, in my own mind I became a true runner.

Five K's led to 10K's and 10K's to marathons and so on. It seemed that almost every weekend started with a race of some sort. I discovered a whole new group of friends who had similar interests. My life had taken on a new dimension. I had accomplished something important and had fun doing it to boot. Was I hooked? You bet!

And now, years later and after well over 100 marathons or ultras, I've learned a lot and have a lot to share. Here are a few of my ideas.

To compete or not compete. Some choose not to run races, but simply to run for the fun of it and the health benefits it offers. Do whatever it takes to satisfy your needs.

If you do choose to run races, find a distance that best suits you. Some runners are more comfortable with 5K's and 10K's, while others prefer marathons or longer. You really have to experiment with different distances to find which is best for you. Marathons and longer have been my forte. The pain lasts longer, but is much less intense than in shorter runs.

Join a running club. It's a great way to meet others with similar abilities and goals. Plus, the friendships will last a lifetime. I joined the Gulf Winds Track Club in Tallahassee, Florida in 1975 and still stay in contact with many of its members.

As for training advice, listen to everyone, but follow no one. Experiment with different ideas and you'll find out which ones works best for you. Trying to follow someone else's workout plan may not serve you best.

Don't be too rigid in your training schedule. Don't feel like you need to stick to a workout if you're not up to it. On the other hand, if you feel unusually good, don't be afraid to do a little more and push it a little.

Don't take yourself too seriously. Don't be disappointed if your race doesn't turn out as well as you wanted. Just let it go and try another day.

Accept the coming of age with grace and dignity. Expect your times to slow down as you get older. Just compare yourself to others in your age group, or better yet, celebrate the fact that you have made the effort. It's an undisputed fact that the health benefits of exercise actually increase as we get older.

Rest. This is an important and often overlooked word. Be careful not to over train. Rest days are just as important as hard days.

Nutrition. I really strive to have a good diet with lots of fruits and vegetables, but with one exception - after long races. At some point, after a marathon or ultra your hunger will kick in. Maybe not right away, but eventually your calorie deficit will have to be repaid and your taste buds will go into overdrive! Your body will tell you what it needs, and it will absorb those nutrients like a sponge. Eat what you crave. You deserve it!

After the Umstead 100 Mile Race in 2007, I ate three hot dogs and drank three large glasses of milk. It was by far the best meal I've ever had in my life! I may go for four of each next time.

Most important of all, however, is the fun factor. If it's not play, not fun, it won't last. If I hadn't thoroughly enjoyed running for all these years, I know I would never have kept it up. I'm certain of that.

So my final piece of advice is simply this: Keep having fun. Keep your running playful, and always remember:

It's never too late to have a happy childhood!

ONE FINE DAY
By Al Barker

As a beginning runner I went through the usual progression of race distances, starting with the mile, then 5Ks and 10Ks and eventually the marathon. My first real thrill was on the track at Florida State University when I finally broke five minutes in the mile. It seemed like I would never get there. The feeling was overwhelming! But it soon faded and I knew it was time to move on. I started to concentrate more on qualifying for Boston.

In those days, just as it is now everyone wanted to someday make it the granddaddy of them all, Beantown! We put in our weekly 20 milers and intervals and eventually, after several attempts most of us made it. And wow, was it worth it! I can still remember the 'lump in my throat' exuberance as if it were yesterday. In reality, it was 1979.

Many years would go by before I would top that experience. I knew there had to be something out there to give me that feeling once again. But what would it be?

My short adventure into trail running proved too dangerous for me. I don't think there was ever a trail race that didn't include blood somewhere on my body! It took two attempts at the Western States 100 to convince me that I should stay on the roads. As much as I love the natural beauty of those types of places, I know now that I should reserve them for hiking, not running.

My running partners Scott Ludwig and Susan Lance had begun doing some interesting 100 milers and 24 hour runs on roads. Maybe this would be a good direction for me as well. So, like a lemming I started following the herd.

At first I was just sort of going along for the ride, not really having much desire to actually stay on my feet that long. The Olander 24 Hour Run in Toledo, Ohio turned out to be a miserable failure for me. It probably had something to do with my seven hour nap midway through the run.

Finally the time came when I realized that if I could run 100 miles in one day it would be something I could really be proud of. Maybe it could be the highlight of all my days of running; my 'magnum opus,' so to speak.

And so the plan began to come to fruition when I decided to join Scott and Susan at the 2005 San Diego 1 Day Run.

There could not be a better opportunity to do it: perfect weather, a well-organized flat course and good aid stations on the one mile loop. All I had to do was run it 100 times before the 'bell' rang!

It turned out to be everything I expected. What a perfect day! I had the good fortune to be in the company of some very experienced ultra runners like Scott, Susan and Andy Velazco. Andy and I ran together for most of the first 50 miles. I won't even venture a guess as to how many ultras he had completed but I know the number was huge. I followed his every word of advice. He told me what to eat and when to eat it. What to drink and when to drink it. And more. 'We'll run to the first light post, then walk to the last one, then start running again.' It seemed like a logical plan to me. 'Just keep doing that and we'll be OK,' he said. And he was right. Being conservative is the key in these long runs.

Somehow, in my mind that day I never doubted I'd be able to finish. This time I believed in myself and that confidence made all the difference. The excitement increased with each mile and the miles began to pile up. As I got closer to my goal I started to look for a nice grassy spot to crash at the end. And crash I did! I spun around and flopped on my back and stayed there for about half an hour. I had finished my 100 miles in only 23 1/2 hours. The clock was still running, but I didn't care. I had done it. This was it! All I needed! Those moments will forever be ingrained in my memory.

It was truly One Fine Day!

PART THREE:
Thanks for the Memories
✦
(The Nineteenth Hole)

THE ETERNAL FINISH LINE

I don't handle death well. Never have, never will.

I've attended countless funerals in my lifetime, and regardless of my relationship with the deceased—immediate family, good friend, co-worker, casual acquaintance or neighbor, I don't handle them well. Never have, never will.

What I turn to for strength in a time of loss are memories. I try my best to remember the good times with that person, the good things about that person, and the good that person brought into the world while they were alive. Trust me; it helps.

You are about to meet four people; four people who provided me a lifetime of memories.

The first is arguably the greatest grandmother a runner could ever want and the greatest one-person support crew *any* runner could ever have.

The second is someone who had a profound impact on my ability to compete as a runner and made a huge difference in the running community.

The third and fourth are my parents, both of whom I lost within a span of 24 days in the fall of 2007. They were my biggest supporters in life and made the biggest impression on who I am today. Lord I miss them.

Please allow me to share my memories of these wonderful people with you.

Chapter Nineteen

Heaven's Aid Station

The first time I met her she greeted me with a smile and handed me some animal crackers and a cup of water. She wasn't officially working as a volunteer at the race I was participating in; she was just being herself—friendly, supportive and extremely generous.

If you've run a marathon in the southeast, the chances are good that she has draped a finisher's medal around your neck. If you've run an ultra in the southeast, the chances are *excellent* that at some point during the race she offered you refreshments, whether they were liquid or solid...but in all probability both. Mercedes...Tybee Island...Big Butt...Chickamauga... Strolling Jim...you name it; she was more than likely lending her support. Up until the fall of 2006, she had helped with every one of our Darkside Running Club events as well.

She thought the world of her grandson Brenton Floyd, and supported him emotionally, physically, and spiritually through countless events of 26.2 miles or more—too many in number to list here. She wrote and spoke frequently about how she was 'spending Brenton's inheritance' doing what they both loved most—running all over the southeast virtually every weekend of the year. Of course, the travel wasn't limited to just that area of the country as they were both 'fully-vested' members of the 50 States Marathon Club, and one does not achieve that honor by limiting themselves to one specific area of the country.

The grandson thought the world of her as well, and I know he misses her dearly. We all do. The face of running in the southeast has definitely changed without her physical presence and support. However, I have no doubt her spirit will still be there, and from that we should all gain a small amount of comfort and support.

In the last E-mail she sent to me, she proudly told me her grandson would be participating in the Darkside Running Club's Way Too Hot 50K, and it would be his 100th lifetime ultra. Alas it was not to be, as her last day of life on earth fell three weeks prior to the event. Her grandson would not be participating after all. In time, however, I have no doubt he will reach his 100th ultra—that is, if he hasn't already. I believe I can say the same for his 200th, if not his 300th as well. After all, she always taught him that quitting—giving anything less than 100%--was not an option. And that, I know, is a lesson he learned well.

Knowing her as I did, I'm certain she is already on duty at the first aid station in heaven. She wouldn't have it any other way.

The first time I met her she greeted me with a smile and handed me some animal crackers and a cup of water. I'm certain that down the road—after I make that one last long run—she'll be there to greet me one more time.

We miss you, Betty Mae Burrell. Thank you for everything you did for so very many of us.

Betty and Brenton

Chapter Twenty
Life in the Fast Lane

Bill McBride is one of the finest runners—and men—I've ever known. Bill and I trained together for several years in the early 1990's, but in time went our separate ways. Bill turned to ironmans (and working on his golf game after his retirement) and I to ultramarathons. Bill developed cancer in 2004 and fought a courageous battle up until the very end. I would see Bill occasionally on my Sunday morning runs—sometimes jogging, but mostly out walking his beloved dog while enjoying the fresh air and beauty of Peachtree City. Bill lost his battle with cancer on August 3, 2008. For a brief moment when I heard the news, time stood still.

At the funeral service for Bill two days later, his good friend Roy Robison said it best when he spoke of Bill's penchant for life and how he was able to squeeze what some would consider a lifetime into each and every year of his life.

Truer words were never spoken.

I first ran into Bill McBride at the Brooks (Georgia) Day 10K in May of 1991. Bill invited me to join him and some of the members of the Peachtree City Running Club (PTCRC) for a casual run the next morning and gave me directions to his home on Raintree Bend—our official starting point.

The next morning—the day after our tough run in Brooks—I met Bill and three of his closest friends, Tom Crofton, Roy Robison and Bob Trombly for a casual run. That is, if you can call 15.7 miles at a 6:45 pace 'casual.'

But that was Bill—living life in the fast lane. I was amazed when he told me he had run a 35:59 at Peachtree the year before...when he was 49. It wasn't long before Bill—15 years my senior—became my running mentor.

At Bill's request I joined the PTCRC, a club which he, Tom, Roy, Bob and several others were responsible for forming. A little over two years later, with Bill's encouragement and endorsement I was elected President of the club.

Back in the early 1990's I was racing almost every Saturday, but I never passed on the opportunity to run with Bill the following Sunday morning. For the two years that Bill and I ran together on Sundays, I always knew what was in store for me—15.7 miles at a 6:45 pace. Sometimes a bit faster, but rarely slower. For me, that was essentially my race pace for that distance.

But there's more. On the Sundays that Bob Trombly would join us we'd all agree before we ran to 'take it easy,' which usually lasted for a good—oh, five or six minutes. After that, Bill and Bob would engage in their usual battle of trying to run as fast as they could so they could make the other one cry uncle. Me? I was usually caught in the middle, trying to pull the two back together as much as possible. Then one day I realized that by staying in the middle, the pace for me wasn't remotely 'casual' and was actually causing me a lot of discomfort.

So one day I decided what the hell: if I'm going to hurt, I'm going to hurt *a lot*. From that point on I would do my best to stay with the frontrunner (it could be either one of them on any given Sunday).

Bill and I traveled to the Atlanta Reservoir one Friday night in August to compete in a 5K race. Fortunately for me, the race was held in two stages: one for the open runners (ages 39 and younger) and one for the masters runners (ages 40 and over). I ran well in the open race, finishing in a respectable 18:10. Bill, however, ran spectacularly in the master's race, finishing in a sizzling 17:41 (at the age of 51).

On Thanksgiving Day 1991 I ran the Atlanta Marathon, convinced that Bill had worked me into good enough shape so that I could finally break three hours on a rather difficult course. It turns out I virtually ran the same pace per mile (6:53) for the marathon that we had been running every Sunday for the last 18 months. Looking back, those 15.7 miles at a 6:45 pace translate pretty well to 26.2 miles (marathon distance) at a 6:53 pace, which meant I had raced virtually every Sunday for two years. If you have already done the math, you know that I missed breaking three hours at the Atlanta Marathon by a mere 20 seconds. However, I promise you I gave it everything I had. After all, I learned from one of the finest: Bill McBride.

I think back to those Sunday runs and realize it was running with Bill, learning from Bill, and being mentored by Bill that led me to run competitively for the Atlanta Track Club Men's Masters Team for eight years.

I also remember how those Sunday runs ended during the hot, summer months. Bill and I would go out to the pool in his backyard. Almost immediately, the two of us would be horizontal, albeit in two entirely different ways:

I would be face up—*flat on my back*--catching my breath by the side of the pool. Bill would be face down--in the water and swimming laps.

After all, that was Bill—living life in the fast lane.

Bill McBride after finishing the 2006
Peachtree City Sprint Triathlon.

Bill McBride

Chapter Twenty-One

Running at Altitude

One of the toughest things for a runner who is not conditioned for it is running at altitude. I guess that's pretty true of most everything in life: if you're not conditioned for it and suddenly have to face it head on, it's going to be difficult to overcome.

Not long ago I came face-to-face with something more difficult than running at 10,000 feet above sea level...or climbing to the top of Mount Everest...or swimming across the English Channel.

On October 30, 2007, I had to swim across the Atlantic Ocean...climb up *and* down Mount Everest...and run at 15,000 feet above sea level. On that day I did all this and more—you see, that was the day I said goodbye to my dad for the last time...the last time I was able to tell him I loved him...the last time he looked me in the eye and silently told me he was proud of who I had become...and the last time he told me he loved me, too.

My father, Harvey Eugene Ludwig, was known as 'Bip' by everyone who knew him. He had battled a myriad of health issues for the past several years. He fought a courageous battle but in time the constant bombardment of aches, pains and disease got the better of him. I was with him in his final hours and for that I am grateful, for I saw him face death with the dignity and courage I would expect of someone I have loved and respected for all of my life. While I regret that he only graced this earth for less than 77 years, I am grateful that he made a lasting and indelible impression on the many people who were close to him. Like me.

Reflecting back on the 53 years he and I shared as father and son, there are a few regrets. But for every regret, there are oh-so-many things for which I am eternally grateful:

- While I **regret** that dad lived in Virginia for the last 35 years of his life and my family lived in Atlanta for the past 28 years and as such dad wasn't able to spend as much time with his two grandsons as he (and they!) would have liked, I am **grateful** that he held my first-born Justin—all two pounds and three ounces of him—in the palms of his hands minutes after birth and had the courage and compassion to weep openly in the waiting room, his joy and apprehension both readily apparent in his tears. I am **grateful** that dad saw his other grandson Josh at age six play in his very first game of Muppet soccer… and see him score five goals. I am also **grateful** that dad lived the last 35 years of his life in his favorite place in the world, Virginia Beach.

- While I **regret** that I never made a career of the U.S. Navy as my dad had hoped (which I now realize is one of the finest careers a person could have), I am **grateful** that my dad saw me realize two successful careers in logistics—24 years with JCPenney Catalog and now with Porsche Logistics. I am **grateful** that he knows I always put my best foot forward, something I saw him do throughout his career in the U.S. Navy.

- While I **regret** that I never took my golf to the next level (whatever that might have meant), I am **grateful** that I played with my dad during the finest round of golf I ever played—a round in which I hit all 18 greens in regulation for the first, last and only time in my life. I am also **grateful** that I played with my dad during *his* finest round of golf (an 87 in Honolulu, Hawaii) and when he made his hole-in-one (one year to the day after I made *my* only hole-in-one—on the very same golf course in Mayport, Florida!).

While I **regret** that dad wasn't around long enough to become a great-grandfather…or to see my first book published…or for he and I to play one last round of golf together, I am **grateful** for so many, many things:

- The first time dad met my future wife Cindy, he told me I found the perfect woman. As always, he was right.
- While driving through Europe in the summer of 1962 in a VW beetle, even though I asked dad 'how many miles' every time we spotted a sign indicating how many kilometers it was to the next city, he never lost his patience…fully aware I had no idea how far a mile was, let alone a kilometer.
- Every time dad left for a six-month tour of duty at sea, he would kiss me goodbye on the forehead while I slept—with tears in his eyes—even though he never knew I was actually awake. Or *did* he?

- Dad wore his gold wedding band on his ring finger for over 55 years. I never saw him without it. Never.
- Dad gave me his full support as a student at the University of Florida, even though it broke his heart that I wasn't attending the U. S. Naval Academy.
- Dad saw me realize my ultimate running accomplishments: a finish at the Badwater Ultramarathon, a USATF 24 Hour National Championship, numerous Boston Marathons, and the first 29 years of my consecutive-days running streak.   And as a dad would, he always worried I was going to 'overdo it.'
- Dad and I posed for a photograph at his 50th wedding anniversary party in 2002—a photograph that is now the most treasured one I own. The photograph currently graces the back cover of this book.

But the thing for which I am most grateful is that I am—and always will be—his son.

Yet, it's still hard for me when I'm running at altitude…

Chapter Twenty-Two

Lifelines and Deadlines

In elementary school I was in the business of creating greeting cards. In middle school, I started writing my first book (loosely based on the old television show 'Voyage to the Bottom of the Sea'). In high school, I started writing (and drawing) comic books. I loved to be creative, and I loved to write.

'You should write a book someday.'

I heard that a lot through the years…from friends, from relatives, but mostly from my mom. Truth be known, I *had* been writing a book…for 28 years, in fact. From the moment I fell in love with running (during the fall of 1978) I wanted to write a book about the sport. In fact in my 1979 running log I made an entry on the day I selected a title for the book: *Footsteps.* However, there is a big distinction between wanting to write a book and actually doing it. That's why I made a public resolution early in 2007 to finish my book and get it published. Once I make my intentions known, they're much easier to carry out.

Perhaps the main reason I made the resolution is because I wanted to make sure my parents—particularly my mom—saw me become a published author. As my dad had been battling blood cancer and several other maladies for a few years, I wanted to make certain that he would see my book in print. Unfortunately he passed away on October 30, 2007. At the time I was exactly where I was 28 years ago: unpublished.

I had been working with a publisher for the better part of the year. The goal he and I had decided on was to have my book published in time for Christmas. We both met our respective production and editing deadlines—and there were many of them--time after time after time. We were on track for a publication date in early December.

However, my mom's health had taken a turn for the worse. She had an emergency colostomy on October 26 and didn't regain consciousness until

264

after my dad had passed. She was unaware that he was gone, although on a higher level I truly believe she knew. After all they had been together for almost 60 years, and they were both to the point they could sense how the other was feeling. Once she regained consciousness she wasn't able to breathe on her own and the doctors feared she had suffered a mild heart attack. The doctors knew mom needed to be told about dad; they just weren't sure when she would be able to withstand hearing he had passed while she was still recovering from surgery.

On November 16 the doctors felt it was time. Their plan was simple: I would tell her about dad and they would be at the ready to provide any needed medical assistance. I was on my own with respect to the verbiage to use; after all, this was a most unusual situation and they didn't have any experience along those lines.

Somehow I found the words to tell her. The doctors weren't needed, although my mom anguished over the news for several hours before finally being able to rest with the help of some medication. My job was complete... and I felt horrible about it.

Several days later, mom showed signs of improvement. But one week later, on November 23 my sister called and said mom had taken a turn for the worse. I returned to my parent's house in Virginia Beach accompanied by my wife Cindy and younger son Josh and met up with my sister Hope. My dad's two sisters and my older son Justin would be joining us shortly.

My sister asked me about the status of my book on November 27 and out of curiosity I did a search on Amazon.com. I couldn't believe it when my book appeared (although I had changed the name of it to *Running through My Mind*). I saw that it had a publication date of November 16 (the day I told mom about dad, and also Justin's 25th birthday). My sister ordered it via overnight delivery, and as far as I know she is the first person to purchase my book. It arrived at my parent's house on November 29 at 1:45 p.m. One hour later we were all off to see my mom with book in hand. At 4:00 p.m. we found my mom resting comfortably, her eyes closed and her face at peace. Hope placed the book next to her pillow. As far as we know, she is the first person to receive a copy of her son's published book.

Before Hope placed the book next to mom, she asked me to write a note on the inside cover. Here is what I wrote:

To mom,

You are the first person to get my book! I hope you and dad enjoy it as much as I enjoyed writing it. I love you both.

Your loving son,

Scott

November 29, 2007

My mom was apart from my dad for 24 days. Throughout their lives, they were virtually inseparable.

Now they always will be.

The Ludwig Family: Bip, Hope, Scott, Cindy, and Gloria

Chapter Twenty-Three

Scratching The Surface

The runners you've met in this book toil…yet *excel* in relative obscurity. They don't do it for the fame. They don't do it for the glory. They do it because they all share a passion for running that is both undeniable and insatiable.

Yet they are just the tip of the iceberg. If there were more time I would have loved to tell you about more of the incredible people who live every day of their lives to the fullest. Just ordinary people doing extraordinary things:

Brenton Floyd of Harrison, Tennessee who ran his first marathon as a 10-year old. When he celebrated his 21st birthday by running his first 100-mile race at the 2006 Umstead Endurance Run, Brenton already had 300 marathons or ultras to his credit. Brenton is also the youngest runner to finish a marathon in all 50 states—a feat he accomplished by the time he was 16.

Mark Covert of Lancaster, California who celebrated the 41-year anniversary of his consecutive-days running streak on July 23, 2009.

Norm Frank of Rochester, New York who has 965 marathons on his impressive running resume.

Wally Herman of Ottawa, Ontario who is the first person to complete a marathon in all 50 states, as well as in 99 different countries around the world.

Ray Scharenbrock of Milwaukee, Wisconsin who has finished a marathon in all 50 states a staggering ten times.

Larry Macon of San Antonio, Texas who established a Guinness World Record in 2008 by completing 105 official marathons.

Paul Morgan of Altamonte Springs, Florida who has completed a marathon, an ultra and climbed the highest mountain or point in all 50 states.

Marshall Ulrich of Idaho Springs, Colorado who, among many other amazing things has completed a solo 586-mile quad crossing of Death Valley (from Badwater to the top of Mount Whitney and back two times within 10 days).

Rob Apple of Murfreesboro, Tennessee who has an impressive total of 547 ultras on his resume.

Sharon Mordorski of Minneapolis, Minnesota who is the first woman to complete a marathon in all 50 states.

Rick Worley of Centerville, Texas who has a Guinness World Record for running a marathon the most consecutive weeks in a row (200 marathons in 156 weeks). In 1997 he was also the first person to complete a marathon in all 50 states in the same calendar year.

Nancy Broadbridge of Birmingham, Michigan who is the first woman to complete a marathon in all 50 states in the same calendar year (1997). Nancy and her husband Tony Lopetrone are the first couple to complete marathons in all 50 states in one calendar year.

Don McNelly of Rochester, New York has completed the most marathons (471) after reaching his 70th birthday, with 175 of those coming after he turned *80*.

Holly Koester of Walton Hills, Ohio is the first person to complete a marathon in all 50 states in a wheelchair. Holly is an Army Captain who lost the use of her legs in a car accident on her way to her military base.

Herbert Fred of Houston, Texas who has run an astounding 236,000 plus miles in his lifetime. At 80 years of age, it is Fred's intention to run 'as long as the good Lord allows' him to.

Steve Boone of Humble, Texas who has over 400 marathon finishes to his credit, with 130 of them in the state of Texas alone.

And finally, one of my personal favorites:

Jill Floyd of Atlanta, Georgia who had never run more than 26.2 miles when she entered an 8-hour run in 2005. Not only did Jill run 43.7 miles, she finished first amongst the women. Three years later an article in a Georgia sports publication was written about Jill entitled '*For Atlantan Jill Floyd, a Marathon is just a Warmup.*' A few months later she completed her first 100 mile run.

Do you know what's even more amazing?

This list…this *book* barely scratches the surface of the stories that are out there waiting to be told.

If only there was more time.

Note: There is no doubt there may be accomplishments out there 'topping' those presented here. This listing is based on months of personal research and years of personal experience; it would be unrealistic to expect this list to be all-inclusive of the many everyday heroes across the globe.

Chapter Twenty-Four

Moving Targets

The portraits you have read in this book were compiled between the spring of 2008 and the spring of 2009. As you can imagine, a lot has happened between now (the summer of 2009) and then that wasn't presented earlier. Keeping up with these 18 people is like trying to hit a moving target: after all, the word 'stop' is not in their vocabularies.

With that in mind, here's what everyone has been up to recently:

ANNE RENTZ is proud of everyone in her training groups who finishes their first marathon, and considers them all as her 'children.' She recounts how most of them transition from doubting they can do it to basking in the satisfaction of completing 26.2 miles. Anne's student who has taken her running the farthest is Susan 'Socks' Kolbinsky (she earned her nickname by showing up for her first training run without socks). Susan completed her 100th marathon/ultra at the Tahoe Rim Trail 50K in July 2009, and has already completed a marathon/ultra in all 50 states. Today Susan works for Jeff Galloway and has been a pace group leader at the ING Georgia Marathon for several years. Cindi Burgess, now 62 started out in Anne's walking program. After walking her first marathon and throwing up at the finish line, Cindi began to get faster and faster; and now leads her own running group. Anne is especially proud of her sister Becky, who was a 'couch potato' when Anne ran her first Peachtree 10K Road Race. Figuring if sis could do it so could she, Becky has since run numerous marathons, adventure races and even a full Ironman event. Becky returned to school and received a degree in Exercise Science and now has a career focused on running and health.

Anne and Bill Cox were married on December 27, 2008. Bill, the man who originally motivated Anne to run, ran his first Peachtree thanks to the motivation provided by Anne. Bill has also walked two marathons and completed several Bike Rides Across Georgia (BRAG). For his selfless and dedicated assistance at races throughout the year, Bill was awarded the Darkside Running Club's 2008 Mama Betty Award (named in honor of Betty Mae Burrell, whom you met earlier in *Heaven's Aid Station*) which is presented annually to the volunteer who goes the extra mile in support of the running community. Anne still dreams of Badwater, Boston and Comrades and will soon complete her 100th marathon/ultra; probably later in 2009.

Bill and Anne, Husband and Wife

AMY YANNI won her age group at the Memphis Marathon in December 2008, and followed that with the Female Grandmaster title at the Tallahassee Marathon in February 2009. Amy may finally get around to running the Mickelson Trail Marathon in 2010. Amy was planning on running it in June 2008, but on June 1 of that year her husband Daniel Jongeling suffered a cardiac arrest. One year later he's doing well, and he and Amy opted to 'reflect and rejoice' and do some of the things that didn't get done earlier in the year...like yard work! *(Daniel was selected as a 2009 Medtronic Global Hero, by the way!)* After this winter Amy and Daniel are interested in moving to Florida; perhaps to Fort Myers. Amy (optimistically) would love to do PR work for the Boston Red Sox or perhaps serve as a running consultant. As for the Red Sox, Amy believes this year's team is one of her favorites. She is especially fond of the way 'Pedey' (Dustin Pedroia) plays the game: 'he plays to win each play, each stolen base, each at bat and never quits...and his uniform is always dirty at the end of the game').

Amy's favorite running memory is running down a hill (which was normally used for sledding) in Balduc Park in Detroit with her brother Bruce one spring day while she was in elementary school. Bruce took Amy's hand and they both 'flew down the hill.' Amy had never run that fast before, and found it to be both scary and exhilarating. Amy loved her brother and wanted him to be proud of her so she held onto his hand for dear life and finished the sprint. She says she can still feel all that and more just thinking about it.

BOBBI GIBB continues to be a member of the Boston Athletic Association, which she says has become her second family. Bobbi has completed several books on a variety of subjects: training for and running the Boston Marathon in 1964, 1965 and 1966; economics (two books, actually); and a compilation of philosophical essays. Bobbi still has her license to practice law in Massachusetts and remains a member of the bar, but most of her time is now spent on medical research, writing, painting and sculpture. She still enjoys running an hour a day along the beaches and through the woods, a time she reserves for personal contemplation and making herself 'feel happy.' Bobbi founded and continues to serve as the President of the Institute for the Study of Natural Systems. She fondly recollects finishing the 1966 Boston Marathon and shaking hands with John Volpe, the Governor of Massachusetts afterwards. On a higher level, Bobbi would like to help raise the consciousness of both men and women towards living lives that are emotionally, mentally, physically and spiritually healthy—in other words to live a life entirely free of substances (alcohol, drugs, cigarettes) of any kind and centered on good exercise, good food and adequate sleep. Bobbi remains an animal lover, and her past litany of pets include two goats (Romeo and Juliet), a bearded collie named Heidi and five white angora cats (Bobbi adds 'try putting on a dark blue lawyer's suit covered with white angora cat hair and driving to work at an upscale Boston Law firm sometime'). Presently Bobbi has a tame seagull who comes to her window and taps; she's taught him to fetch a stick, turn around in a circle and come when called (she adds that it's a thrill to give a call and see a free-flying white bird circling way up in the sky and come down and land next to you).

Bobbi's most precious running memory is running with her dog across the upland valleys of Nevada. She would spot a pale blue mountain peak off in the distance and spend hours running to the top of it. The sense she had of being on our amazing planet was overwhelming, and provided her a sense of being immersed in some kind of 'gigantic love that no one ever notices' and it reminded her of the miracle of existence and how we often take it for granted when in reality it is 'a gift of immense proportions.' She remembers how she would run in solitude and enjoy the silence, hearing only the sound of the wind and the gentle waving of the grass.

SUSAN LANCE wants to run the Western States Endurance Run once she reaches the age of 50, and plans on giving it everything she's got to win her age group. Susan continues to rescue stray animals (on a personal note, the 4th feline to join the Ludwig household, Moe—a beautiful orange tabby was a project of Susan's), but in all honesty she's lost track of how many. At home Susan currently plays 'mom' to four dogs, nine cats, three horses, one goat (Rupert, who still thinks he's a horse), seven chickens, three finches, three cockatiels and one small parrot. On the immediate horizon Susan will be competing in two 100-mile events in 2009: Burning River (Ohio) and Heartland (Kansas). Susan posted the 34th fastest 50 mile time in the country in 2008.

Susan's fondest memory is circling the track in Auburn, California in 2007 with her friends, running mentors and significant other Ken as she completed her first Western States.

ELIZABETH HURDMAN and her husband Jeff took a trip to India in December 2008. They particularly enjoyed their morning runs in South India as they would venture into a variety of landscapes: rustic farm villages, rice paddies, fishing villages and tea plantations. In March 2009 Elizabeth ran Around the Bay, a race which contends for the honor of being the first official running race in Canada/United States. It poured rain, and Elizabeth 'bumped' into Amie Chong, the woman who mentored her in her early years of running. They provided one another updates of their respective lives for the entire 30 kilometers of the race.

Elizabeth has embarked on two new adventures in learning: one in the dotty language of Braille and the other in the fine art of swimming. Elizabeth has signed up for several sprint triathlons and hopes her swimming lessons will pay off (and that she won't drown; for some reason she says swimming 'just won't take' with her). In July 2009 Elizabeth successfully completed her first triathlon...in spite of aquatic anxiety!). To celebrate their 25th wedding anniversary, Elizabeth and Jeff will be going to England for a 'running tour' of the Cotswolds, where they will cover about 100 miles in six days. In August 2009 Elizabeth will return to Lean Horse, only this time she will be running the 50 mile version while Jeff will tackle 100 miles for the first time. Elizabeth will return to the 100 mile distance at the Heartlands 100 in October 2009.

Elizabeth's favorite running memory is always the run she just completed. But if she was forced to select just one run, it would be the second half of the 2008 Lean Horse 100 where she was paced by her husband. Running alongside Jeff when a huge deer leapt into the path in front of them, so close that they could feel its heavy hoofs hit the ground and feel the cool breeze created by its proximity to them is one of the happiest moments of Elizabeth's life.

AMY COSTA officially launched the new Jacksonville Outward Bound Center on April 25, 2009, a project very close to her heart which she had been working on for the past six years. Amy reports that Jacksonville offers a beautiful river running through town that connects and ties everyone together as well as many beautiful wilderness areas. Her goal: to improve the quality of life of the local youth, college students and professionals in the corporate and educational fields. The mission of the Outward Bound Center is to inspire character development and self-discovery and on a higher level, to make Jacksonville and the world a better place. On the running scene, in 2008 Amy posted the 90th fastest 50K, the 7th fastest 50 miler and the 3rd fastest 100 miler in the country. Her 100 miler also happened to be the 8th fastest time in the world in 2008!

Amy competed in the Florida Keys 100 in May 2009 and despite battling a stomach flu for over 80 miles found herself in first place amongst the women until her ailment got the best of her, as she was falling in and out of consciousness. After 81 miles an EMT (correctly) insisted she receive fluids intravenously at the local hospital, which in hindsight Amy says 'I guess it was just not my day; there are always more races.'

Amy is proud of her healthy and energetic children. Micayla is running cross country and track for the Bolles School in Jacksonville. She has started running half marathons at the age of 15 and is already leaving mom 'in the dust.' Jordyn is running a little cross country in middle school and enjoys swimming in the Bolles swim program. While swimming takes up most of her time, she is always up for a 5K or 10K on a holiday and can be found running alongside mom at many of mom's longer races. Amy says that Jordyn never complains about waking up early and is very dedicated to her training programs. Josh loves all sports, although swimming and soccer are his main events these days. Josh plays on a traveling soccer team and devotes a large amount of time to swimming at the Bolles School where he is a distance swimmer in both the freestyle and the butterfly. Husband Joe is the head of Urology at Shands Hospital in Jacksonville, but still manages to find time to remain an avid runner. The Costa family—all five of them, will be competing in the Wild West (200 mile) Relay in August 2009: the ultimate family adventure!

Hands down, Amy's favorite running memory continues to be sharing her love for running with her family. She loves seeing her children run races, and being there beside her in ultra races. Amy fondly recalls competing in the 2009 Florida Keys 100 and having all three of her children taking turns running side by side with her in the dark wearing headlamps.

KELLY MURZYNSKY will return to the ultra arena in December 2009 at the Tallahassee Ultra Distance Classic 50K. She is proud her daughters share her passion for running: Sara is the recipient of a scholarship in cross country at Drury University in Springfield, Missouri and Danielle is running cross country and track as a junior in high school. Kelly has recently started working for Fusion, a glass art gallery in Seaside, Florida.

Kelly says the most important part of her running career has been her official 'hold my stuff guy,' husband Joe. Joe has traveled from coast to coast…waited hours in the pouring rain…cheered and smiled when Kelly was at her worst…and never complains about her extensive training or disgusting toenails. Joe has always encouraged Kelly to do her best, and she considers him to be a huge part of her training and racing success.

JANICE ANDERSON reports that membership in GUTS is quickly approaching 300 members, and the club boasts a repertoire of six events. Within the next year, Janice hopes to add one or two more. Janice has been experiencing leg problems which has caused a lot of 'compensation issues,' and at the moment finds it difficult to ramp up training for competitive running although she is still able to enjoy running distances from 50 kilometers to

50 miles 'just for fun.' Janice has taken her running to a different arena, as she is presently training several other runners. She enjoys encouraging those who think they can't do it. Janice finds that everyone with the interest also has the ability if they put their hearts and minds into it. Janice was a crew member for Kathy Youngren, a fellow friend and runner at the Badwater Ultramarathon in July 2009.

Janice's favorite running memories go back to the fall of her high school days, running at the local cross country park and enjoying the wonderful smell of waxy cut grass and feeling as if she could fly. It reminds her of why she fell in love with running in the first place.

SARAH LOWELL has set her sights on a return to the Western States Endurance Run (hopefully) in 2010. She would love to break 24 hours and 'be done with it.' Down the road Sarah would like to run all of the arctic ultras including the Alaska ultra that follows the Iditarod Trail all the way to Nome (both the 'shorter' 350 mile version…and then the 1,100 mile version). Sarah is proud to report that Daniel just started first grade in May 2009. Daniel has finished his chemo and his scans are indicating that he is clear of cancer! He will be a second grader in the fall. Sarah adds that Daniel is adorable and hilarious, 'a true hero after all he has been through.' Appropriately, Sarah is a national semi-finalist for the Energizer Bunny Award for her efforts in support of Daniel's battle.

Sarah's favorite running memory is one she shared with her sister. Sarah completed the 1998 Coldfoot (Alaska) 100 Mile Race in her best time ever (19:22:20) and her sister was there to capture most of the race on video she took while riding in the support vehicle. Sarah watches the video occasionally and fondly remembers running way beyond what she thought possible. Having her sister there to share the experience made it feel like a dream.

LLOYD YOUNG entered the 85-89 age group in the summer of 2008. In the first ten weeks after celebrating his 85th birthday, Lloyd ran some spectacular times: a 5K in 27:35; 5 miles in 45:10 (on his birthday, as a matter of fact); 10K in 56:59; two 10-milers (1:31:48 and 1:33:39); a half marathon in 2:11:38, and what he considered a 'disappointing' marathon (Twin Cities) in 5:00:35. Lloyd battled throat cancer for the first half of 2009 and with the worst behind him he hopes to return to Peachtree City in November 2010 to run a 50K road race. Lloyd is also writing a book of short stories he anticipates collaborating on with his daughter, and is looking forward to the day he turns 90 (July 18, 2013) so he can begin his assault on another tier of age group records.

Lloyd's favorite memory was at Grandma's Marathon in Duluth, Minnesota when, at the age of 79 he was asked what time he would like to run prior to the event. He replied that he'd like to run an hour slower than his personal best; 'something around 4 hours and 10 minutes.' His finishing time? Four hours, 10 minutes...and two seconds.

TOM ADAIR proudly reports that he now has 10 grandchildren with the recent addition of Declan Simon Adair, who entered this world on June 9, 2009 and weighed in at six pounds and five ounces and measured 19 ¾ inches long. The 50 States Marathon Club now has 438 members (out of 1,852 total members) who have completed a marathon in all 50 states. Tom is proud to report that he completed his 300th lifetime marathon and/or ultra with a marathon in Peachtree City, Georgia on Memorial Day 2009. Earlier in the year Tom was experiencing lumbar back problems which posed a serious threat towards accomplishing his milestone; however the stimulation and anticipation of completing # 300 allowed his to overcome his adversity. Kevin Hatfield provided Tom with bib #300 for the event, and throughout the 26.2 miles Tom ran with many of his friends who he found to be very encouraging and supporting.

Tom's favorite running memories are his two 100-mile finishes (Umstead and Lean Horse) in 2006. He considers them his favorites not only because he finished but because both events allowed him to bond with his son-in-law Chris Lowery, whose friendship and support he considers 'priceless.' Tom and Chris fought the battles of fatigue, pain, exhaustion and dehydration (and for Tom, hallucination)...and won. Tom truly believes it was Chris' encouragement and companionship that allowed him to finish both races.

JACK McDERMOTT and Laura Reardon were married on October 25, 2008 in Niagara Falls, New York. The next day they ran the Niagara Falls International Marathon together. As Laura is a schoolteacher they did not have what they consider an 'official' honeymoon, but they took an extended trip to Oregon this summer (of course, a marathon was on the agenda) and at some point they will take an extended trip to Norway for their honeymoon (most likely in the summer of 2010). The 2009 Tallahassee Marathon had 204 finishers and continues to grow. While Jack's immediate goal is getting adjusted to married life, he would like to help Laura qualify for the Boston Marathon. On the personal level, Jack is slowly trudging toward his goal of a marathon in all 50 states (St. George, Utah in October 2009, where he hopes to run a personal best will be # 34). His other 'pipe dreams' include taking a shot at the Masters course record at the Tallahassee Ultra 50 Mile Run in December 2009 (Jack ran the 52nd fastest 50 mile time in the country in 2008) and finishing a 100 mile race somewhere down the road. Jack plans on continuing his two 'marathon streaks,' having run every Boston Marathon since 2002 and every First Light Marathon (Mobile, Alabama) since 2001.

Jack's favorite memory is qualifying for the Boston Marathon for the first time. In his sixth marathon (Mardi Gras Marathon in New Orleans, Louisiana in February 2001) Jack ran 3:06:15 which not only qualified him for Boston; it lowered his personal best by 15 minutes.

BOB DALTON, at the age of 56 ran 37:41 at the prestigious Peachtree 10K Road Race on Independence Day 2009, placing him third in the competitive 50-59 age group. In 2008 the Harvest Baptist 5K attracted 260 runners but more importantly the event raised over $20,000 for the HeartCry Ministry which supports orphans. Bob's son David is a musician with several Christian bands and travels throughout the southeast as a Christian worship leader. Bob still admits he would like to be the 'Bill Thorn of the US 10K Classic (Thorn has now run all 40 editions of the Peachtree 10K Road Race). When Bob crosses the finish line of the US 10K Classic in September 2009 he will have competed in all 16 years of the event. Bob feels privileged to have been blessed with a 'little bit of running talent,' a gift which he is grateful for every day. Bob has always been more than willing to supplement his gift with a lot of hard work Bob's high school coach Hal Cochran, whom Bob greatly admires presented him with a scripture for graduation which has served as Bob's 'life verse' ever since:

Trust in the Lord with all your heart, and lean not on your own understanding, in all your ways acknowledge Him and He shall direct your paths. (Proverbs 3:5-6).

Bob's favorite running memory is winning the 1988 Peachtree City Classic 15K 'in front of the hometown crowd.' Setting a state age group record was simply icing on the cake.

ANDY VELAZCO has been plagued by a nagging right hip ache that won't seem to go away ('It sucks getting old,' he says). With that in mind he's set his sights on a 'more realistic' goal of 50 miles per event. Most recently he ran 50.2 miles in June 2009 at the FANS 24 Hour Run in Minnesota. Over the next few months he will be tackling that distance at three different events. Wife Kathy has started playing golf and working out. Son Geoffrey still works for BMW and has opened the Alibi Bar and Grill in Los Angeles. Daughter Kati (who still thinks her dad is insane, incidentally) is working on the Ocean Exhibit at the Smithsonian. Son Alec is training so he'll be able to pace dear old dad over the next several months and is now a senior at the University of Colorado. Daughters Kristin and Kari still work for ABC and LA Fitness, respectively. One thing that hasn't changed: the Velazco family still runs.

Andy's fondest memories are his trips to Death Valley to both participate and crew in 'the toughest footrace on the planet,' the Badwater Ultramarathon. A close second would be 'watching the last runners go all out to try to beat the clock' at Comrades...after he had beaten the clock first, of course.

CRAIG SNAPP ran the Boston Marathon as an 'official qualifier' seven times, and once more in 1996 (the 100th anniversary of the event) as an 'official lottery selection.' Craig has added another running streak to his resume: he has run 10 or more miles every day beginning with the San Diego Marathon in May 2008, a streak which he hopes to maintain until the publication of this book. A short-term goal for Craig and his running partner Debbie is to complete a marathon at a 'nine-something minute pace.' A long-term goal is to run his 100,000th lifetime mile (which at his current rate would be in early 2011). Craig is grateful that he has been fortunate enough to honestly enjoy the act of running; any numerical and statistical results are merely a bonus and if he were forced to stop running tomorrow, his 'regrets scorecard' would indicate 'zero.'

Craig favorite memory is completing 26.2 miles on a self-measured course on the 29th day of his running career when he was 26 years old to win a bet. He also fondly remembers a day 12 years before that when he saw Jim Ryun shatter the high school mile record, beating Olympic 800 and 1500 meter champion Peter Snell in the process.

GARY GRIFFIN was honored for his outstanding efforts in 2008 by being named the Gulf Winds Track Club's Male Runner of the Year. Appropriately so, his wife Peg was inducted into the club's Hall of Fame as well. Gary was also bestowed with the Darkside Running Club's 2008 Best in Performance Award. Gary was cited in *Ultrarunning* magazine for winning an ultramarathon (the Darkside 8 Hour Run) after reaching 50 years of age. His 100 mile finish was also the 58th fastest time in the country in 2008.

Gary's favorite running memory is completing the Comrades Marathon in South Africa. He feels honored to have been able to run in one of the most prestigious events in the ultra community. In June 2009 Gary, at the age of 59 participated in the Western States Endurance Run. While severe blisters on the balls of both feet forced Gary to drop out of the race after 80 miles, he feels privileged to have been able to participate in the most famous ultramarathons in both South Africa and the United States.

JERRY DUNN reports that participation for the 2009 Mickelson Trail Marathon increased by 300 from the year before. Jerry is particularly proud of the runners' comments indicating that the race is a 'must do' on most runners' lists. The Lean Horse Hundred and Half Hundred enters its fifth year in 2009, and continues to draw good numbers as well. Jerry plans on launching a new website (lean horse) which will be a fun website for blogging, podcasts, running advice and storytelling. Always on the go, Jerry is in the process of creating a fund raising program (similar to Team in Training) to benefit either Habitat for Humanity or the East Coast Greenway. While Guinness never recognized Jerry's accomplishments during his mega-marathon years, he is proud of his body of work and admits the media gave him all the recognition he needed. Besides, he adds, 'when's the last time you saw anyone reading the *Guinness Book of World Records* on a plane or in a coffee shop?'

Jerry's favorite experience is the 18th day of his 26 consecutive runs of the Boston Marathon course in 1996. *NBC Today* scheduled their on-air reporter to run six miles with Jerry for an exclusive interview. An unexpected and rather heavy snow storm blew into Hopkinton and the entire Boston area, and the reporter showed up at the starting line and asked Jerry if he would still be running. Jerry's reply: Well of course; let's go.' So they did.

AL BARKER continues to experience great success at the St. George Marathon. In 2008 he ran an impressive 3:30:58, finishing 4th in his age group (out of 634) amongst a very competitive field. On Thanksgiving Day 2008 Al and I commemorated the 15th year of our friendship by running the (*what else?*) Atlanta Marathon together. In April 2009 Al and I ran the first 50 miles of the Umstead 100 Mile Endurance Run together, but Al eventually stopped after 75 miles and afterwards he and I both swore it would be our last 100 mile event…but then again, we've said that before. Many times. The first half of the title of this book, *A Passion for Running*, was Al's idea. When he suggested it while we were running one morning I instantly knew it was meant to be. Every single person portrayed in this book has it and their words and actions personify that passion. The second half of the title, *Portraits of the Everyday Runner* is my personal tip-of-the-hat to Al Barker the *artist*: his passion for art is arguably as impressive as his running.

Al's favorite running memory is running his first Boston Marathon in 1978. On Patriot's Day 2010—32 years later—he'll toe the starting line in Hopkinton for the 12th time. After all, running is his passion.

• •

A passion for running is shared by all 18 amazing runners portrayed in this book. With a collective running portfolio featuring five hundred years of running experience and more than one million miles ran (including 5,000 races, with almost 2,400 of them being marathons or ultras), they have all personified the spirit of the sport for the better part of their lives. *(If you're interested, the women had more running experience than the men, 254 years to 246 years, while the men ran more miles than the women, 524,000 to 490,000).*

When Al Barker is lining in the starting corral for the 2010 Boston Marathon, I'll be right there with him.

Acknowledgements

First I would like to say thank you to **Stephanie Robinson**, who has once again helped me compile incredible amounts of information and somehow manage to present them in some semblance of order between the covers of this book. *(Steph—don't go anywhere; I've got at least three more books in me.)*

Al Barker, you've been a great friend and confidant for over 15 years. Here's to 15 more (and then 15 after that). I hope this book has fulfilled your wish that it be your 'legacy' to our sport, as well as something your family and friends—and *you* will be proud of.

Mom, I can still hear you say *'you should write a book someday.'* Now you know I was listening. It brings a smile to my face remembering the last time I saw you smile: the day I told you my (first) book was being printed.

Dad, you always pushed me to be the best I could be. I hope you know you were successful; I couldn't be prouder of this book.

You may be wondering why I chose to portray 18 runners in this book. Or perhaps how the subtitles of the three parts of the book were chosen (*The Front Nine, The Back Nine and the Nineteenth Hole*, respectively). All are references to the game of golf, and is a salute to my dad for that last round of golf he and I were never able to play together.

Cindy, you've run ten half-marathons over the past three years. Being there for all of them, it's been a blast; I think my heroes and I are rubbing off on you. I couldn't be happier. Once you get to this point in reading this book I hope you now have the passion to add 'finishing a marathon' to your bucket list.

I want to express my eternal gratitude to **my personal heroes** who were willing to be part of this book. I am honored you allowed me to be the one to tell your stories, and believe me when I say it was my pleasure. May your stories forever live and inspire others to run. I appreciate your willingness to

283

share, I thank you for your friendship and inspiration, and I'm astounded all of you were patient with me during the 18 months it took to put this book together. You're the greatest. You're all my heroes.

Finally I'd like end with one last update: Cindy and I are now the proud grandparents of **Krischan James**. Our grandson entered this world on March 24, 2009. I hope one day he will read this book and it will inspire him to pursue his passions in life—whatever they may be. After all, this book is part of my legacy to him…and to everyone else who has the ambition, discipline and dedication to pursue *their* passions in life.

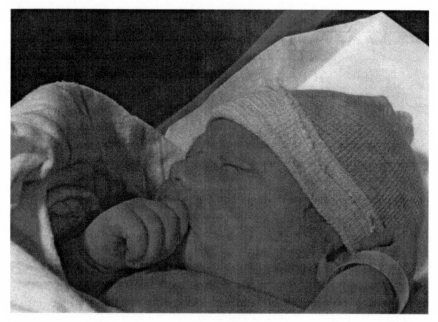

Krischan James